DEMON POSSESSION AND ALLIED THEMES

BEING AN INDUCTIVE STUDY OF

PHENOMENA OF OUR OWN TIMES

BY REV. JOHN L. NEVIUS, D. D

For Forty Years a Missionary to the Chinese

WITH AN INTRODUCTION

BY REV. F. F. ELLINWOOD, D. D.

Secretary of the Board of Foreign Missions of the Presbyterian Church,
U. S. A., and author of "Oriental Religions and Christianity."

WITH AN INDEX: BIBLIOGRAPHICAL, BIBLICAL,

PATHOLOGICAL, AND GENERAL

LONDON

GEORGE REDWAY

1897

INTRODUCTORY NOTE

BY REV. F. F. ELLINWOOD, D.D.

For several years I have been aware that Rev. Dr. John L. Nevius of Chefoo, China, was giving careful attention to certain strange psychical phenomena which were presented from time to time in the interior districts of the Shantung Province. I became more interested in the progress of his inquiries from the fact that upon an acquaintance continued for more than a quarter of a century I regarded him as a man peculiarly fitted to examine so intricate and difficult a subject.

His philosophic insight, his judicial fairness of mind, his caution and his conscientious thoroughness, appeared to me admirable qualifications for such a study. Moreover his thorough mastery of the Chinese language spoken and written, his intimate sympathy with the people, and his correspondingly truer interpretation of their innermost thought and life, have rendered him still more capable of ascertaining the real facts in the case, and of forming accurate judgments upon them.

Antecedently to any knowledge of the New Testament the people of North China believed fully in the possession of the minds and bodies of men by evil spirits. This belief is a part of that *animism*, or spirit worship, which has existed in China—as in many other countries—from the very beginning of history or tradition. It has always been understood that the personality of the evil spirit usurped, or for the time being supplanted that of the unwilling victim and acted through his organs and faculties. Physical suffering and sometimes violent paroxysms attended the presence and active influence of the spirit, and not only the particular demoniac but all his household were filled with more or less anxiety and distress.

When therefore Christianity was introduced into China, and the narratives of demoniacal possession given in the New Testament were read, the correspondence that was at once recognized by the native Christians seemed complete.

In relation to this particular form of New Testament miracles there has never been any difficulty on the part of Chinese Christians, if indeed among the heathen portion of the community. And what is very striking in the accounts given by Dr. Nevius, is their uniform confidence shown in the power of Jesus, or even of an appeal to His name to expel the spirits and set the victims free. According to the testimony of many witnesses no earnest Christian believer has ever continued to be afflicted. This seems to be a generally accepted fact, by the heathen who have known the circumstances, as well as by believers.

It will be observed that nearly all the incidents related are given on the testimony not of missionaries, but of native Christians—mostly native pastors. The cases have been carefully investigated, however, by several different missionaries, who have shared in the interest taken by Dr. Nevius, and no one of them appears to have any doubt of the veracity of the witnesses.

Some of the facts also have passed under their own immediate observation.

Missionaries in China have all proceeded with great caution in this matter. Dr. Nevius and others have avoided any measures which might lead the people to suppose that they claim the power to cast out devils even in Jesus' name. Nor does it appear that any native minister has claimed any such power. The most that has been done has been to kneel down and pray to Jesus to relieve the sufferer, at the same time inviting all present to unite in the prayer; and it seems a well established fact that in nearly or quite every instance, the person afflicted, speaking apparently in a different personality and with a different voice has confessed the power of Jesus and has departed.

Whatever theory we may adopt by way of explaining these mysterious phenomena, the idea of intentional fraud on the part either of the afflicted, or of the Christian witnesses and sympathizers, is excluded.

The absence of all motive to deceive, the great number of instances, the well tried character of the witnesses, and all the circumstances connected with their minute and consistent narratives, establish beyond reasonable doubt their entire sincerity. Whatever the world at large may think the native Christians of Shantung are as fully convinced both of the reality of demoniacal possessions, and of the available power of Jesus to remedy them, as were the disciples in the apostolic church. And the number of coincidences which Dr. Nevius has pointed out between these cases and those described in the Gospels and the Acts of the Apostles is certainly remarkable. In regard to them each reader of the book must form his own conclusions. The author does not insist upon any particular interpretation, or any final conclusion. He is evidently impressed with the gravity of his subject and the possibility of erroneous speculations. But in his extended researches he has found such speculations already rife, and he has considered them briefly in some of the later chapters of his book.

A belief in demoniacal possession has existed in

many lands and throughout the ages, and many and conflicting theories of explanation have been advanced by anthropologists and writers on psychology, hypnotism, etc. Some of these Dr. Nevius has answered, and, as I think, successfully; and on the whole his mind seems inclined to the view that as yet no theory has been advanced which so well accords with the facts as the simple and unquestioning conclusion so universally held by the Christians of Shantung, viz: that evil spirits do in many instances possess or control the mind and will of human beings.

Hypnotism, making due allowance for a thousand extravagances which have attended it, does seem to show that one strong and magnetic human will may so control the mind and will of its subject as by a mere silent volition to direct his words and acts. Who shall say then that a disembodied spirit may not do the same?

Professor Shaler of Harvard in his *Interpretation of Nature* has pointed out the fact of a strong reaction against the materialism which seemed confident of dominion a few years ago. Certain biological investigators, flushed with the success of their researches, were very confident that if they had not been able to discover the human soul with the microscope, they had at least identified it very closely with the substance of the brain and nerves. But now, as the professor shows, science is beginning to discover realms of spirit lying beyond the physical, and of which we have as yet but the barest glimpses of knowledge. Evidently human research has not yet finished its work and is not ready to rest its case upon any dogmatic verdict.

Over against materialistic speculation are the vagaries of spiritualists, theosophists and all apostles of Oriental or Occidental occultism. Their theories are on the opposite extreme, and it is one of their chief claims for recognition that they hope to save society from the deadening influence of materialism.

Dr. Nevius, after considering both of these extremes, finds no better account of man's spiritual nature than that which is given in the Word of God:—No more rational view of his conflicts with evil, no more satisfactory and all sufficient remedy for that evil. While he does not dogmatize in regard to the mysterious maladies suffered in Shantung he deems it wise to state the facts, nor does he disguise the leanings of his own mind, in regard to them.

F. F. ELLINWOOD.

October 5, 1893.

Postscript: Since the above was written Dr. Nevius has gone to that world of unseen spirits where he no longer sees "through a glass darkly." He died peacefully, though without a moment's warning, at his house in Chefoo, Oct. 19, 1893.

PREFACE.

In this age of superabounding literature, an author in presenting a new book to the public, often feels called upon to give his reasons for so doing. Good and sufficient reasons will no doubt be thought especially called for in again raising the question: Is there such a thing as Demon-Possession in this latter part of the Nineteenth Century?

The author's apology is, that in the prosecution of his missionary work in China this subject was repeatedly forced upon his attention, so that it became absolutely necessary to examine it, and to form an intelligent opinion respecting it.

In this investigation, in intervals of leisure during the past twelve years, facts have been elicited which seem to have more than a local and temporary interest, as they are nearly related to some of the most important questions of the day, viz.; the Authenticity and Inspiration of the Bible; Spiritualism; and Materialism. A somewhat exceptional opportunity for observation, and one which may prove transient, is an additional reason for making facts which have come to light the common possession of all who are interested in them.

As the matter contained in this volume is largely connected with the writer's individual experiences, an effort to suppress his own personality, would be a useless affectation. It is hoped that this consideration will be regarded as a sufficient reason for using the first personal pronoun more frequently than would otherwise be necessary.

Some of the readers of these pages will in all probability be disappointed in finding the characters and doings of spirits much less interesting and creditable than they are as represented in the familiar writings of Milton and Dante. It must be borne in mind, however, that this is not a work of the imagination, and that the author is not responsible for the characters which he introduces. His object is to present a truthful statement of facts, confident that from such a course, nothing but good can come to the cause either of science or religion.

I wish here to express my thanks to my friend Henry W. Rankin, Esq., son of Rev. Henry V. Rankin, formerly my beloved colleague in Ningpo, for his kindly undertaking, on my leaving for China, to see this work through the Press, and also preparing the accompanying Index.

JOHN L. NEVIUS.

August, 1892.

CONTENTS.

[1]

CHAPTER X.

SUPPLEMENT.

NOTE OF EXPLANATION.

In August, 1892, Dr. Nevius finished his work upon this book, placed it in the hands of the present writer to arrange for its publication, and returned to China. He had thought of adding another chapter, in which his principal argument, and its applications, should be stated more at large and concluded less abruptly; but time and health did not permit.

The unique foundations of his book lie in a collection of indisputable facts drawn from no libraries but from life.

Yet he spent much time searching in libraries, and towards the last he did this when he greatly needed rest. Still other features which would add to the completeness of the book he would gladly have supplied, but he felt that his own work must cease, and that this must be done, if done at all, by other hands. Accepting the offer of a friend to prepare an index, he subsequently expressed the desire that this friend, bound to him by life-long ties of love and reverence, and by sympathy with his convictions in this theme, should do more if he would, than read the proof and prepare the index.

He desired the correction of any obvious in-accuracy of language or quotation, and the addition of such bibliographical or other notes as might further elucidate the subject, or en-hance the value of the book for students. With diffidence this editorial function was assumed, and with the hope of submitting results to his approval before the volume should take on its final form. The further examination of the re-lated literature, and the verification of refer-ence and quotations, insensibly grew to a larger task than was foreseen. It consumed much time, while still more delay was occasioned by illness and by other cares.

Then came the sad news of the author's death, sad for the many hearts bereaved, though for him it meant a glad translation into the immediate presence of that Master whom he had served with devotion and delight. He had rounded out his forty years of missionary life, rich in manifold experience and priceless fruits. Dr. Nevius stood in the first rank of modern mis-sionaries as an evangelist, pastor, educator, or-ganizer, and founder of Christian literature in a pagan tongue. He was a man of rare versa-tility, and adaptability to untoward conditions, and there are many who knew him best as a successful promoter of the material interests of the great land of his labors and adoption. The number is also large of those who will look eagerly for the story of his life which his widow is eminently fitted to prepare. *

He was one of those all-around men of whom no class has furnished so many or so illustrious examples as the missionaries of the Cross of Jesus Christ from St. Paul down. As a writer he was a prolific author of important works in the Chinese language. In matters pertaining to China no man was better informed than Dr. Nevius. A book written by him some years ago as a general account of the land and people is still as good an introduction to the subject as can be found. It was called *China and the Chinese*, and was published by Harper Bros. in New York in 1868.

It was no great pleasure in the subject that led him to prepare the present volume, but a deep sense of responsibility. Experiences unwelcome, as they were unsought, opened his mind to the significance of a much neglected class of facts; neglected by many who otherwise would be best qualified to interpret them, and who most need to understand them. But the facts, once known in their integrity, speak plainly for themselves, while the noble quality of this author's mind, his evident fairness, thoroughness and soberness of argument, and his magnanimity towards all opponents of his views, are as unmistakable as they are rare and beautiful wherever found.

* Issued by F. H. Revell Co., in 1895.

Some will think the missionary has beaten the professional scientist on his own ground, and exhibited a model of inductive study, tested premises, and conclusions covered by the premises, such as is seldom met. On the other hand, to many, so offensive are the views maintained in this volume that a response from such persons of apathy or contempt may be naturally expected. But from all the pain of incurring such a reception for his faithful work he has been spared.

As the bibliographical material accumulated, it seemed best to make a separate chapter of nearly all that part of it which had to do with books and writers not referred to by our author himself. And as these dealt with the entire class of those phenomena of which some varieties are more particularly treated in this volume, it was thought proper to introduce the description of books by some general remarks upon the class.

The term *occult* was preferred to other designations of this class as a whole for reasons which appear in the chapter, and for this eighteenth chapter on *The Facts and Literature of the Occult* the present writer is alone responsible; so also for the statements of the *Bibliographical Index* that succeeds it, for some scattered footnotes of a similar sort, and for that portion of the *Appendix* not concerned with Chinese instances.

In these additions the aim has been to fulfill, so far as might be, the desires of the author, to make the book more useful to every reader, **and,** in some degree, to furnish for the student the critical apparatus that would facilitate original researches in this field. But the editor's work may be justly open to severer judgment than that done by the author.

Debarred from the latter's counsel by long distance, then by his death, having to work alone, without the stimulus of companionship in dealing with a gloomy and oppressive theme, in much bodily weakness, and with insufficient access to books, it would not be surprising if at some points the bounds of prudence were exceeded, or errors committed unawares. He can but hope that such errors, should they exist, may be charged to their proper source, and that nothing which he may have said or omitted shall impair the due effect of the author's words, or lessen the respectful attention which they receive.

HENRY W. RANKIN.

E. Northfield, Mass.
June 23, 1894.

Note for the Second Edition: For this edition corrections have been made in the type and text, material has been added to the footnotes and Appendix II., and a Supplementary Chapter, followed by extracts from reviews of the first edition.

May, 1896.

DEMON-POSSESSION

CHAPTER I

FIRST IMPRESSIONS AND EXPERIENCES

My first home in China was in the city of
Ningpo, in the province of Che-kiang, which
place we reached in the spring of 1854. My
first work was of course that of acquiring the
language. A native scholar, Mr. Tu, was engaged to serve me as a teacher. He was a
strong believer in the "supernatural," and when
we could understand each other through the
medium of his vernacular, spiritual manifestations and possessions formed a frequent subject of conversation. I brought with me to
China a strong conviction that a belief in demons, and communications with spiritual beings,
belongs exclusively to a barbarous and superstitious age, and at present can consist only
with mental weakness and want of culture. I
indulged Mr. Tu, however, in talking on his
favorite topics, because he did so with peculiar
fluency and zest, and thus elements of variety
and novelty were utilized in our severe and otherwise monotonous studies. But Mr. Tu's mar-

velous stories soon lost the charm of novelty. I
used my best endeavors, though with little success, to convince him that his views were the
combined result of ignorance and imagination.
I could not but notice, however, the striking resemblance between some of his statements of
alleged facts and the demonology of Scripture.
This resemblance I accounted for as only apparent or accidental, though it still left in my mind
an unpleasant regret that it was so strong, and
I should also add a feeling amounting almost to
a regret that such detailed statements should
have been recorded in the Bible.

In the summer of 1861, we removed from
Ningpo to the province of Shantung in northern
China.   There again I met with many evidences
of this same popular belief, which constantly
confronted us in the prosecution of our missionary work.

The first event in connection with this subject in Shantung, which I recall to mind, occurred in a country station of one of my col-
leagues, about the year 1868.   This colleague
was desirous of renting a native house to be
used as a chapel in the market town of Chang-
kia chwang, about thirty milles from Chefoo.
After many fruitless attempts to secure such a
place, he was surprised by the unexpected offer of
an excellent building in a very desirable location,
and on very reasonable terms.   Fearing that

delay might give rise to difficulties and obstructions he concluded the bargain at once. The articles of agreement were drawn up, and native Christians in his employ were immediately assigned to occupy and take charge of the premises. The next morning the new occupants found a crowd of curious neighbors awaiting their first appearance on the street, and were asked with an air of mysterious interest how they had slept, and if they had passed a comfortable night. It soon transpired that the Christians had been sleeping in a "haunted house." No one in the village had for some years dared to use the building for any purpose, which fact accounted for its having been so readily obtained.

So far there was nothing very remarkable in our having come into possession of a house supposed to be haunted, but the matter did not end here. Before night the occupants of a neighboring compound* came to see the Christians, informing them that the spirit had taken possession of one of the women in their family, and insisted upon taking up its abode with them, as it had been driven away from its former dwelling place by the presence of Christians, with whom it could not live. This family seemed to think they had a right to complain of this un-

* *Compound.* [Malay, *kompung*, a village.] In China and the East Indies an inclosure, containing a house, outbuildings &c. Webster,

welcome visitor having been thus foisted upon them. The native Christians replied that they would do what they could to rid the complainants of the spirit, and returned with them to their home taking with them a New Testament, and a Prayer printed in large characters as a placard. After they had prayed and read the Scriptures the woman supposed to be possessed, was restored to her normal condition. The Prayer was posted on the walls, and the frightened inmates of the house were exhorted to withstand and drive out the spirit in the name of Jesus. They were not troubled afterward, though the spirit was heard of trying to gain an entrance into other families in the neighborhood.

In the above statements the villagers generally, and the native preacher, and the persons principally concerned (some of whom have since become Christians) all concur. The event excited some interest in our mission circle for a time. It was accounted for as due, like other cases of "haunted houses," to fear and hallucination, and the subject was dismissed from our thoughts as unworthy of serious attention.

In the year 1871, or 1872, the following experiences were met with in the village of Chumao in the district of Ping-tu. There was a native school there in which was a boy named Liu, about twelve years of age, who was supposed to be at times possessed by an evil spirit. When the attacks occurred he would start and cry out with fear, as if conscious of some unseen presence, and then fall down insensible. On these occasions a woman in the village who was believed to be a spirit-medium, or exorcist, was immediately sent for. On the recurrence of one of these attacks another of the pupils ran to call the exorcist. On his way he met a man named Liu Chong-ho, who had recently been to Teng-chow fu, as an "enquirer," and had, after studying the Scriptures there for a month or more, been baptized. On learning the boy's errand he told him not to summon the exorcist, and at once returned with him to the school. Requiring all the pupils to kneel with him, he earnestly called on Jesus for help. Then turning to the prostrate boy he said in almost Scriptural words: "I command you in the name of Jesus Christ to come out of him!" The boy uttering a piercing cry, was at once restored to consciousness. I can say from personal knowledge that he never had another of those attacks from that day to this. Some years since he graduated from the high-school at Teng-chow fu; and is now a useful and efficient man. Both his parents have become Christians. Liu Chong--ho died in the autumn of 1888 of cholera. He had for more than fifteen years sustained the character of a worthy, steadfast Christian, and at the time of his death was an elder in the Chu-mao church. The teacher of the school, Li Ching-pu, who afterward became a Christian, fully corroborated the story.

It may be well to state that no Protestant missionary, so far as I know, has ever given native converts instructions as to casting out spirits; and few, if any, have dreamed that their converts would have the disposition, the ability, or the opportunity to do so. When converts have undertaken to do it, it has always been from an unsuggested spontaneous impulse, the natural result of reading the Scriptures and applying its teachings to their actual circumstances.

When the boy above referred to was interrogated as to the reason for his crying out, he said it was because the spirit in leaving him hurt him; and he showed the place on his side where he was injured. Those present at the time still declare that they saw the spot, and believed that it originated as represented. This event, though somewhat startling, was not regarded as furnishing in itself any conclusive evidence of spirit-possession, and but little importance was attached to it. We supposed the boy to be suffering from epileptic fits, or something of that nature.

During the few years immediately following we were from time to time perplexed by similar occurrences, noticeably by one related to me by the native teacher Li Ching-pu above referred to, and confirmed by many independent witnesses. It will be found given at length in Appendix A. This and other cases brought the subject of demon-possessions into practical relation with our work as missionaries. The question to be considered was, do cases of possession actually exist in China? If they do not, how are the phenomena to be accounted for, and by what means shall we convince the native Christians of their delusion? What attitude shall we instruct them to take with reference to the whole matter?

I made enquiries of the more intelligent of our converts and found that the most of them believed in the reality of these manifestations, and could give more or less definite information of cases in their families, or among their neighbors, of which they had been eye-witnesses. I determined in my evangelistic tours in the interior to investigate the matter as opportunities offered. In the district of Ping-tu, 150 miles southwest from Chefoo, the Christians pointed out village after village which had either persons supposed to be "possessed," or exorcists. I had thought it would be easy to obtain the information I required. But unexpected difficulties presented themselves. On making enquiries in the different villages, every person applied to declined giving information, and most of them declared their absolute ignorance of what I was talking about. I soon learned the reason of this. To have a case of spirit-possession in a family is, as a rule, regarded as not only a great misfortune, but also a disgrace. A man would be almost as unwilling to give information of this kind about a neighbor, especially to a foreigner, as to accuse him of theft without any personal grudge leading him to do so. Moreover, in this case he would not only fear the resentment of his neighbors, but still more that of the avenging demon. So I found the object of my pursuit a very *ignis-fatuus*, ever eluding my grasp as I approached it. I again, and not unwillingly, discontinued the investigation of the subject. It however often obtruded itself in the course of ensuing years; and in such a way as to make the reconsideration of it imperative.

CHAPTER II

EXPERIENCES IN CENTRAL SHANTUNG

In the spring of 1877 I took part in the work of famine-relief in Central Shantung, after which my mission-tours were extended farther westward, over the district covered by this famine.

During the summer of 1878 I received a letter from a native assistant, Mr. Leng, relating some experiences which he had met with in the mountainous district of Ling-ku; his account of which, in his own words, is as follows:

"While visiting the enquirers at 'Twin-Mountain Stream' I was told of a young man, of the family name Kwo, living in the village of Hingkia, who was suffering all sorts of inflictions from an evil spirit. I desired to see the man, and it was arranged that we should pay him a visit. We found Mr. Kwo at work in the fields, where I had a conversation with him, which was as follows: 'I have heard that you are troubled by an evil spirit.' He replied: 'It is true, and most humiliating. That I, a man in the full vigor of health, should be a slave to this demon, is the trial of my life; but there is no help for it.' I said: 'I assure you there is help.' 'What do you mean?' he asked. I replied: 'I will tell you. I am associated with a foreign teacher of Christianity, who often visits the region east of you. His object is to urge all men to worship the one true God, and to believe in Jesus Christ, the only heaven-appointed Saviour. Jesus Christ is all-merciful and all-powerful. It is His purpose to deliver us from the dominion of evil spirits; and they flee before Him.' 'But,' said Kwo, 'I have tried every thing, and in vain.' I said: 'You have not tried believing and trusting Jesus, and I assure you that if you will do this, and take Jesus to be your Saviour, the demon will leave you.' He replied: 'If what you say is true then I will believe in Jesus.' Seeing that he was sincere, I further exhorted and encouraged him. In the meantime we had reached his house, and he pointed out to me the shrine where he worshiped the demon. I then told him that the first thing to do was to tear away this shrine. To this he readily consented. After this we all knelt down praying the Saviour to protect and save him. I then gave Mr. Kwo directions how to acquire further knowledge of Christianity; and leaving with him a few Christian books I took my leave. As we separated he thanked us warmly for our visit."

After receiving this account from my native

helper, I looked forward with no little interest to seeing this man.

In the month of March, 1879, on my way to the village of the "Twin-Mountain Stream," Mr. Kwo, hearing of my approach, came out some distance on the road to meet me, and invited me to his house. Leaving my conveyance and luggage to go on to the inn by the main road, I accompanied him across the hills to his mountain home. On my way I learned further particulars of his previous life. He had never attended school, and until recently had been unable to read. Moreover, (and this is very unusual in China,) not a person in his village could read. He was a hardy mountaineer, thirty-eight years of age, bright and entertaining, with nothing in his appearance which could be regarded as unhealthy, or abnormal. It was late in the afternoon when I reached his home. I was at once introduced into the reception-room, which was the place where the evil spirit had formerly been worshiped.

I had scarcely seated myself when he called his little daughter, about ten years of age, to recite to me what she had learned. This bright child, who had never seen a foreigner, stood before me without the slightest appearance of shyness, and repeated page after page of a catechism specially prepared for Chinese enquirers, both question and answer, as fast as her tongue could go, evidently understanding what she said, on, on, half through the book, including the Ten Commandments, and the Lord's Prayer. Then she repeated selected passages of Scripture, and various forms of prayer, and also a number of hymns. When she could go no farther she stopped suddenly, saying: "That is as far as I have got!" When she had finished her recitation, her mother, a pleasant intelligent young woman with a child in her arms, came in, and she in turn went over the same lessons, and with the same correctness. On examining Mr. Kwo himself, I found that he had got on still further in these same studies.

This was only six months after Mr. Kwo had first heard of the religion of Jesus. Remembering his ignorance of the written language, and also that no one in his village could read, I enquired how it was possible for him to learn all this. The reply was: "On Sundays I go to worship with the Christians at the Shen-jen kwo (Home of the Genii) or at the 'Twin-Mountain Stream,' and sometimes one of the Christians comes to spend a day or two with me. Whenever I meet those who can teach me, I learn a little; and what I learn I teach my wife and daughter." He then went on to say: "I told my wife and daughter that I intended to ask you for baptism on this visit. They said: 'But you must not leave us behind.

We too wish to be baptized.' Now we are all here before you, and we request baptism." Having said this, he anxiously waited my decision. The answer immediately suggested to my mind was: "Can any man forbid water that these should not be baptized?"* And with no hesitation, though with some anxiety, I baptized the father, mother, little girl, and infant. The reception to the church of this family, under these novel circumstances, was an event of great interest to me. As the sun was setting I wended my way across the hills to the village of the "Twin-Mountain Stream," Kwo accompanying me as my guide.

After the services of the next day, which was Sunday, I requested Mr. Kwo to accompany me to the next preaching place; and then drew from him a fuller history of his experiences from the time when he first came under the control, as he supposed, of the evil spirit. I afterward had long conversations with his wife, and also conversed on the same subject at length with his father. All the different accounts supplement and confirm his own, and agree in every important particular. I give these statements as I received them. I offer no opinion of my own respecting the phenomena presented. Of course Mr. Kwo's statements respecting what he said and did when he was in a state of unconsciousness depend on the testimony of those

* Acts x; 47.

about him.   The story, in his own words, is as follows:

"Near the close of year before last (1877) I bought a number of pictures, including one of Wang Mu-niang, the wife of Yu-hwang, (the chief divinity of China). For the goddess Wang Mu-niang I selected the most honorable position in the house; the others I pasted on the walls here and there, as ornaments.   On the second day of the first month I proposed worshiping the goddess; but my wife objected.   The next night a spirit came, apparently in a dream, and said to me: 'I am Wang Mu-niang, of Yuin-men san, (the name of a neighboring mountain). I have taken up my abode in your house.'   It said this repeatedly.   I had awakened and was conscious of the presence of the spirit.   I knew it was a *shie-kwei*, (evil spirit), and as such I resisted it, and cursed it, saying: 'I will have nothing to do with you.'   This my wife heard, and begged to know what it meant, and I told her.   After this all was quiet, and I was not disturbed for some days.   About a week afterward a feeling of uneasiness and restlessness came over me, which I could not control.   At night I went to bed as usual, but grew more and more restless.   At last, seized by an irresistible impulse, I arose from my bed and went straight to a gambler's den in Kao-kia, where I lost at once 16,000 cash, (sixteen dollars, a large sum for a peasant Chinaman). I started for home, and lost my way. But when it grew light I got back to my house. At that time I was conscious of what I was doing and saying, but I did things mechanically, and soon forgot what I had said. I did not care to eat, and only did so when urged to. After some days a gambler from Kao-kia came and asked me to go with him, which I did; and this time I lost 25,000 cash. On the fifteenth and sixteenth of the first month, I went to Pe-ta where there was a theatre. The same night I again lost 13,000 cash in gambling. The next morning I returned home, and just as I was entering my village I fell down frothing at the mouth and unconscious; and was carried to my house. Medicine was given me which partially restored me to consciousness. The next day I dressed myself and attempted to run away from home, but I soon found myself staggering; everything grew dark, and I rushed back to my room. I soon became violent, attacking all who ventured near me. My father hearing the state of things came from his home to see me. As he entered I seized a fowling-piece, which I had secreted under my bed, and fired it at him. Fortunately the charge went over his head into the ceiling. With the help of the neighbors my father bound me with chains, and took me to his home in Chang-yiu. A doctor was called who, after giving me large doses of medicine without effect, left, refusing to have anything more to do with me. For five or six days I raved wildly, and my friends were in great distress. They proposed giving me more medicine, but the demon, speaking through me, replied: 'Any amount of medicine will be of no use.' My mother then asked: 'If medicine is of no use, what shall we do?' The demon replied: 'Burn incense to me, and submit yourself to me, and all will be well.' My parents promised to do this, and knelt down and worshiped the demon, begging it to torment me no longer. Thus the matter was arranged, I all the time remaining in a state of unconsciousness. About midnight I attempted to leave the house. The attendants followed me, brought me back, and bound me again. Then my parents a second time worshiped the demon, begging it to relieve me from my sufferings, and renewing their promise that I myself should hereafter worship and serve it. I then recovered consciousness, and my mother told me all that had happened, and of the promise they had made for me. On my refusing consent to this, I again lost all consciousness. My mother besought the favor of the demon, renewing her promise to insist upon my obedience, and I again recovered consciousness. In their great distress my father and mother implored me to fulfill their promise, and worship the evil spirit;

and at last I reluctantly consented. The demon had directed that we should call a certain woman in Kao-chao who was a spirit-medium, to give us directions in putting in order our place for worship. So all was arranged, and on the first and fifteenth of each month we burnt incense, offered food, and made the required prostrations before the shrine on which the picture of the goddess was placed. The spirit came at intervals, sometimes every few days, and sometimes after a period of a month or more. At these times I felt a fluttering of the heart, and a sense of fear and inability to control myself, and was obliged to sit or lie down. I would tell my wife when these symptoms came on, and she would run for a neighboring woman less timid than herself, and they two burned incense to the demon in my stead, and received its directions, which they afterward communicated to me, for though spoken by my lips I had been entirely unconscious of them. The demon often bade us not to be afraid of it, saying it would not injure us, but that, on the contrary, it would help us in various ways; that it would instruct me in the healing art, so that people would flock to me to be cured of their diseases. This proved to be true; and soon from my own village the people came bringing their children to be healed by the aid of the demon. Sometimes it would cure the sick instantaneously, and with-

out the use of medicine. Sometimes it would
not respond when first summoned, and when it
did appear would say it had been absent in such
and such places; but it never said on what
business. Many diseases were not under its
control, and it seemed as if it could perfectly
cure only such as were inflicted by spirits. My
own child had long been ill, and I invoked the
demon, but it did not come. The child died.

"The demon said he had many inferior
spirits subject to him. He also frequently indicated his plan for my future life and employ-
ment. It was that through his assistance I
should grow more and more skilled in healing
diseases. The people would soon be willing to
make a return for my services. In time of
harvest I should go about from family to family
getting contributions of grain, and these contributions as they accumulated should be applied
to the support of the neighboring temple."

I would remark that Mr. Kwo's own account
of Leng's visit exactly corresponded with that
given above. Mr. Kwo, however, added the
following. Said he: "The death of our child
occurred a few days after we had torn down the
spirit's shrine. My wife was much distressed,
believing it was in consequence of my having
offended the demon. She urged me to restore
the shrine and resume the worship. I told her
that whatever might happen I would not break

my vow to worship and trust in Jesus. A few days after that the demon returned and, speaking through me, of course, a conversation ensued between it and my wife, which was as follows: 'We understood that you were not to return. How is it that you have come back again?' The demon replied: 'I have returned but for one visit. If your husband is determined to be a Christian this is no place for me. But I wish to tell you I had nothing to do with the death of your child.' 'What do you know of Jesus Christ'? they asked. The answer was: 'Jesus Christ is the great Lord over all; and now I am going away and you will not see me again.' This, said Mr. Kwo, was actually the last visit; and we have not been troubled since."

The above is a full account of Mr. Kwo's case up to the spring of 1879. In October of that year I visited him again. Arriving at his house after a long and tiresome journey I requested him after our evening meal to conduct the usual family worship. He opened the Bible and read with fluency and accuracy the fourteenth chapter of St. John's Gospel; and then followed a prayer, the simplicity, appropriateness, and earnestness of which surprised me greatly. On the next day, which was Sunday, I baptized nine adults in his house. They were from neighboring villages and had received their instruction in Christianity chiefly from him. His home had already become an independent centre of religious interest.

I have given this case particularly, because I am familiarly acquainted with the persons concerned in it; and to show its intimate connection with the progress of Christianity in that neighborhood.

It is now (1892) fourteen years since Mr. Kwo was baptized. Persecutions have tried the faith of the whole company of Christians in that neighborhood. Mr. Kwo's father, after suffering severe losses in business, took to strong drink, and died, leaving his family in considerably reduced circumstances. Under the combined influence of old habits, evil and idolatrous associations, persecutions, and poverty, many of the Christians in that vicinity grew cold, and gave up the outward observance of Christian duties; though most of them still profess to be believers in Christianity. Mr. Kwo continued to be one of the most reliable and useful men in that region. He also grew more familiar with the Bible and Christian truth. He has his faults, as others have, but he is a decided and outspoken Christian, and his is a happy Christian home. Neither he nor his neighbors think of doubting that he was rescued from the dominion of an evil spirit through faith and trust in Christ.

During the last two years, interest in Christianity has greatly revived in Mr. Kwo's neighborhood, and there have been large accessions to the church, not a few of whom received their first religious impressions in the church in Mr. Kwo's house.

In 1889, Mr. Kwo, in company with many other emigrants from Central Shantung, removed with his family to the province of Shen-Si to take up cheap lands left vacant by the ravages of the famine of 1877. His leaving was a matter of much regret on the part of his foreign teachers, and the native Christians associated with him. For many months we could obtain no information concerning him, and fears were entertained that he had perished by the way as many of the emigrants did. We received letters from him in 1890 stating that he had found a new home, that he wanted for nothing; and that he had commenced a new work for Christ, and had a little company of neighbors, and newly formed acquaintances, **worshiping with him in his house every Sunday.**

CHAPTER III

EXPERIENCES IN SHANTUNG: CONTINUED

Early in the summer of 1879 I heard from the native assistant, Leng, of a case of supposed "possession," in which he had failed to afford relief. This failure he attributed to want of faith. At my request he gave me an account of the case, which, in his own words, is as follows:

"This spring when I was at Tse-kia chwang, in the district of Shiu-kwang, I was giving the Christians there an account of the case of Mr. Kwo at Hing-kia, when an enquirer present said: 'We have a similar case here.' It was that of a woman, also named Kwo. She was thirty-two years of age, and had suffered from this infliction eight years. It happened that at the time of my visit the woman was suffering more than usual. Her husband, in the hope that the demon would not disturb his wife in the house of a Christian, had brought her to the home of his brother-in-law, Mr. Sen, who had lately professed Christianity. On my arrival they said to me: 'She is here, on the opposite side of the court,' and they begged me to cast out the spirit; as they had tried every method they knew of without effect. Then without waiting for my assent, they brought the woman into the room where I was. I said: 'I have no power to do anything of myself. We must ask God to help us.' While we knelt in prayer the woman was lying on the *k'ang*, apparently unconscious. When the prayer was finished she was sitting up, her eyes closed, with a fluttering motion of the eyelids, her countenance like one weeping, and the fingers of both hands tightly clenched. She would allow no one to straighten her closed fingers. I then, hardly expecting an answer, as the woman had hitherto been speechless, said to the demon: 'Have you no fear of God? Why do you come here to afflict this woman?' To this I received instantly the following reply:

'Tien-fu Yia-su puh kwan an,
Wo tsai che-li tsih pa nian,
Ni iao nien wo, nan shang nan,
Pi iao keh wo pa-shin ngan.'

[Translation]:

'God and Christ will not interfere. I have been here seven or eight years; and I claim this as my resting-place. You cannot get rid of me.'

She continued for some time uttering a succession of rhymes similar to the above, without

* The earthen bed of North China.

the slightest pause; the purport of them all being: 'I want a resting-place, and I'll not leave this one.' The utterances were so rapid that the verse given above was the only one I could remember perfectly. I can recall another line: 'You are men, but I am *shien*,' (i. e. one of the genii). After repeating these verses, evidently extemporized for the occasion, a person present dragged her back to her apartments—the demon not having been exorcised.

Mr. Leng revisited this region in the month of August. His further, and more satisfactory experiences in connection with this case, I also give in his own words:

"I was attending service one Sunday at a village called Wu-kia-miao-ts, two miles from Tse-kia chwang, and Mr. Sen from the latter village was present. Noticing in Mr. Sen's hand a paper parcel I enquired what it contained, and was told that it contained cinnabar. This is a medicine which is much used for the purpose of expelling evil spirits. Mr. Sen said he had procured it to administer to the possessed woman, Mrs. Kwo, who was suffering from her malady very severely. I then spoke to the Christians present as follows: 'We are worshipers of the true God. We ought not to use the world's methods for exorcising demons, but rather appeal to God only. The reason why we did not succeed before was our want of faith. This is our sin.' I went on to tell them how willing God is to answer prayer, referring to my own experience in the famine region, when, reduced almost to starvation, I prayed to God for help, and was heard and rescued. I asked those present if they would join me in prayer for Mrs. Kwo, and they all did so. After this I set out for Tse-kia chwang in company with two other Christians.

"While this was transpiring at Wu-kia-miao-ts the Christians at Tse-kia chwang were attempting to hold their customary Sunday service; but Mrs. Kwo (or the demon possessing her) was determined to prevent it. She raved wildly, and springing upon the table threw the Bibles and hymn-books on the floor. The wife of a younger Mr. Sen, who was a Christian, then became similarly affected; and the two women were raving together. They were heard saying to each other: 'Those three men are coming here, and have got as far as the stream.' Some one asked: 'Who are coming?' The woman replied with great emphasis: 'One of them is that man Leng.' As I was not expected to visit that place until a few days later, a daughter of the family said: 'He will not be here to-day.' To which the demon replied: 'If he does not come here to-day, then I am no *shien*. They are now crossing the stream, and will reach here when the sun is about so high,'

3 *Demon*

and she pointed to the west. No one could
have known, in the ordinary way, that we were
coming, as our visit was not thought of until
just before starting. Moreover the two men
who went with me were from different villages,
at a considerable distance in opposite directions,
and had had no previous intention of accompanying me. When we arrived at the village a
large company were assembled at Mr. Sen's
house, attracted by the disturbance, and curious to see the result of it. After a time I went
into the north building where the two raving
women were sitting together on the *k'ang*. I
addressed the demon possessing them as follows: 'Do you not know that the members of
this family are believers in the true God, and
that this is a place used for his worship? You
are not only disturbing the peace of this house,
but you are fighting against God. If you do not
leave, we will immediately call upon God to
drive you out.' The younger of the two women
then said to the other: 'Let us go—let us go!'
The other drew back on the *k'ang* angrily saying: 'I'll not go! I'll stay and be the death of
this woman!' I then said with great vehe-
mence: 'You evil, malignant spirit! You have
not the power of life and death; and you cannot intimidate us by your vain threats. We will
now call upon God to drive you out.' So the
Christians all knelt to pray. The bystanders

say that during the prayer the two possessed persons, awakening as if from sleep, looked about, and seeing us kneeling, quietly got down from the *k'ang* and knelt beside us. When we rose from prayer we saw the women still kneeling; and soon after Mrs. Kwo arose and came forward greeting us naturally and politely, evidently quite restored." Here ends Mr. Leng's narrative.

I myself visited the place in the month of October in company with Rev. J. A. Leyenberger, at which time Mrs. Kwo asked for baptism. As she gave evidence of sincerity and faith in Christ, she was baptized, together with thirteen others. As far as I know she has had no return of her malady.

The statements of Mr. Leng, as given above, were confirmed by minute examinations of all the parties concerned, and their testimony was clear and consistent. No one in the village or neighborhood doubts the truth of the story; nor do they regard it as anything specially strange or remarkable.

Mrs. Kwo is highly esteemed in her neighborhood, and has, since her baptism, been regarded by all who know her as an intelligent and consistent Christian. She is a woman of pleasing manners, and a retiring disposition, apparently in good health, and there is nothing unnatural or peculiar in her appearance. For nearly two

years after her baptism, threatened returns of
her old malady gave her and her friends no little
anxiety. She says that she was frequently conscious of the presence of the evil spirit seeking
to gain his former control over her, and was
almost powerless to resist the unseen influence
which she felt threatening her. At such times
she at once fell on her knees and appealed to
Christ for help, which she never failed to receive. She says that these returns of the demon
became less and less frequent and persistent,
and after a time ceased altogether. Mrs. Kwo
has never in her normal condition shown any
aptitude for improvising verses, and I presume
could not now compose a single stanza.

The morning following the baptism of Mrs.
Kwo, one of the Christians in the village informed my traveling companion, Mr. Leyenberger, and myself, that a woman living in a
neighboring house, who was a spirit-medium,
was then under the influence of a demon, and
was improvising verses referring to us. We
enquired the character and history of the woman,
and received the following reply: "She was in
your audience yesterday morning. She has
frequently come to our services, and was for a
time much interested in hearing about Christianity. But she said that she always felt distressed after being at our meetings, and on that
account she had ceased attending them. There

had been a struggle in her mind between a desire to be a Christian, and the influence of the demon which controlled her; between a sense of right and duty, and her unwillingness to give up the gains of her business as a spirit-medium. She spends her time going about among the villages in the neighborhood telling fortunes, and healing diseases, and in this way makes a good deal of money for the support of herself and family."

We were desirous of seeing this woman, especially as her case resembled Mrs. Kwo's in the particular of extemporising verses. After some hesitation and delay we were allowed to enter. As we approached we heard the measured cadences of the woman's monotonous chant, which, we were told, had already continued for more than an hour. Entering the house we saw her lying on the *k'ang*. Her appearance was that of a corpse; the face expressionless, and no part of the body stirred except the lips and tongue; which were giving forth utterances with the rapidity and uniformity of clockwork. Everything she said was in measured verse, and was chanted to an unvarying tune. The first half of each verse seemed like the meaningless chants heard in Buddhist temples; but the latter half was evidently impromptu, and referred to us, and the Christian religion, and our work as missionaries. Her voice never faltered, and she never hesitated an instant for a word. The rapid, prefectly uniform, and long continued utterances, seemed to us such as could not possibly be counterfeited, or premeditated. Her daughter-in-law, at our suggestion, tried to arouse her, calling her loudly by name. But it seemed like talking to the dead. Her respiration was natural, and her pulse full and regular, the skin neither dry nor moist; and there was not the slightest evidence of fever or excitement. Her arm when lifted fell down again entirely limp. After watching her for some minutes we went to attend morning prayers with the Christians. On our return she presented exactly the same appearance, but her utterances had ceased, and she was speechless, motionless, and apparently unconscious. Her daughter-in-law told us that it was useless trying to awaken her; but that sooner or later she would come back to consciousness herself. We were told that later in the day she roused and went about her work. Not many months after this she died.

On the eleventh of October, 1879, at Shin-tsai, in the district of Ling-ku, I was conversing with a simple-minded countryman who was an applicant for baptism, when the subject of demoniacal possessions was brought up very incidentally and unexpectedly. I asked the enquirer: "Have you met any opposition in your family in consequence of your desire to be a

Christian?" He replied: "I have from one source; my sister-in-law has for many years been possessed by a demon, and the demon objects to my being a Christian, and so my sister-in-law is afraid, and advises me against it." "What does the demon say?" I asked. He replied: "It said: 'If you believe in, and worship Jesus, this is no place for me. I must leave.' I said to it: 'I was not aware that I was interfering with you, or your interests. I believe Christianity to be the true doctrine; and I trust in Christ for salvation and eternal life; and I do not want to give up Christianity.' The demon replied: 'It may be very good for you; but it is very bad for us!'"

Then I went on to question the man; "How do you know that it was a *demon*?" "Why," he replied, "it spoke!" "Was it not your sister-in-law who spoke?" "No, my sister-in-law knew nothing about it; she was unconscious. She was frightened when she heard of it." "Had not the demon been in the habit of speaking?" I asked. He replied: "Only once—years ago. Then it told her that when she arrived at the age of thirty-six, it wanted her to heal diseases." I asked again: "If she did not speak when the demon came to her, what did she do?" He answered: "She only breathed hard, and was unconscious."

The narrator of this incident was a few months

later baptized.   Some years after the sister-in-law and her husband were also admitted to church-membership.   There has been no return of the malady—whatever it was.   Though extremely poor, they are intelligent and sincere Christians.

CHAPTER IV

CIRCULAR LETTER AND RESPONSES

The experiences detailed in the preceding chapters made more imperative the duty of forming an intelligent opinion respecting these manifestations, in order to determine what position should be taken with reference to them in my intercourse with native Christians and helpers. With the view of gaining information and assistance from missionaries in other parts of China, the following Circular was issued, and sent to the various Protestant missions. A corresponding Circular in Chinese was sent to the native Christians.

To Protestant Missionaries engaged in the work of Christ, Greeting: Dear Brethren:
The subject of demon-possession has for some years past been constantly forced upon my attention in connection with missionary work, and the founding of Christian churches. I am desirous of learning from missionaries in other fields how far their experience corresponds with my own in this part of China; what the real nature of these manifestations is; and what les-

sons we are to learn from them. I should be much obliged for answers to the following questions, or for general information, either in English or Chinese, bearing on this subject. Will you kindly forward the enclosed Chinese circulars to any intelligent and reliable native Christians, who, you think, would be able and disposed to assist in this matter.

I. Are cases of supposed demoniacal possession common in your locality or not?

II. Are the subjects of them persons constitutionally weak and unhealthy, or those in whom the functions of body and mind are in other respects normal?

III. Do you know cases in which these manifestations are certainly involuntary, or where the subject is averse to them, and strives to be free from them?

IV. Please state minutely the symptoms of these cases.

V. Are these manifestations uniform, or do they vary? And if they vary, how may they be distinguished and classified?

VI. To what agent or agents are they ascribed?

VII. In supposed cases of demon-possession in which the subject gives forth utterances apparently proceeding from a different personality, is there any conclusive proof that this is really the case? Does the subject retain a recollection, after passing from one of these abnormal states, of what he has said or done while in it?

VIII. What are the methods by which heathen Chinese exorcise demons; and how far are they effectual?

IX. In what way do Christians cast out spirits; and how far are they successful?

X. Is this undertaken by Christians generally, or only by certain individuals, who seem specially disposed and enabled to do it? If this is done by a particular sort of Christians, how do they differ from others?

XI. Do you know cases in which excluded church-members, or those who have afterwards been excluded, have cast out evil spirits? *

XII. Where cases of supposed demon-possession have occurred, has their influence on the church appeared to be injurious or the contrary?

XIII. Do you know of exemplary Christians who have been the subject of supposed demon-possession?

Will you be so good as to give in detail the history of any supposed case or cases of demon-possession, bringing out the answers to the above questions, or presenting other phases of the subject not suggested by them; giving names of persons, and places, and dates?

I especially desire distinct and authentic statements from eye and ear witnesses.

Hoping that you will favor me with the re-

---

* This question refers to the statements in Matt. VII; 22, 23.

sults of your observations and experience in this matter,

I remain yours in the fellowship of the Gospel,

JOHN L. NEVIUS.

Chefoo, September 1879.

In answer to this circular communications were received from all parts of China; of which a selection giving a good representation of the .whole, will be found in this and the following chapters. The number connected with a paragraph designates it as an answer to the question of the same number in the above circular.

REV. J. L. NEVIUS, D.D.

Dear Bro:—

In accordance with your recent circular I send you enclosed a paper prepared by my native teacher, on the subject of demon-possession; which I hope will give you the desired information with regard to that matter here. It (i. e. supposed demon-possession) is very common in our mission field, especially that part with which I have been recently connected; and, had I the requisite time, I would write out what I know of the matter. However, I may be able to send you other papers on the subject from well-informed natives here. I am very busy in view of a contemplated visit to the United States in a few weeks.

I remain in haste,

Very sincerely yours,

W. J. PLUMB.

Missionary of the American Methodist Board.

Literal translation of the communication from Mr. Plumb's teacher, Chen Sin Ling.

"To the Teacher Ni Greetings:

I write in reply to a circular asking for information respecting possessions by spirits. I am a native of the district city of Chang-lo. I was reared in the provincial capital (Fu-chow). From a child I have attended school, and given myself to study. I was first a Confucianist, and afterward entered the religion of Jesus. Of late years I have been connected with different foreign missionaries as a scribe. Being quite willing to communicate anything I know on the subject, I hereby give you a statement of what I have myself seen and heard; following the order of your questions.

I. As to cases of possession in the province of Fukien in general, I know but little, and have no opportunity of knowing. In the city of Fu-chow cases are met with occasionally. They are more numerous in the villages. In the district of Tu-ch'ing they are exceedingly common. There are many also in the district of Chang-lo.

These cases are familiarly called Fan Hu-li (In-flictions by the fox). *

II.　When a man is thus afflicted, the spirit (*kwei*) takes possession of his body without re-gard to his being strong or weak in health. It is not easy to resist the demon's power. Though without bodily ailments, possessed persons ap-pear as if ill. When under the spell of the de-mon they seem different from their ordinary selves.

III.　In most cases the spirit takes posssesion of man's body contrary to his will, and he is helpless in the matter. The *kwei* has the power of driving out the man's spirit, as in sleep or dreams. When the subject awakes to con-sciousness he has not the slightest knowledge of what has transpired.

IV.　The actions of possessed persons vary exceedingly. They leap about and toss their arms, and then the demon tells them what par-ticular spirit he is, deceitfully calling himself a god, or one of the genii come down to the abodes of mortals. Or it professes to be the spirit of a deceased husband or wife, or a *hu-sien ye* (one of the fox fraternity.) There are also *kwei* (demons) of the quiet sort who talk and laugh like other people, only that the voice is changed. Some have a voice like a bird. Some speak

* It is believed by the Chinese that demons are specially fond of pos-sessing the bodies of foxes and weasels, and that demons possessing men are also connected with foxes. So in Japan. See p. 104.

Mandarin, * and some the local dialect; but though the speech proceeds from the mouth of the man, what is said does not appear to come from him. The outward appearance and manner are also changed.

In Fu-chow there is a class of persons who collect in large numbers, and make use of incense, pictures, candles, and lamps, to establish what are called "Incense-tables." Tao-ist priests are engaged to attend to the ceremonies, and they also make use of "mediums." The Tao-ist writes a charm for the medium, who taking the incense stick in his hand stands still like a graven image, thus signifying his willingness to have the demon come and take possession of him. Afterwards the charm is burned, and the demon is worshiped and invoked, the priest in the meanwhile going on with his chanting. After a while the medium begins to tremble, and then speaks and announces what spirit has descended, and asks what is wanted of him. Then whoever has requests to make, takes incense sticks, worships, and makes prostrations, speaking of himself as "*ti-ts*," (follower or pupil) and asks a response respecting some disease, or for protection from calamity, etc. In winter the same performances are carried on to a great extent by gambling companies. If some of the responses hit the mark a large number of people are

* Mandarin is the spoken language of the northern provinces of China, and is quite different from the language of the province of Fukien from which this communication comes.

attracted.   They also establish a shrine and offer sacrifices, and appoint days calling upon people from every quarter to come and consult the demon respecting diseases, etc.

There is another practice called *Kiang-lan*. *
They take a forked branch of a willow, attach to it a pencil, and place beneath it a large platter covered with sand. There are two persons supporting the branch, one on each side, for the purpose of writing. They then burn charms, and worship, and invoke the demon; after which the pen moves tracing characters on the sand.

There is also a class of men, who establish what they call a "Hall of Revelations." At the present time there are many engaged in this practice. They are for the most part literary men of great ability. The people in large numbers apply to them for responses. The mediums spoken of above are also numerous. All the above practices are not spirits seeking to possess men, but men seeking spirits to possess them, and allowing themselves to be voluntarily used as their instruments.

V.   As to the outward appearance of persons when possessed, of course they are the same persons as to outward form, as at ordinary times; but the color of the countenance may change, the demon may cause the subject to assume a threatening air, and a fierce, violent

---

* This is nearly equivalent to Planchette. Compare Proceedings of the Psychical Society, 1888, and Epes Sargent's book *Planchette*.

manner. The muscles stand out on the face, the eyes are closed, or they protrude with a frightful stare. Sometimes the possessed person pierces his face with an awl, or cuts his tongue with a knife. In all these mad performances the object of the demon is to frighten people. Their actions need to be carefully watched in order rightly to interpret them.

VI. As to the question: "Who are those spirits supposed to be?" The names by which they are called are very numerous, and it is difficult to give a full account of them. Some are called Shin (gods); as for instance U-hwang, or Tai-san, or Ching-hwang, and in fact any of the whole host of deities. Others are called genii, and their names are associated with Tao-ism, as for instance Lu-tsu and a great many others. Beside this they falsely assume the name of the god of medicine, or of deities who preside over cattle and horses, etc., etc. When they take possession of a man, if they personate a scholar, they affect a mild and graceful literary air; if they personate men of warlike reputation, they assume an air of resolution and authority. They first announce their name, and then act so that men will recognize them, as being what they profess to be.

VII. The words spoken certainly proceed from the mouths of the persons possessed; but what is said does not appear to come from their

4 *Demon*

minds or wills, but rather from some other personality, often accompanied by a change of voice; of this there can be no doubt. When the subject returns to consciousness he invariably declares himself ignorant of what he has said.

VIII. The Chinese make use of various methods to cast out demons. They are so vexed and troubled by inflictions affecting bodily health, or it may be the moving about or destruction of family utensils, that they are driven to call in the services of some respected scholar, or Taoist priest, to offer sacrifices, or chant sacred books, and pray for protection and exemption from suffering. Some make use of sacrifices and offerings of paper clothes and money in order to induce the demon to go back to the gloomy region of "Yang-chow." Or a more thorough method is adopted; as for instance using peach branches and willow branches, or the blood of different animals, and charmed water to drive them away. Some also profess to seize them and confine them in bottles. As to whether these methods have any effect, I do not know. As a rule, when demons are not very troublesome, the families afflicted by them generally think it best to keep them quiet by sacrifices, and burning incense to them.

IX. Christians are occasionally invited to families where there are possessed persons, where they simply read the Scriptures, sing hymns, and pray to God. They know of no other method of expelling demons. When this is done the afflicted person gains relief for the time, though it is not certain that the cure will be permanent. But if he sincerely believes the truth, and enters the Christian religion, there is very little fear of the demon's giving him further trouble. In the district of Tu-ching the number of those who for this cause have become Christians is very great. They speak of the demons from which they have suffered as "Spirits of mad foxes." As to whether they are right in this supposition, I do not know.

X. As to there being any difference among Christians as to their ability to cast out devils, I suppose they are all alike. It is simply this: If any Christian prays to God with true faith in Christ, the desired help will be granted.

XI. I presume unworthy Christians and those who have been excommunicated would not be able to cast out demons, though I do not know much about this.

XII. In the spread of the Gospel, if cases of possession are met with, and Christians are able through faith in Christ to cast out the demons, the effect would certainly be favorable to Christianity.

XIII. Near my home there have certainly been cases of possessed persons becoming Christians. As to whether they will continue true and faithful it is impossible to say—God only knows. I have heard that in the district of Tu-ching there are many of this class. In my native district, Chang-lo, there is a man who was formerly possessed by a demon. He believed in Christ, and entered the Christian religion, and was entirely relieved from the control of the demon. He afterwards turned aside from the truth, gave up his Christian profession, and the demon returned and tormented him until his death."

Other communications received from different provinces containing full answers to the several questions of the circular so closely resemble the preceding that they need not be given in full. Some extracts from them may be of interest as presenting new phases of the subject, or giving further Chinese testimony on some points of special interest.

Extracts from Wang Wu-Fang's answer to the circular.

(Mr. Wang Wu-Fang is a well-known and greatly respected native helper connected with the English Baptist Mission of Shan-tung.)

II. Cases of demon-possession are found among persons of robust health, as well as those who are weak and sickly.

III. In many unquestionable cases of possession the unwilling subjects have resisted; but have been obliged to submit themselves to the control of the demon.

IV.   In many cases of possession the first symptoms occur during sleep, in dreams.   The subject is given to weeping.   When asked a question he answers in a word or two, and then falls to weeping again.   He perhaps asks that incense, or paper money may be burned, or for other sacrificial offerings; or he complains of heat or cold.   When you give the demon what it wants the patient recovers.   In a majority of cases of possession the beginning of the malady is a fit of grief or anger.   The outward manifestations are apt to be fierce and violent.   It may be that the subject alternately talks and laughs; he walks awhile and then sits; or he rolls on the ground, or leaps about; or exhibits contortions of the body, and twistings of the neck. Before we became Christians, it was common among us to send for exorcists who made use of written charms, or chanted verses, or punctured the body with needles.   These are the Chinese methods of cure.

V.   Demons are of different kinds.   There are those which clearly declare themselves, and those who work in secret.   There are those which are cast out with difficulty, and others with ease.

VI.   In cases of possession by demons what is said by the subject certainly does not proceed from his own will.   When the demon has gone out, and the subject recovers consciousness, he has no recollection whatever of what he has said or done.   This is true invariably.

VII.   The methods by which Chinese cast out demons are, enticing them to leave by burning charms, and paper money; or by begging and exhorting them; or by frightening them with magic spells and incantations; or driving them away by pricking with needles, or pinching with the fingers, in which case they cry out and promise to go.

VIII.   I was formerly accustomed to drive out demons by means of needles.   At that time cases of possession by evil-spirits were very common in our village, and my services were in frequent demand.   After I became a Christian these cases rapidly diminished, and finally almost disappeared.   When persons from adjacent villages called upon me as before to cast out spirits, it was difficult to know what I ought to do.   I could not, as a Christian, follow the former method, so I declined to go.   But the elders of the villages would not let me off.   On one occasion I told them the demon might perhaps be cast out merely by prayer for God's help.   They replied that they were quite willing I should use whatever method I preferred.   I was not sure that I should be successful, but I determined to try.   When I arrived at the man's house I commenced singing a hymn; and the person possessed immediately cried out, and covered his head. Before the close of the prayer which followed he had recovered.

There was another case which I met with on the twenty-fifth day of the first month of the present year (1880). The subject, who was twenty-three years old, was the wife of the second son of Li Mao-lin. When under the influence of the demon she was wild and unmanageable. This continued six days without intermission. The family applied to "*Wu-po*" (mediums, literally female magicians,) and persons who effected cures by needles; but without success. They were at their wits' end, and, all other means having failed, a person named Li Tso-yuen came and applied to me. I declined going, but he urged me at least to go and look at her, which I consented to do. When we entered the house, she was surrounded by a crowd of people and her noisy demonstrations had not ceased. When they learned that we were approaching, the people present opened a way for us, and the possessed woman at once took a seat, began adjusting her hair and wonderingly asked: "Why are there so many people here?" Her husband told her what she had been doing for several days past. She exclaimed in a surprised way: "I know nothing about it." The people thought it very remarkable that she should be restored as soon as I entered the house; and I, of course, was very thankful for the result. From this time the fame of Christianity rapidly spread, and there were many accessions to the church.

More than ten days after this, the woman had another attack; and they again sent for me. I went to the place accompanied by another Christian. As we entered, she recovered as before, and sat up; to all appearances quite well. We availed ourselves of this opportunity to preach to the family for a long time. On our way home my friend delightedly exclaimed: "Even the devils are subject to us!" *

Ten days afterward, during the night, we heard a loud knocking at the door. It was a messenger from Li Tsoyuen, who informed us that the possessed woman was worse than ever; that her face was purple, her body rigid, her skin cold, her respiration difficult, and her life almost extinct. I called a Bible student who was near by to accompany me. He was an earnest Christian, and I supposed that on our arrival at the house the demon would leave as before. To our surprise the woman remained rigid and motionless, as dead. The sight frightened us, and we betook ourselves to prayer. Presently she turned her head away from us, seeing which, the family were delighted, and cried out together: "She has come to life again!" We then sang a hymn. When we had finished,

* Luke x, 17.

the woman drew a long breath, and was soon restored. Her sister-in-law asked her many questions. She had no recollection of what had occurred. The sister-in-law said to me: "The demon knew your name, and said, the previous time, that when you came it would leave; and when you should return home, it would come back again: How is this?" I replied: "Believers in Christ can cast out devils. If you should believe, the demon would be afraid of you." The family then asked for Christian books, which I promised, and afterward sent them. After this time the demon did not return. This is an account of my own experience.

IX. As to excommunicated church-members casting out spirits, I know nothing. If they have not entire faith, they certainly cannot.

X. In our preaching, to be able to tell people that in our holy religion there is the power to cast out demons, and heal diseases, thus manifesting the love and mercy of God, is certainly a great help to the spread of the Gospel.

XI. In the village of Ta Wang-kia there is a man named Wang Pan-hu who was possessed of an evil spirit; but was entirely relieved after becoming a Christian. I know also other similar cases, of which I cannot now make a full record. These have all come under my personal knowledge."

Translation of extracts from a communication of Wang Yung-ngen of Peking.

After referring briefly to a case of possession which he had met with, he adds:

I.   "I have known many other cases which it is unnecessary to record in full.   It may be said in general of possessed persons, that sometimes people who cannot sing, are able when possessed to do so; others who ordinarily cannot write verses, when possessed compose in rhyme with ease.   Northern men will speak languages of the south, and those of the east the language of the west; and when they awake to consciousness they are utterly oblivious of what they have done.

IV.   Cases of possession are less frequent in peaceful times, and more frequent in times of civil commotion; less frequent in prosperous families, more so in unlucky ones; less frequent among educated people, and more so among the ignorant.

V.   The varieties of outward manifestations of demons are very numerous, and their transformations remarkable.   The same demon will transform itself into any number of manifestations; so that it is very difficult to comprehend them.   This is what they are specially noted for."

Below are given translations of a few extracts from a communication from an excommunicated church-member, and former preacher, Chung Yuen-shing.   This man is believed by native

Christians who know him to have in former years cast out devils. These extracts taken from his paper are given principally to present his views on question eleven.

XI. "If imperfect Christians or excommunicated persons meet with cases of possession, there is no reason why they should not cast them out, as well as others; for we read of those who cast out devils in Christ's name who did not follow Him." *

Mr. Chung, in the paper from which the above is taken expresses the belief that evil spirits sometimes connect themselves with idols, or graven images; giving them a certain efficacy, and thus deluding their worshipers through them. This is the belief of many native Christians.

* Refers to Luke IX, 49, 50, a passage, however, that should be differently understood.

CHAPTER V

RESPONSES TO CIRCULAR: CONTINUED

The following letter, though only a private one, is of special interest, as relating to the region beyond the border of China proper.

Letter from Rev. James Gilmour, of the London Missionary Society, and author of *Life in Mongolia.*

"My dear Dr. Nevius:

I send you four diabolical communications which I hope you will find useful. If everybody sends you as many as I do, you'll have plenty of "demoniacal possessions," by the time you are finished. I am glad I can give you no personal experience in this line, though I must say with one of old referring to Satan, that 'I am not ignorant of his devices.' *

In Mongolia I find more or less belief— generally more—in demoniacal possessions, but I have never had a case put into my hands to treat; and the Monguls are so thoroughly imbued, one and all, with the spirit of lying, that I have found it useless to repeat what the most

* 2 Cor. II, 11.

60

respectable say; even when they have no conceivable motive for not telling the truth. Perhaps their free and untrammeled life accustoms
them to such absence of restraint that they cannot confine themselves to truth. Seriously (and
perhaps you think it time) I have often had the
subject of possession called up to my mind during ten years residence in Mongolia and China
by witnessing the transports of passion into
which children and grown people are sometimes
thrown by quite inadequate causes; and I shall
await with much interest the result of your investigations. Wishing you prosperity in all your
interests,

   Believe me faithfully yours,

       James Gilmour.

P. S. Hsu Chung-ki is a steady-going man,
a Christian of some four or five years' standing.
The other two "Ma" and "Wau," are recent converts of whom nothing can be said. J. G."

*Translation of a communication from Hsu
Chung-ki.*

"Thirty-four li west of my home is a small
village called Ho-kia-chwang. In it lived a Mr.
Chin, who was very wealthy, and had a large
family. He was also a noted scholar, and had
many disciples. All at once his home became
the scene of very strange manifestations. Doors
would open of their own accord, and suddenly
shut, or would shut and suddenly open. The

rattling of plates and bowls was often very annoying. Foot-falls were sometimes heard, as of persons walking in the house, although no one could be seen. Often straw was found mixed with the millet, and filth with the wheat. Plates, bowls, and the teapot would suddenly rise from the table into the air; and the servants would stretch out their hands to catch them. These were constant occurrences. Various persons were called to the house to put an end to these disturbances. Efforts were made to propitiate the spirits by burning incense to them, and by vows and offerings. Mr. Chin entered a protest against the spirits in the Tung-Yoh Temple. All possible means were tried, but with no avail. This state of things continued for two years. The wealth of the family mysteriously disappeared. Mr. Chin died, and now all his descendants are in extreme poverty."

The other three papers, sent by Mr. Gilmour, I have not thought it necessary to insert.

The following are extracts from a paper written by Rev. Timothy Richard, Missionary of the English Baptist Church. It was sent me in response to my circular, though originally prepared for a social and literary meeting of the foreign residents in Chefoo.

"The Chinese orthodox definition of spirit is, 'The soul of the departed;' some of the best of whom are raised to the rank of gods. Officials who have conducted themselves with considerable credit, so as to obtain a good name from the people, and favor in the sight of the emperor, when they die are deified by the emperor, and temples are erected to their memory; and their images are placed in the temples that the people may worship them, and copy their noble examples. These in process of time become the people's guardian angels, and lastly their gods. All those spirits which are not so fortunate as to appear in the Imperial Edict, or to be deified by the universal consent of the people, have their lot cast among a class called 'demons,' who, however, vary indefinitely, as the good spirits do, in their powers. . . . . Having dwelt on demons in general let us now proceed to a special class of human phenomena which the Chinese attribute to the influence of demons. We shall commence where this influence is least, and end where it is greatest. First then, as to their power to produce diseases. There is no disease to which the Chinese are ordinarily subject that may not be caused by demons. In this case the mind is untouched; it is only the body that suffers; and the Chinese endeavor to get rid of the demon by vows and offerings to the gods. The subjection in this case is an involuntary one.

"Next come those *possessed* by the evil spirit. These the Chinese distinguish from lunatics both by their appearance and language. There is more of the cringing nature in the possessed, and the patient is perfectly consistent with the new consciousness, which is said to be the demon's. When questioned as to his home the demon answers that it is in the mountains, or desert—generally in some cave. Sometimes he says the person whom he had possession of before is dead; and having no other abode he takes up his quarters with the new victim. Sometimes he says he is traveling, or is only come to pay a visit to a brother or sister, to a father or mother, and that after a short stay he will go away. Persons possessed range between fifteen and fifty years of age, quite irrespective of sex. This infliction comes on very suddenly, sometimes in the day, sometimes in the night. The demoniac talks madly, smashes everything near him, acquires unusual strength, tears his clothes into rags, and rushes into the street, or to the mountains, or kills himself unless prevented. After this violent possession the demoniac calms down and submits to his fate; but under the most heart-rending protests. These mad spells which are experienced on the demon's entrance, return at intervals, and increase in frequency, and generally also in intensity, so that death at last ensues from their violence.

"A Chefoo boy of fifteen was going on an errand. His path led through fields where men were working at their crops.   When he came up to the men, and had exchanged a word or two with them, he suddenly began to rave violently; his eyes rolled, then he made for a pond which was near by.   Seeing this, the people ran up to him, stopped him from drowning himself, and took him home to his parents. *   When he got home he sprang up from the ground to such a height as manifested almost superhuman strength.   After a few days he calmed down and became unusually quiet and gentle; but his own consciousness was lost.   The demon spoke of its friends in Nan King.   After six months the demon departed, and the boy recovered. He has been in the service of several foreigners in Chefoo since.   In this case no worship was offered to the demon.

"Now we proceed to those who, though involuntarily possessed, yield to, and worship the demon.   The demon says he will cease tormenting the demoniac, if he worships him, and will reward him by increasing his riches.   But if not he will punish his victim; make heavier his torments; and rob him of his property.   People find that their food is cursed.   They cannot prepare any, but filth and dirt comes down from the air to render it uneatable.   Their wells are likewise cursed; their wardrobe is set on fire; and their money very mysteriously disappears.   Hence

* Compare Matt. XVII, 15.

5 *Demon.*

arose the custom of cutting off the head of a string of cash, that it might not run away. . . . When all efforts to rid themselves of the demon fail, they yield to it, and say: 'Hold! Cease thy tormenting, and we will worship thee!' A picture is pasted upon the wall, sometimes of a woman, and sometimes of a man, and incense is burned, and prostrations made to it twice a month. Being thus reverenced, money now comes in mysteriously, instead of going out.

"Even mill-stones are made to move at the demon's orders, and the family becomes rich at once. But it is said that no luck attends such families, and they will eventually be reduced to poverty. Officials believe these things. Palaces are known to have been built by them for those demons, who, however, are obliged to be satisfied with a humbler shrine from the poor.

"A further stage is reached when the demon says: 'It is not enough that you worship me privately at your own house; you must go about to declare my power, and influence your neighbors.' By this time the demoniac's will is almost powerless: he therefore goes forth immediately. Hitherto if he worshiped a demon, he would scarcely own it except with shame. Now he boasts of his power. He professes to heal diseases by the demon's aid.

"In seeking the aid of demons, the suppliant takes with him incense and paper money, besides valuable presents of bread, red cloth, and red silks, which are presented in connection with offerings and prostrations. This class neither dance nor beat drums, nor ring bells, but sit and commence a slow shaking as from ague, then yawn, gape, and at last shake so violently that their teeth chatter. Then they fall into a fit like the former class. They tell the suppliant to return home and place a cup outside the window, and the right medicine for the sick person will be put into it by a spirit. The suppliant is at the same time made to vow that he will contribute to the worship of the particular demon whose power and intervention he now invokes; and that he will also contribute towards some temple in the neighborhood.

"Somewhat simliar to this class is another small one which has power to enter the lower regions. These are the opposite of necromancers, for instead of calling up the dead, and learning of them about the future destiny of the individual in whose behalf they are engaged, they lie in a trance for two days, when their spirits are said to have gone to the Prince of Darkness to enquire how long the sick person shall be left among the living. . . . . .

"Let us now note the different methods adopted to cast out the evil spirits from the demoniacs. Doctors are called to do it. They use needles to puncture the tips of the fingers, the nose, the neck. They also use a certain pill, and apply it in the following manner: The thumbs of the two hands are tied tightly together, and the two big toes are tied to each other in the same manner. Then one pill is put on the two big toes at the root of the nail, and the other at the root of the thumb nails. At the same instant the two pills are set on fire, and there they are kept till the flesh is burned. In the application of the pills, or in the piercing of the needle, the invariable cry is: 'I am going; I am going immediately. I'll never dare to come back again. Oh have mercy on me this once. I'll never return!'

"When doctors fail, they call on people who practice spiritualism. They themselves cannot drive the demon away, but they call another demon to do it. Both Confucianists and Taoists practice this method. They write a charm and burn it. They also burn incense and prostrate themselves. If the burnt charm has not the name of a particular spirit written upon it, the nearest spirit will come. Sometimes the spirits are very ungovernable. Tables are turned, chairs are rattled, and a general noise of smashing is heard, until the very mediums' themselves tremble with fear. If of this dreadful character, they quickly write another charm with the name of the particular spirit whose quiet disposition is known to them. Lu-tsu is a favorite one of this kind. After the burning of the charm and incense and when prostrations are made, a little frame is procured to which a Chinese pencil is attached. Two men on each side hold it on a table spread with sand or millet. Sometimes a prescription is written, the pencil moving of its own accord. They buy the medicine prescribed, and give it to the possessed. Sometimes the demon writes a charm which they are to copy, and paste upon the door or window, or make the demoniac carry about like a talisman; or he may have to burn it, and take its ashes in a cup. Should this fail the relatives may go to the temples, worship a particular god, and then get his name written on a tablet, and take it home, burn incense, offer sacrifices, and promise unusual devotion, in case their prayers should be heard. Should this fail again, they go and prosecute the demon before the tutelar deity of the district to which the demoniac belongs. This they do by writing their complaint against the evil spirit in full. This charge they take and burn in the presence of the idol within the city walls. As soon as burnt, this is supposed to appear in the presence of the god, in the spiritual world. But fearing the god will not take up the case, they never fail to burn heaps of paper money along with it.

"Should they find that this again fails to liberate the poor victim, they may call in conjurors such as the Taoists, who sit on mats, and are carried by invisible power from place to place. They ascend to a height of twenty or fifty feet, and are carried to a distance of four or five *li*.* Of this class are those who in Manchuria call down fire from the sky in those funerals where the corpse is burnt. These conjurors not only use charms, but recite incantations, make magic signs, and use some of those strange substances which the astrologers use to keep away evil influences.

"These exorcists may belong to any of the three religions of China. The dragon-procession, on the fifteenth of the first month, is said by some to commemorate a Buddhist priest's victory over evil spirits. Some of these may make use of the astrologist's mysterious articles; such as vermilion ore, a black mule's hoof, a black dog's blood, or the sword of the seven stars. In addition to these they use many charms and recite incantations or prayers. They paste up charms on windows and doors, and on the body of the demoniac, and conjure the demon never to return. The evil spirit answers: 'I'll never return! You need not take the trouble of pasting all these charms upon the doors and windows.'

"Exorcists are specially hated by the evil spirits.† Sometimes they feel themselves beaten fearfully; but no hand is seen. Bricks and stones may fall on them from the sky or housetops. On the road

---

*A *li* is one-third of a mile. †See Acts. xix, 14-17.

they may without any warning be plastered over, from head to foot, with mud or filth; or may be seized, when approaching a river, and held under the water and drowned. Owing to the great danger to which these exorcists are exposed, they never venture anywhere without having charms, talismans, and all kinds of 'abracadabras' about them. Weak people cannot do these things; hence all of this class are men in the strength of manhood.

"Lastly, Christians may be called in to cast out the devils. Both Roman Catholic and Protestant missionaries are in possession of a thousand instances, in which after all other efforts are found unavailing, a prayer offered by a Christian, foreign or native; or even the possessor of a New Testament, or a portion of the Bible; or even proximity to a Christian place of worship, has driven away the demon, and restored the demoniac to a sound mind, praising God.

"Thus in considering this subject, one feels himself transported back to the days of the Apostles; and is compelled to believe that the dominion of Satan is by no means broken yet.

"In closing we may remark that most of these evil spirits are said to be foxes, weasels, or snakes. But they are by no means confined to these. The *Liao-chai*, a book published a century ago, (1765) is the production of a scholar whose style is held up as the pattern for every student. In it birds, fishes, beasts, stones, flowers, and in fact almost everything in its turn, is represented as instinct with spirit; and as sometimes appearing in human form. Scholars invariably say such things are not true; but when questioned further they admit that there are similar stories believed by people who have never heard of *Liao-chai*. The truth seems to be that the author of this book gathered together all sorts of legends which were current among the people; some of which were general, while others were only known to a few persons, or in particular localities."

One hundred and sixty four of the best stories contained in the *Liaochai* have been translated into English by Herbert A. Giles, of H. M.'s consular service. The translation is in two volumes, 8 vo pp. 434, 404; and was published in 1880 by Thos. De La Rue & Co. 110 Bunhill Row, London. Mr. Giles says the book is known to the Chinese as the *Liao-Chai-Chih-I*, or more familiarly as the *Liao-Chai*. The author was *P'u Sung-Ling*, who completed his collection of tales in 1679, though it was not printed until 1740. Since then many editions and commentaries have been made, of which the best appeared in 1842, in sixteen small 8vo volumes of about 160 pages each. It is an invaluable repertory of Chinese folk lore.

CHAPTER VI

Letter from Mr. W. D. Rudland of the China Inland Mission.

Tai-Chow, July 8, 1881.

"My dear Dr. Nevius:

You may think it strange that I have not before answered your note asking for information respecting demoniacal possessions in this part of China. The main reason for my delay is that I wished to investigate on the spot a case which the enclosed letter refers to. The letter I think speaks for itself; and needs no further explanation. It was written by a very reliable native helper, in whom I had good reason to confide, and was sent to Mr. Williamson, who was superintending the work here during my absence in England. A copy of the letter was sent to the editor of 'China's Millions,' but was not thought fit for publication. On my return to China in the autumn of 1876 Mr. Williamson kindly gave me a copy of the letter, and we visited the place together, making what enquiries we could about the matter. Since then, having a station there,

73

I have frequently visited the place, and become well acquainted with all the parties concerned. I have visited the place since receiving your note and took the opportunity of investigating the case in the house where it occurred. I heard an account of the facts from several different persons who were present, and all agree in their statements. To my mind, it is as clear a case as it is possible to conceive of. The natives here all believe most firmly that the woman was possessed of a devil; and that the reading of God's word was the means of its being cast out. The young man mentioned as having been converted at the time was baptized by Mr. Williamson, and is now one of our junior native helpers. Just now he is here for study during the week, and supplying a station on Sunday. About three years ago I baptized the mother and the elder brother and sister together, so that of a family of six, five are now Christians. But strange to say, the woman who was possessed is not converted, nor is her husband. They both say they believe, but have made no profession. The woman is perfectly well. As I can vouch for the facts, you can make what use you like of this letter, and put my name to it if you wish. The portion of Scriptures read, was the first ten verses of St. John's Gospel."

A translation made by Rev. Wm. A. Wills of the Chinese paper above referred to, written by Chang Ah-liang.

"At Yang-fu-Miao, forty *li* S. E. of Tai-chao,
is a family consisting of an elderly woman, two
sons, and the elder son's wife; all of whom live
together. The eldest son was a zealous Buddhist, and leader in the idolatrous ceremonies in
the neighboring temple; the younger a Christian, and a member of the Tai-chao church.

In June 1876 the son's wife was seized with
violent pain in the chest. The Christian brother
went to a place seven miles distant, to get advice about it. After his departure she swooned
for an hour, then revived and said her husband's
first wife (long since dead) had come to take her
and her husband away. The friends present
were much alarmed, and promised the demon
that if it would leave the woman they would call
six priests to chant the classics for three days.
The answer was: 'Not sufficient.' They then
said they would burn a quantity of paper, over
which the name of Buddha had been repeated
many times. The answer as before was: 'Not
sufficient.' The husband brought the classics,
chanted several, and placed the book on her
heart, hoping by this means to get rid of the
demon. She said: 'You can't get rid of me by
this means.' Then a fishing net was spread
over the woman, and she said: 'You can't catch
me with this.' After several methods had been
tried the Christian brother returned, to whom
they related all that had passed. He said to

her: 'Why do you talk in this foolish, confused manner.' She replied: 'I am not confused; I am your deceased sister-in-law.' He said: 'You are an evil spirit; leave her!' He read the New Testament to her, but she turned away, and did not want to hear. After two or three verses had been read, she said: 'Your reading pains me to death. Don't read! Don't read. I will go.' The woman then got up and attended to her duties; and until the time I left Tai-chao, at the end of 1878 was well in body and mind. The husband was convinced of the power of God, and professed to believe in Christianity. The neighbors were greatly astonished, and one young man present also believed."

Letter from Rev. H. V. Noyes of the American Presbyterian Mission, Canton.

"I do not know that anything I send you now in regard to demoniacal posssesions will be in time to be of any service. I have not personally seen much of it; but there have been occasional instances here, and especially some years ago, of the native preachers' casting out devils—as the natives call it. I send you an account of two instances, as I happen to know the native preachers well. Some time in the year 1868, in the fourth month of the Chinese year, Ho-kao, a preacher of the London Mission, was preaching in Fatshan, and a portion of his discourse referred to Jesus casting out devils. After the service a man came and asked Ho-kao if he could cast out devils, stating that he had a son thus possessed; and if Ho-kao could give him relief he would be very grateful. Ho-kao replied that he could not; but Jesus did of old, and could now if He chose to do so. All that he himself could do would be to pray to Jesus; and that he would be very willing to do. Ho-kao then went with the man to his home in a village not far from Fatshan, and found that his son, a grown up man, had been disordered for ten or more days, attacking people with knives, and making attempts to set fire to the house; so that he had been chained to a tree, with a little mat-shed near him to protect him when it rained. The people were afraid of him. Ho-kao asked the family and friends all to kneel down; and some one forced the man himself down on his knees. Ho-kao then prayed. As soon as the prayer was finished the chained man gave one or two leaps as high as he could, and then Ho-kao said: 'Take off the chains!' They were all afraid to do this, so Ho-kao himself took them off, and led the man into the house. He was quiet and seemed much exhausted, and soon fell asleep. The family wished to burn incense, etc., etc., but were told to do nothing of the kind. The father of the demoniac tore down everything pertaining to idol-worship in his house, and would have nothing more to do with it thereafter. He soon joined the church, and has been in connection with it ever since. The demoniac has never had any return of his trouble. The man Ho-kao who prayed with him is an earnest preacher, and a very good man. He is, I suppose, now about fifty years of age. Ho-kao afterwards had a somewhat similar experience with some other cases, but I am not acquainted with the particulars.

"I know of another instance which occurred early in the autumn of 1872. A native assistant, of the English Wesleyan Mission, was passing along one of the streets of his native village, when he saw a small company making sport of a man, who they said, was possessed of a devil. They called to the native assistant and challenged him to come and cast out the demon; as he claimed that the God of the Christians had such power. He went and prayed with the man, who then became much more quiet. The assistant visited him for two or three days, when he appeared to be perfectly well and, seemed to form an exceedingly strong attachment for the native assistant who had prayed for him. The circumstance led to the formation of a class which met every evening for the study of the Bible, and some were converted. I omitted to mention in connection with the case at Fatshan that the effect seemed to be good in drawing favorable attention to the work going on in connection with the chapel there.

"A man who came back from California some years ago, a member of the Presbyterian church, was said to be able to exorcise evil spirits; but was one hundred and fifty miles from here, and I am not acquainted with the particulars."

In July 1880 Mr. Noyes wrote again as follows: "There is a case of the supposed casting out of evil spirits which I have not mentioned. It happened ten years ago at Hin-kong, in the Hai-ping district. A returned Californian named Chao Tsi-ming prayed in the name of Jesus for a slave girl who had been afflicted as they said, by an evil spirit, for eight or nine years; and she recovered and has been well ever since. One of our native preachers went there afterwards, and found a great deal of interest taken by the villagers in the circumstances. I have obtained from Ho Yuing-she, the preacher of the London Mission, a written statement of his experience in Fatshan in casting out spirits and enclose it herewith."

Translation of Communication from Ho Yuing-she.

"I was stationed in the city of Fu-san, and engaged in chapel preaching, when I was visited by a man from the neighborhood of Shin-Tsuen, about twenty *li* distant. He said that his elder brother Tsai Se-hiang had been for several months afflicted by an evil spirit; and they had made use of every kind of magic for expelling demons, and had exhausted all the forms of idol-worship without the slightest result. He said that night and day they were borne down by this calamity, and found themselves absolutely powerless; that they had heard that Jesus was the Saviour of the world, and that by His name evil spirits might be cast out; and therefore they had come to beg the disciples of Jesus to visit them, and in the name of Jesus cast out the demon. I said: 'Your determining to come and invite a disciple of Jesus to your home to cast out the devil by prayer, is certainly an excellent thing; but it is not certain that the members of your family will be willing to trust and follow us. Please enquire particularly whether his wife, children, and brothers are willing to give up all idolatrous practices, and reverencethe true God. If they are willing to do this, bring me word again, and I will gladly go.' The next day the man came again, and said all were willing to comply with the Christian customs, and begged me to come. I then with a companion went back with him to his home. Arriving at his house I saw Tsai Se-hiang's wife, children and relatives all very sad and distressed. I asked the wife about her husband's malady. She said: 'My husband has been afflicted for a long time; we have wasted our substance on physicians;

but without avail. All the day long he moans
and mutters; he has almost ceased to be a man.
In the night his malady is still more severe. In
our extremity we have besought you two gentle-
men to visit our humble home, and pray for
him; and in the name of Christ cast out the
evil spirit. It depends on you to bring back
peace and happiness to our family; and our
grateful remembrance of you shall have no end.'
I said to the woman: 'Do you believe in Christ?'
She replied: 'I believe.' I said: 'If you believe kneel with me and pray.' After prayer
we looked at Tsai Se-hiang and saw that his
countenance was peaceful and natural. All the
family were wild with delight, and their astonishment knew no bounds. We then bade them
adieu, and came away. Very strangely and unexpectedly about ten days afterwards Mrs. Tsai
Se-hiang again worshiped idols; and from that
time her husband's malady returned. She immediately sent her brother in-law to inform me
of what had happened. He told me that his sister-in-law had not kept her promise, that she
had disobeyed the commands of our religion,
and gone to the temple to worship idols; and
the evil spirit had returned. 'So,' said he, 'we
are obliged to come and trouble you again, and
if you will come and pray for him our gratitude
will be more than we can express.' This time
we ourselves did not go, but told the messenger

6 *Demon*

to return and tell his sister-in-law that she her-self ought in sincere repentance and reformation to trust in the power of Jesus, and in simple faith pray without ceasing; and she might hope that her husband would again be restored to health. The wife followed my direction, and continued in earnest prayer night and day; and the evil spirit was driven away and entirely left her hus-band. From that time he was completely cured. In the eighth month he came to the chapel with gifts and offerings to express his gratitude. I very gladly accepted his thanks, and acknowl-edgments, but declined his gifts."

The following communication was forwarded to me by Rev. J. Innocent, of the English Methodist Mission in Tien-tsin. He says in his letter dated Feburary 1, 1881: "I have obtained the enclosed account from one of our catechists who was stationed at the place where, and at the time when, the event narrated took place. I fear it lacks detail."

[Translation]

"In the province of Shantung, Wu-ting fu, Shang-ho-hien, in the village Yang-kia lo, there is a family named Yang, in which a woman was grievously tormented by evil spirits, and had been for fifteen years. She frequently appeared on the streets declaring to the people that the teachings of the Christian religion came from heaven; and that men ought to believe and reverence this religion. She was asked: 'Has not the Mi-mi religion (a local sect) power to cast you out?' She replied: 'The Mi-mi kiao is a religion of demons; how could it cast me out? I am also a demon (mo-kwei).' Some of the native Christians heard this and said: 'When Jesus was in the world He healed diseases, and cast out demons. Why cannot we who believe in Christ do the same?' Whereupon those present, Yang Ching-tsue, Yang Shing-kung, and Yang Shiu-ching earnestly prayed for God's help in casting out this demon. After prayer they proceeded to the afflicted woman's house. Before they reached it the woman said: 'There are three believers in the heavenly doctrine coming.' On their arrival she called each one by name, and asked them to be seated. She then said: 'You are the disciples and servants of the God whom I greatly fear.' They then asked: 'What is your name?' The answer was: 'My name is Kyuin (Legion).' The three men then charged the demon to leave the woman's body. The demon replied: 'I have helped this woman fifteen years. She has not an ornament on her head or her feet which she has not obtained by my assistance.' After a violent fit of weeping the demon promised to leave the woman on the tenth day of the first month. And on that day agreeably to its promise, it left." *

* Compare Acts, XVI, 16-18, and Luke VIII, 30. Mk. iii, 23. i Cor. x, 20,

CHAPTER VII

OTHER COMMUNICATIONS FROM VARIOUS
SOURCES IN CHINA

The following is taken from the "Christian Herald and Signs of the Times" of August 4, 1880.

"A Chinese demon-possessed woman becoming a Bible-woman."

"The Rev. W. R. Stuart, of the Foochow Mission in China, (English Church Missionary Society) in his report of work during the past year, furnished the following marvelous cure of a demon-possessed woman.

"·One Sunday morning, about a year ago, a woman with her husband and four children came to my house here, and asked to be taken in and taught 'the doctrine.' We replied that we had no place where they could reside, and no means whereby to support them. The poor people fell down before us, knocking their heads on the ground, beseeching that we would have pity on them, and teach them the doctrine, (i. e. Christianity) for that the woman was possessed by an evil spirit, and had come a very long way at considerable expense, in obedience to a dream commanding her, if she would get rid of the evil spirit, to go to Foochow, and learn the doctrine of Jesus. Still we replied that it was quite impossible that we should take them in. However, just at that time the students of our Theological College were in need of a cook, and hearing of this family they sent over word that they themselves would take the man as their cook, and subscribe among themselves sufficient to support the family for a while; allowing them to occupy an empty room underneath the college. To this we agreed; the entire expense being borne by the students.

"Some few days afterwards I was suddenly summoned by a message that the woman was in one of her fits, and I immediately went down with Dr. Taylor. We found her sitting on her bed, waving her arms about, and talking in an excited manner. She evidently had no control over herself, and was not conscious of what she was saying. Dr. Taylor, in order to ascertain whether it was merely a hysterical fit, or something over which she had control, called for a large dinner knife, and baring her arm laid the edge against the skin, as though he intended to cut; but the woman seemed to take no heed whatever. He then threw a cupful of water in her face; but she seemed to mind this as little as the knife; never for a moment stopping in her loud talk; and strange to say, as far as I could follow it, it was entirely about God and Christ and the Holy Spirit; and that she believed in the Son of God.

"This was the more strange, seeing that, as far as we could reason, the woman never had any opportunity whatever of learning the doctrine. Holding her hand I induced her to stop for one moment, and said: 'Who is this Son of God; do you know?' She replied at once in the same wild way as before: 'Yes, I know, He is Jesus: Jesus is the Son of God.' *

"A few moments afterwards she shivered all over three times in a strange way. I caught her hands thinking she was about to fall. But she seemed to get better, and lay quietly down on the bed. The next day or two she remained in bed, and on Saturday night following she again had a dream. The evil spirit seemed to seize her by the neck, commanding her to leave Foo-chow at once, and return to her home, or it would kill her. However instead of obeying she ran by herself Sunday morning to the church, and while there the pain which she had been feeling all the morning in her neck left her, and she experienced a strangely happy sensation; and since that day she has had no return of those attacks which she had been subject to continually for three years previously, and to obtain a cure for which she, poor woman, had pre-

* Compare Mark III, II.

sented many costly offerings to the idols. Now for a year she has been working with Mrs. Stuart, and nothing could exceed her diligence and earnest desire to learn the way of God more perfectly. Just lately she has returned home well able to read the New Testament, and parts of the Old Testament, burning with a desire to teach her relations and friends at Chia-Sioh, none of whom, as yet, know anything of the truth."

Further particulars connected with this case are given in an account of it written by Mrs. Stuart, and published in "Woman's Work," May, 1880. After alluding to the happy experience referred to above Mrs. Stuart says:

"All the Christians there, both men and women, had been praying very earnestly for her, and were greatly rejoiced when they heard of this happy result.

"Soon after this she joined our class of Christian women, who came to our house daily to study, and was most remarkable for her great diligence and eager desire to learn. She learned quickly and easily, and seemed to take great delight in it. Her great anxiety was to learn enough herself to be able to teach her relations and friends, especially her parents; for she was so afraid that they might die before she had taught them to know and love the Saviour.

"Her relations, hearing that she was cured, were

very much astonished, and sent her messages several times asking her to come back and teach them about the Christian's God; for they believed He must have greater power than their idols. She remained with us however until she had learned to read the colloquial New Testament very fairly; and a short time ago the whole family returned to their native village, taking with them a well instructed Christian woman to help them in teaching their heathen relations and friends. She begged us to remember them in prayer that God would give them wisdom and incline the hearts of the people to listen to them; for she felt she must obey the Saviour's command given of old to one in a similar position: 'Return unto thine own house and show how great things God hath done unto thee.'"*

The following are extracts from an account of a supposed case of "possession" in the province of Kwang-tung, which was published in 1880. Many interesting details relating to Chinese social life and customs are omitted.

"How a Familiar Spirit was Ejected from the Yong Family."

Translated from the verbal narrative of Mrs. Yong, by Miss A. M. Field, author of "Pagoda Shadows."

"'The first thing that I remember in my life is the distress of extreme poverty. . . . . . When I was fifteen years old my mother was attacked

* Compare Luke VIII, 38, 39.

by a demon, and she could not drive it away. Christians have only to resist the devil and he flees from them; * but people who know nothing about God have only their own strength with which to meet demons, and they have to succumb to them. My mother had violent palpitations of the heart, spasmodic contractions of the muscles, and foaming at the mouth. Then she would speak whatever the demon told her to say, and would do whatever he impelled her to do. My father told her that it was very bad to be a spirit-medium; but if she was going to be one she must be an honest one, and never give other than good advice, nor take more than fair pay for her services. She never took more than two or three cents from any one who came to her for a consultation with the demon. There were several spirit-mediums in our village, but none was so popular as my mother became. . . . When I was twenty-two my father died, and shortly after, the two young women that my mother had taken as wives for two of my brothers, died, within twenty days. My brothers then said that my mother's familiar spirit was a harmful one, and that they would no longer live in the house with it. The two elder boys went away and became the sons of a well-to-do kinsman; the third set up housekeeping apart from us; and the youngest hired himself out to a petty official. My mother was greatly distressed

* Jas. IV, 7.

by all this, and thought she would try to rid herself of her possessor; but the demon told her that if she tried to evict him she would be the worse for it; and she then dared to do nothing for her own salvation."

Then follows a long account of the manner in which the family heard of Christianity which they finally embraced. Then the story proceeds as follows: "As the Holy Spirit entered my mother's heart the demon went out. When she knew about the true God, and trusted in Jesus, she no longer feared the demon, and when he came and agitated her heart and twisted her muscles, she prayed to God till the demon left her. The idols were all put out of the house, and the other members of the family began to believe.

All the neighbors protested against my mother's ceasing to interpret the will of the gods to them. When they saw that my brother Po-hing and I were determined to be Christians they urged my mother to separate from us, and continue her old occupation. But we held to our mother, and finally brought her heart and all with us. We have less money than we had when my mother was a spirit-medium; but we have what is worth more than money, a knowledge of the truth, and the joy that comes from the consciousness that we are in the way to Heaven. . . . . . .

The familiar spirit troubles my mother no more. Every member of our household is a believer, and several of our neighbors come to our house for Sunday worship."

At the end of the above translation Miss Field adds the following remarks:

"This old woman, named Lotus, was, when I first saw her, the least hope-inspiring of all the women who have come under my instruction. Her son and daughter had urged her to come out here to see me, hoping I might lead her to the Saviour, but not daring to present other motives for her coming than that of "seeing the Teacheress' pretty foreign pictures and furniture." She came with them, saying she did not care about hearing any preaching, but as she had not been away from home for a long time she would go and see the Teacheress. She seemed such a wreck as a demon might make of a woman. Her hands shook so that she could scarcely hold a book; her head vibrated incessantly from palsy; and her split tongue, slashed often in her frenzies to draw blood for medicine, appeared like a forked one, about to fly out of her mouth as she talked. Her mind was completely saturated with heathenism. I wondered whether the rays of Divine light would ever penetrate the great depth of paganism in which her soul was sunk; and whether they would ever so quicken it that it would burst the tangled coils of the superstitions which bound it. That was three years ago. To-day that old woman is a Christian, singularly quick in apprehending the highest spiritual truths, and with a great love for the Bible, which she delights in reading to herself and others.

"Had I stood beside the Lord in Judea when he healed the demoniac that raged among the tombs, and with my mortal eyes had seen that man sitting at the feet of Jesus, clothed and in his right mind, the miracle would have appeared to me no greater than this one, and no more truly the work of His hand." (Swatow, China, 1880.)

My readers will probably think that the cases of supposed demon-possession already given are quite sufficient for a fair presentation of the whole subject, and that a continuation of these cases, which might be indefinitely multiplied, would be not only useless, but monotonous and wearisome.

As some persons, however, may be specially interested in further details, and especially in new phases of these phenomena, other cases from our Shantung stations and other places in North China, may be found in the Appendix. These coming from familiar acquaintances, who could be questioned and cross-questioned, are specially accompanied with circumstantial details. Similar facts and experiences from other eastern nations, and from European nations, are given in the chapters immediately following.

Before closing this chapter I think it well to make some reference to the experience and testimony of Roman Catholic missionaries in China, on this subject. It would not be difficult to multiply evidence from this source to almost any extent. I will content myself with introducing an extract from the letter of D. M. St. Martin, a translation of which was kindly sent me by S. Wells Williams, LL. D. This communication is important, as showing how common supposed cases of demon-possession were in China more then half a century ago; and how missionaries of this church have dealt with them.

Translation.

"Experience moreover has proved that religion spreads the more it is persecuted. Those who had no knowledge of this before, astonished at the faithfulness and intrepidity of the confessors of this faith, acknowledged at least that there was in it something more than human. They then longed to be instructed in the truth. As simply as possible were taught to them the doctrines of the gospel; and with the same simplicity they believed.

Strongest of proofs for them was the fact, always remaining, of the Christian's power over demons. It is amazing how much these poor infidels are tormented by them. From them they can discover no remedy save in the prayers of the Christians, by whose assistance they are delivered and converted. I am at this moment awaiting the outcome of an event that bids fair to turn to the advantage of religion. There is at a distance of seven or eight leagues from here the home of certain pagans which, during a month past, has been infested with demons. They maltreat all there who oppose them, and have been seen from time to time setting the house on fire; so that the wretched occupants are kept ever on the alert. They have had recourse to all kinds of superstition; having called upon their Bonzes, who are the priests of the country; but the Bonzes could do naught. The *pater familias*, at whose house we reside, proposed to go thither; and upon accepting his suggestion I gave him what instruction was necessary, and he went. He is a man of most admirable faith. He was converted some five or six months ago, and has himself converted all his family, which is an unusually large one. He has worked many marvelous cures, saying to the sick: 'Believe, and thou shalt be made whole,' and this practice is usually attended with success. He has already been persecuted for the faith, and borne his sufferings with the greatest constancy. My trust in God's compassion is such that I know his journey will be a perfect success."

Letters of D. M. Saint Martin.

CHAPTER VIII

DEMON-POSSESSION IN INDIA, JAPAN AND OTHER LANDS.

The "Contemporary Review," February, 1876, contains an article from the pen of a well-known English missionary in India, the Rev. Robert C. Cardwell, D.D., now missionary bishop, which gives the observations and conclusions of one who is well qualified to speak on this subject. The article is entitled "Demonolatry, Devil Dancing, and Demoniacal Possession." Extracts only can be given here, as the paper is too long to be presented entire.

Dr. Cardwell says: "I have examined several of the phases of modern devil worship, but must confess that I am in a state of considerable perplexity. I daresay I have seen almost as much of the *cultus* of evil spirits in the East as any living man has; but still, although I am far from being credulous, I should like to be convinced fully and finally of the unreality of several of the manifestations and phenomena which have come before my notice. . . .

"I write of that I have seen. And I ask calmly

and advisedly, the strange startling question: *Does devil-possession, in the sense in which it is referred to in the New Testament, exist at this present time amongst the least civilized of the nations of the globe?* I have met several men of the widest learning, and deepest experience, who never would answer me fully and frankly this question. It is one of the easiest things in the world to sneer at the very mention of such a proposition. . . . .

"At the outset of this enquiry a question arises which in itself is open to endless argument: What was the nature of demoniacal possession in the time of our Lord and Saviour Jesus Christ? No doubt the simplest answer would be an absolute negation of the premise, by affirming that there never was such a thing as devils entering into men, and indeed that devils do not exist. Into such a realm of controversy it is impossible for me to follow the reasoner. I am a Christian in my fixed beliefs, and credit the plain sense of the sacred narrative. The God incarnate cast out demons who seem to have done their best to become themselves incarnate. Evil spirits dwelt in the bodies of men and exercised tyrannical influence over their victims. By the mouths of men they spoke, though with them they could not become corporate. They had the power of inflicting bodily punishment. They rent some; others they made to gnash with their

teeth. They hurried them hither and thither.
They bore them away from the society of their
fellows. They hurled living beings headlong to
self-destruction. In a word they appear to have
had a distinct spiritual personality. If I believe
rightly it was not merely hysteria, epilepsy,
mania, or various kinds of raving madness that
Christ cured; He 'cast out evil spirits' which
had 'taken possession' of the bodies of men.
These spirits were the emissaries of Satan; as
God He had power over them and prevailed.
This appears to me to be part of a Gospel which
is not against, but beyond reason, and must as
such be humbly received.

"But let my view be ever so incorrect, it only
partially affects my main argument. I contend
that it appears that certain demonolators of the
present day, as far as the outward evidence of
their affliction goes, display as plain signs of
demoniacal possession as ever were displayed
eighteen hundred years ago. I hold that—as
far as sense can be trusted, and history relied
upon—several *peyâdis*, or devil-dancers, could
be produced to-morrow in Southern India, who,
as far as can be ascertained, are as truly possessed
of evil agencies as was the man who was forced
by the fiends within him to howl that he was
not himself, but that his name was Legion. Not
a few of the persons I refer to are, on ordinary
occasions calm. They have their avocations,

7 *Demon*

and often pursue them diligently. Sometimes they have their wives and children; they possess their inherited hut, small plantation garden, well, and score of palmyras. They eschew bhang as a rule, and the juice of the poppy, and arrack. They are quiet, sleepy men and women who occupy much of their time in staring over the yellow drifting sands at the quailflocks, as they flit hither and thither, or at the gaunt solitary wolves which skulk under the shade of thorny thickets, waiting for an unwary goat to pass by. But evening draws near; the sunset reddens over the Ghauts; the deep mellow notes of the wood-pigeons grow fainter, and they cease; fire-flies twinkle out; great bats flap by lazily overhead; then comes the dull tuck of the tom-tom; the fire before the rustic devil-temple is lit; the crowd gathers and waits for the priest. He is there! His lethargy has been thrown aside, the laugh of the fiend is in his mouth. He stands before the people, the oracle of the demon, the devil-possessed!. . . . He believes he is possessed of the local demon whom he continually treats just as if it were a divinity; and the people believe in his hallucination. They shudder, they bow, they pray, they worship. The devil-dancer is not drunk; he has eschewed arrack, and is not suffering from the effects of *Ganja, abin mayakham*, as the Tamil poet calls it. He has not been seized with epilepsy; the sequel shows that. He is not attacked with a fit of hysteria; although within an hour after he has begun his dancing, half of his audience are thoroughly hysterical. He can scarcely be mad, for the moment the dance is over he speaks sanely, and quietly and calmly. What is it then? You ask him. He simply answers: 'The devil seized me, sir.' You ask the bystanders. They simply answer: 'The devil must have seized him.' What is the most reasonable inference to draw from all this? Of one thing I am assured—the devil-dancer never 'shams' excitement. . . . . Whether this be devil-possession or not, I cannot help remarking that it appears to me that it would certainly have been regarded as such in New Testament times. It is an extremely difficult thing for a European to witness a devil-dance. As a rule he must go disguised, and he must be able to speak the language like a native, before he is likely to be admitted into the charmed circle of fascinated devotees, each eager to press near the possessed priest, to ask him questions about the future, whilst the divine afflatus is in its full force upon him." (See Virgil's account of the Sibyl, p. 430.)

The author closes a long and graphic description of the phenomena of devil-dancing in the following words:

"Shrieks, vows, imprecations, prayers, and exclamations of thankful praise rise up all blended together in one infernal hub-bub. Above all rise the ghastly guttural laughter of the devil-dancer, and his stentorian howls: 'I am God! I am the only true God!' He cuts and hacks and hews himself, and not very infrequently kills himself then and there. His answers to the queries put to him are generally incoherent. Sometimes he is sullenly silent, and sometimes whilst the blood from his self-inflicted wounds mingles freely with that of his sacrifice, he is most benign, and showers his divine favors of health and prosperity all round him. Hours pass by. The trembling crowd stand rooted to the spot. Suddenly the dancer gives a great bound in the air. When he descends he is motionless. The fiendish look has vanished from his eyes. His demoniacal laughter is still. He speaks to this and to that neighbor quietly and reasonably. He lays aside his garb, washes his face at the nearest rivulet and, walks soberly home a modest well-conducted man. . . . .

"After all has been said and described, the prime question remains: Do there exist in the present day such instances of demoniacal possession as those which elicited the marvelous intervention of Christ? If the case now-a-days of the demonolators of Southern India differs from that of the Hebrews, who in the time of Christ were possessed with devils, will any one point out to me the exact bound and limit of the difference? The question I raise is surely one which Christians of all creeds may fairly and calmly consider and argue. Is there such a thing as 'demoniacal possession' in the present day, amongst barbarous and uncivilized tribes? And if it does exist, does it materially differ from the kindred afflictions which the Great Physician, in His infinite mercy, deigned to cure, whilst He walked as man amongst men?"

An article in the "Nineteenth Century," October, 1880, on "Demoniacal Possessions in India," by W. Knighton, Esq., is interesting and important as giving the views and observations of an English official in India. Here again we have room only for the following extracts:

"In conversation with an intelligent Talukdar, Abdul-kurim by name, when I was a magistrate in Oudh, I learned that this Satanic or demoniacal possession was commonly believed in not only by the peasantry of Hindustan proper, but also by the higher classes, the nobility, and learned proprietors. . . .

"The exorcists have their own method of procedure, but violence and the infliction of pain to cast out the devils are the most common. When the cure is not effected, the devil is said to be vicious and obstinate. Then severe beating is resorted to, and in some instances cotton wicks soaked in oil are lighted and stuffed up the nostrils, etc. . . . Both Hindus and Mohamme-

dans resort to the Dongah at Ghonspore, bringing with them their afflicted relations to be exorcised—idiots, lunatics, hysterical patients, all
are brought; for the ignorant villagers class
them all under the same category; they are all
equally possessed with devils, and Ghonspore is
the place to have the demons cast out. Cures
must of course sometimes be effected or the
superstition could not survive; cures doubtless
the result of the action of pain or unwonted excitement to diseased nerves. Faith in Ghonspore and its efficacy in the cure of the possessed
with devils is spread all over the adjoining
country."

In the article from which the above extracts
are taken, Mr. Knighton gives a detailed account
of a case which he examined into particularly.

It was that of a young woman named Melata,
the wife of a man named Ahir, who was a culti-
vator in the employ of Abdul-Kurim above mentioned, Mr. Knighton said he saw the woman
after the supposed exorcism of the devil. "A
well formed, active, intelligent woman with large
lustrous black eyes. When her father and
mother died she sank into melancholy. Then
it was that she became possessed. Neither she
nor her husband had any doubt of the fact. . .
"I conversed with several villagers on the subject.
Possession by an evil spirit was plain to all of
them, and the old hag, her enemy, who lived

opposite to her, was accused as the cause. . .
She became morbid, sullen, taciturn. At length
her disease culminated in dumbness.

"The woman was taken to the shrine at Ghonspore and treated at first by beating, questioning,
and enchantments; but all in vain. Then 'by
the ojah's command,' said Gemganarain, 'I tied
her hands behind her. I tied her feet. Cotton
wicks steeped in oil were prepared. They were
lighted and stuffed up her nostrils and into her
ears. It cured her. It drove out the devil.
She shrieked and spoke. She was convulsed
and became insensible. She is well now. The
devil has left her. And it was true. In three
days she returned with me; and the old hag
died; and she has been well ever since. The
darkness of hell was in our home before; now
we have the light of heaven.' All the villagers
confirm this; none more readily than Melata
herself." (See pp. 193-4 in this volume.)

In a visit to Japan in the summer of 1890 I
found on inquiry that the beliefs and experiences
of the natives of Japan with regard to demon-
possession are not unlike those of the Chinese.
I had a conversation and some correspondence
with one of the professors in the Imperial University in Tokyo, who is making a special investigation of this subject, and we may hope
that the results of his enquiries will be made
known to the public at no distant date. In the

meantime we have some very interesting statements relating to demonology in a recent work entitled "Things Japanese," by Basil Hall Chamberlain, professor of Japanese and Philology in the Imperial University of Japan. It was published in 1890.

Professor Chamberlain says: "Chinese notions concerning the superhuman power of the fox, and in a lesser degree of the badger and the dog, entered Japan during the early Middle Ages. One or two mentions of the magic foxes occur in the Uji Jui, a story of the eleventh century, and since that time the belief has spread, and grown, till there is not an old woman in the land —or, for the matter of that, not a man either— who has not a circumstantial fox story to relate, as having happened to some one who is at least an acquaintance to an acquaintance. . . The name of such tales is legion. More curious and interesting is the power with which these demon foxes are credited of taking up their abode in human beings in a manner similar to the phenomena of possession by evil spirits so often referred to in the New Testament. Dr. Baelz, of the Imperial University of Japan, who has had special opportunities for studying these cases in the hospital under his charge, has kindly communicated to us some remarks, of which the following is a *résumé:*

"Possession by foxes (kitsuni-tsuki) is a form

of nervous disorder or delusion not uncommonly observed in Japan. Having entered the human being, sometimes through the breast, more often through the space between the finger nails and the flesh, the fox lives a life of his own, apart from the proper self of the person who is harboring him. There thus results a sort of double entity or double consciousness. The person possessed hears and understands everything that the fox inside says or thinks, and the two often engage in a loud and violent dispute, the fox speaking in a voice altogether different from that which is natural to the individual. The only difference between the cases of possession mentioned in the Bible and those observed in Japan is that it is almost exclusively women that are attacked, mostly women of the lower classes. Among the predisposing conditions may be mentioned a weak intellect, a superstitious turn of mind, and such debilitating diseases, as, for instance, typhoid fever. Possession never occurs except in such subjects as have heard of it already and believe in the reality of its existence.

"To mention one among several cases. I was once called in to a girl with typhoid fever. She recovered; but during her convalescence, she heard the women around her talk of another woman who had a fox and who would doubtless do her best to pass it on to some one else in order to get rid of it. At that moment the girl experienced an extraordinary sensation. The fox had taken possession of her. All her efforts to get rid of him were vain. 'He is coming! he is coming!' she would cry as a fit of the fox drew near. 'Oh! what shall I do? Here he is.' And then in a strange, dry, cracked voice the fox would speak, and mock his unfortunate hostess. Thus matters continued for three weeks, till a priest of the Nichiren sect was sent for. The priest upbraided the fox sternly. The fox, (always of course speaking through the girl's mouth) argued on the other side. At last he said 'I am tired of her. I ask no better than to leave her. What will you give me for doing so?' The priest asked what he would take. The fox replied, naming certain cakes and other things, which, said he, must be placed before the altar of such and such a temple, at 4 P. M. on such and such a day. The girl was conscious of the words her lips were made to frame but was powerless to say anything in her own person. When the day and hour arrived, the offerings bargained for were taken by her relatives to the place indicated, and the fox quitted the girl at that very hour."

Dr. Baelz' theory for explaining these phenomena will be given in a subsequent chapter.

While the guest of Dr. D. B. McCartee, in Tokyo, July 23, 1890, I had a conversation on this subject with his scribe and literary assistant whose name is Ga-ma-no uchi. He stated that he had heard of no cases of demon-possession in Tokyo, but that they were not infrequent in his home in Ki shiu, in the district Wa-ka-ya maken. He gave in detail a case he knew, of a boy about fourteen years old named Mo-ri Sa-no ki-chi, possessed as was asserted by a person calling himself by a name which Mr. Ga-ma-no uchi had forgotten, whose home was in Sendai. Mr. Ga-ma-no uchi said that he held long conversations with this new personality, who described accurately his former home Sendai, which place the boy had never visited. The boy was sometimes his original self, and at other times the new personality spoke through him. There were not two co-existing personalities, (the boy and the supposed spirit conversing together) but only one personality at a time. When a physician was called, the boy often resumed his original consciousness. He was cured by priests who held a service over him, upbraiding the spirit and commanding it to leave. The spirit promised to leave on condition of certain offerings being made. When they were made the boy Mo-ri Sa-no ki-chi, was restored to consciousness, and by degrees gained his strength and became well again.

Mr. Ga-ma-no uchi is a man of intelligence and literary culture, and by profession a physician. When asked how he explained these facts and conversations, he replied that they might be explained by either of the three following hypotheses.

1. Fever and brain excitement.

2. Nervous disorder or insanity.

3. Being frightened, excited, and deceived by the priests.

When asked how the boy knew about a place he had never visited he said that the boy's accounts were only true in general, and not in minute particulars, and that he might have learned what he knew from studying geography.

It may be observed here that Mr. Ga-ma-no uchi's testimony respecting demon-possession in Japan differs from that of Dr. Baelz as regards sex, the fox, and a double personality.

Additional cases of a similar character might be obtained to an indefinite extent from semi-civilized nations of the past and present. A full and interesting compilation of facts on this and kindred subjects may be found in Dorman's "Origin of Primitive Superstitions," and Tylor's "Primitive Culture." These authors give not only facts but theories to account for them. It is sufficient to state here that the facts given in the above mentioned volumes correspond throughout to those presented in the preceding chapters; showing the remarkable uniformity which, notwithstanding variations in minor particulars, resulting from race peculiarities and difference of culture, have characterized these manifestations always and everywhere.

Some of the facts collected by Dr. Tylor will appear incidentally in a subsequent chapter, in considering his theories for accounting for these facts.

Rev. J. Leighton Wilson, D. D., formerly a missionary in Africa, in speaking of demon-possession in that land, says: "Demoniacal possessions are common, and the feats performed by those who are supposed to be under such influences are certainly not unlike those described in the New Testament."*

Rev. Thaddeus McRae, author of "Lectures on Satan," quoting the testimony of a late missionary in India, says: "The Rev. Dr. Ramsey remarks in his work 'A Satanic Delusion,' that the most of our missionaries in the heathen world have witnessed such scenes as correspond very well with the Scriptural account of demoniacal possessions, and if they are not in reality demoniacal possessions, it will be very difficult to account for them on any other theory. He gives some cases, and adds that 'the Christians who have witnessed them, so far as I have known their views, agree in regarding them as veritable possessions.' Dr. Ramsey cites the testimony of other missionaries to the same effect."†

* Western Africa p. 217.
† Lectures on Satan, p. 138.

In January, 1883, in a lecture upon *Zöllner*, showing him to be "a Biblical demonologist," Joseph Cook spoke as follows:

"Prof. Phelps has published an article with the title: 'Ought the Pulpit to ignore Spiritualism?' and his answer is 'No.'* I showed that article to no less a man than Prof. Christlieb, who brought it back to me and said: 'I endorse every word of it.' I have heard him teach his own theological students that demoniacal possession is a modern fact. I am giving his opinion, not mine. 'Keep your eyes open,' he said to me, 'and when you are in India study the topics of magic and sorcery, and demoniacal possession. Ask veteran missionaries whether they do not think there is something like demoniacal possession on the earth to-day?' I have done that, and I have found that about seven out of ten of these acutest students of paganism do believe in demoniacal possession, and affirm that they can distinguish cases of it from nervous disease. About three out of ten have told me that such cases collapse on investigation."†

* See *My Portfolio*, (p, 150). By Austin Phelps, D. D. C. Scribner's Sons. N. Y. 1882.

† See *Occident*, (p. 143). By Joseph Cook. Boston. H. M. & Co, 1884.

CHAPTER IX.

DEMON-POSSESSION IN CHRISTIAN COUNTRIES.

The phenomena we have been considering are certainly seldom met with in western and nominally Christian lands. But though rare they are not wholly wanting. Perhaps they may be more common than is generally supposed.

A remarkable case of what was regarded as "possession" by demons is given in the "Biography of Rev. John Christopher Blumhardt" published in Germany in 1880.

Blumhardt was born in 1805 and died in 1880. His first pastorate was in Iptingen in Würtemberg, then in Möttlingen, also in Würtemberg. At the latter place he became famous for his "prayer cures," relieving applicants not only from physical ills, but especially from spiritual and mental disorders of various kinds, and all and only by prayer.

Among other cases brought to him for healing was that of Gottliebin Dittus who was believed to be possessed of demons. The account of this case, and the manner and success of the treatment, occupies forty-five pages of the memoir.

After he had cured Gottliebin Dittus, complaints were made to the government against Blumhardt, averring that he dealt in magic arts, etc. In his own defence he then wrote a pamphlet giving all the facts in the case.

The department of Public Worship, Instruction, etc., after investigation decided that Blumhardt was blameless, and expressed itself satisfied of his piety, and the simple means he employed in effecting Gottliebin's cure.

I am indebted to the late Theodore Christlieb, D. D., Ph. D., Professor of Theology, and University Preacher, Bonn, Prussia, for calling my attention to this case; and to a German friend for the selection and translation into English of the extracts which follow.

"Gottliebin Dittus was a young unmarried woman belonging to the laboring class. At the first meal after removing to Möttlingen in Würtemberg, while the blessing in the words, "Come Lord Jesus, be our guest," was being pronounced a sudden rustling noise was heard, as though made by a woman's dress, and Gottliebin fell senseless to the floor. She is described as sickly, shy, and not prepossessing in her appearance, and as very religious. When Blumhardt first prayed with her, and she folded her hands to accompany him, her hands were suddenly torn apart, as she said, by some external force. She told Blumhardt that she saw a vision of a woman with a dead child in her arms (a person who had been dead two years), who said, 'I want rest,' and, 'Give me a piece of paper; and I will not come again.' Blumhardt advised Gottliebin not to hold any conversation with the apparition, nor accede to its demands. He then requested a woman to sleep with Gottliebin. This woman also heard noises, etc.

"A committee of prominent citizens, including the Burgomaster and Blumhardt, made a thorough investigation. Persons were stationed all around the house and in the various rooms, and several in Gottliebin's chamber. Noises were heard which gradually increased in violence. They were heard by all the watchers, and seemed to concentrate in Gottliebin's room. Chairs sprang up, windows rattled, plaster fell from the ceiling, etc. When prayer was offered the noises increased. Nothing was discovered to account for these manifestations.

"The young woman was then removed to another house to live with a family. Noises etc., continued for a while in the house where she formerly lived, and then commenced in that to which she had been removed. Every time she saw the vision she fell into convulsions, which sometimes lasted as long as four hours.

"One evening several persons besides Blumhardt being in her room while she had convulsions, he conceived a sudden purpose; 'I stepped

8 *Demon*

resolutely forward,' he says, 'grasped her firmly by both hands, and with a loud voice calling her by name, I said: 'Put your hands together and pray Lord Jesus help me. We have seen long enough what the devil can do. Now we will see what Jesus can do!' She spoke the words, and immediately all convulsions ceased. This happened several times. She often made a threatening motion to strike Blumhardt, when he pronounced the name Jesus. After recovering consciousness she invariably said she had no recollection of what had happened. Every time Blumhardt visited her he took with him prominent citizens, the mayor, physicians, and others, all of whom corroborate everything he says. Another time when he invoked the name of Jesus the patient shivered, and a voice proceeded from her entirely different from her own, which was recognized by those in the room as that of the aforesaid widow, saying: 'That name I cannot bear.' Blumhardt questioned the spirit as follows: 'Have you no rest in the grave?' It answered: 'No.' 'Why?' 'On account of my evil deeds.' 'Did you not confess all to me when you died?' 'No; I murdered two children, and buried them secretly.' 'Can you not pray to Jesus?' 'No; I cannot bear that name.' 'Are you alone?' 'No.' 'Who is with you?' 'The worst of all.'

"On a subsequent visit the mayor received a

blow as if from an unseen hand. Blumhardt, however, though threatened, was himself never touched.

"On one occasion after prayer, which was continued longer than usual, the demon suddenly broke forth in the following words: 'All is now lost. Our plans are destroyed. You have shattered our bond, and put everything into confusion. You with your everlasting prayers—you scatter us entirely. We are 1,067 in number; but there are still multitudes of living men, and you should warn them lest they be like us forever lost and cursed of God.' The demons attributed their misfortunes to Blumhardt, and in the same breath cursed him and bemoaned their own vicious lives; all the time ejaculating: 'Oh, if only there were no God in heaven!'

"Blumhardt held conversations with several of the demons, one of whom proclaimed himself a perjurer, and yelled again and again: 'Oh man think of eternity. Waste not the time of mercy; for the day of judgment is at hand.' These demons spoke in all the different European languages, and in some which Blumhardt and others present did not recognize.

"The end came between the second and twenty-eighth of December, 1843. After continued fasting and prayer on the part of Blumhardt, the demons seemed gradually to forsake Gottliebin, and instead took possession of her sister and brother.   The first struggle took place in the person of her sister Catherine, who at times was possessed of such super-human strength that it took several men to hold her.   One night after hours of prayer Blumhardt commanded the demon to come forth, when a fearful outcry was heard by hundreds of people penetrating to a great distance, and the demon avowed himself an emissary of Satan.   The struggle lasted all night, and then yelling: 'Jesus is victor' the demon departed.   After this time the three persons afflicted had no recurrence of the 'possession.'   Gottliebin's health was restored. Several physicians testify that a deformed limb and other maladies which they had attempted in vain to relieve her of, were suddenly cured."

The book states that three men who witnessed the phenomena, including two sons of Blumhardt, were still living (in 1880), and could testify to the truth of the statements above made.

W. Griesinger, M.D., Professor of Clinical Medicine and of Mental Science in the University of Berlin: Honorary Member of the Medico-Psychological Association: Membre Associé Etrangér De La Société Médico-Psychologique de Paris, etc. etc., gives in his work entitled "Mental Pathology and Therapeutics" a description of cases in Germany of what he calls Demono-melancholia and Demonomania.   He gives also references to still more numerous cases of the same kind in France.* The extracts which follow are taken from pages 168—171 of the American edition of the above named work, published in New York by William Wood & Co., 1882.

The English translators, C. Lockhart Robertson, M. D. Cantab, and James Rutherford, M. D. Edin. give their estimate of Professor Griesinger as a medical authority, and of the character of the book translated in these words: "Professor Griesinger is essentially the representative, and the acknowledged leader, of the modern German school of Medical Psychology. As such his work must be an object of deep interest to every student in Medical Science."

Extracts: "In the vast majority of cases those religious delusions of the melancholic are to be regarded as symptoms merely of an already existing disease, and not as the causes of the affections.

"The symptoms are also similar in that interesting form of melancholia in which the sentiment of being governed and overcome manifests itself in the idea of demoniacal posession, the so-called demono-melancholia which is met with in all

*M. Macario, "Etudes cliniques sur la Démonomanie," Annal Méd. Psychol. i, 1843, p. 400; Esquirol, translated by Bernhard, i, p. 280. See also on this subject—Calmeil, 'De la Folie,' Paris 1845, i p. 85; Albers Archiv. f. Physiol. Heilk, XIII 1854, p.224; Portal, 'Mem. sur plusieurs Maladies,' II, p. 110; Moreau, Du Hachich,' etc. pp. 336 and 354; Baillarger, Annal.Méd. Psychol. VI, p. 152; Schutzenberger, ib. VIII, p. 261.

countries (in France particularly it is by no means rare) and of which recently in our own country, ignorance and the grossest superstition have used to the worst ends.

"In this form this foreign evil power, by which the patient imagines himself to be governed, assumes different demoniacal shapes, according to the prevailing superstitions and beliefs of the epoch and country(devils, witches, etc.)to which, as he may probably at the same time experience some abnormal sensations in different parts of his body, a very limited seat is assigned by the patient, sometimes one half of his body, sometimes his head, his back, or his chest, etc. It is not uncommon to see along with this, convulsions of the voluntary muscles, contractions of the larynx which alter the voice in a striking manner, anaesthesia of different important organs, hallucinations of sight and hearing. This delirium is at times accompanied with intermittent paroxysms of violent convulsions, evidently analogous to epileptic, or still more frequently to hysterical attacks, which are separated by intervals of perfect lucidity."

"Since the publication of the first edition of this work I have had the opportunity of studying several cases of demonomania in various stages, of which I shall here give two interesting examples.*

* The theory adopted by Prof. Griesinger, to account for the facts of the cases which he adduces, is considered in a subsequent chapter.

"*Example XV. Attacks of mental disorder, occurring every two or three days, presenting particularly the character of ideas of opposition.* M— S—, a peasant, at fifty-four, had, when twenty-two years of age every night for three months, an attack of violent nightmare and hallucinations of hearing. . . . . When she was between thirty and forty years of age there gradually appeared a disease occurring in paroxysms, attacks occurred every two or three days, and in the interval the patient was perfectly well. They commenced with pains in the head, loins and neck; palpitation, anxiety, great exhaustion; occasionally symptoms of globus and hysterical convulsions. She was obliged to lie in bed, became completely apathetic, could no longer connect her thoughts, and there was manifested as a mental anomaly, an internal contradiction against her own thoughts and conclusions —a constant immediate opposition against all which she thought and did. An inward voice which she, however, did not hear in her ear, opposed everything which she herself would do (for example, even against the mere lying in bed, which her condition renders necessary), especially, however, against all elevation of the sentiments—praying, etc. The voice is always wicked when the patient would do good, and sometimes calls to her, but without being heard externally: "Take a knife and kill yourself."

The patient, who is a clever woman, says on this subject, that she almost believes that a strange being, a demon, is within her, so certain is she that it is not herself who does this. I took the patient into the clinique at Tübingen, and there had frequent opportunities of observing the attacks. During them she seemed much heated, congested, had an obscure and confused expression, was not feverish (temperature normal). The attack lasted from twenty-four to forty-eight hours. On one occasion at the commencement, when the head was much congested, venesection to a small amount was performed, which only temporarily relieved her.

"*Example XVI. Chronic demonomania.* C. S——, an unmarried peasant, at forty-eight, voluntarily presented herself at the clinique, because she was possessed by spirits. Her father became a little strange as he advanced in years; her sister and sister's son are insane. The patient had a child at the age of nineteen; she nursed it for three years, and fell into a state anaemia, with extended pains of the limbs, and sometimes convulsions. For a long time she had convulsive movements of the mouth. Three years after the first appearance of the disease (about thirteen years ago) 'the speaking out of her' commenced. From that moment, all kinds of thoughts and words were expressed unintentionally by the patient, and sometimes with a voice different from her usual. At first it seems to have been not so much opposing, as quite indifferent and even reasonable remarks which accompanied the thoughts and language of the patient: for example "it" said: 'Go to the doctor.' 'Go to the priest,' or 'Thus, thus you must do it,' etc. Gradually these indifferent remarks were succeeded by others more negative, and at one time the voice sometimes simply confirms what is said by the patient, at another it derides and mocks it: for example when the patient says anything which is right, the voice says after her, 'You, that is a lie; you, that you must keep to yourself.' The tone of the voice in this speaking of 'the spirit,' is always somewhat, sometimes entirely, different from the ordinary voice of the patient, and she looks upon the fact of her having another voice as a leading proof of the reality of the spirit. 'The spirit' often commences to speak with a deep bass voice, then passes to a pitch lower or higher than the ordinary tone of the patient; occasionally it passes into a sharp shrill cry, which is followed by a short ironical laugh. I have myself often observed this. Besides these words spoken by "the spirit" the patient heard inwardly and almost incessantly, a great number of spirits speaking. Sometimes she had actual hallucinations of hearing, but never of sight. Praying rendered the state which we have described still worse; it increased the restlesness.   In church, however, she could, from awe of the congregation and clergyman, restrain the voice of the spirit; she could also read aloud from the prayer-book without being disturbed.   Sometimes her discourse had a slight taint of nymphomania; she said that the spirit caused her to have obscene thoughts, and to express them. The patient never knows until it is spoken what the spirit would say.   Sometimes the power of speech is altogether denied her for a certain time.   In all the phenomena which we have described, the greatest and invariable uniformity prevailed, and her condition, which for a long time had been fixed and stationary, continued the same during the short period during which she was under treatment.

"*Example XVII.   Convulsive attacks with ideas of possession, and plurality of the personality, of short duration, in a child.* Margaret B— at eleven, of lively disposition, but a godly, pious child was on the nineteenth of January, 1829, without having been previously ill, seized with convulsive attacks, which continued with few and short intermissions for two days.   The child remained unconscious so long as the convulsive attacks continued.   She rolled her eyes, made grimaces, and performed all kinds of curious movements with her arms.   On Monday, the twenty-first of January she assumed a deep bass voice, and kept repeating the words 'I pray earnestly for you!' When the girl came to her senses she felt tired and exhausted. She was perfectly unconscious of what had passed, and merely said that she had been dreaming. On the evening of the twenty-second of January another commenced to speak in a tone distinctly different from the aforementioned bass voice. This voice spoke almost without intermission as long as the crisis lasted, that is, for half hours, hours, and even longer; and was only occasionally interrupted by the bass voice which still repeated the aforementioned words. In a moment this voice would represent a person different from that of the patient, and perfectly distinct from her, speaking of her always objectively and in the third person. There was no confusion or incoherence in the words of the voice, but great consistency was shown in answering all the questions logically, or in skilfully evading them. But that which principally distinguished these sayings was their moral, or rather their immoral character. They expressed pride, arrogance, mockery, or hatred of truth, of God and of Christ. The voice would say, 'I am the Son of God, the Saviour of the world—you must adore me,' and immediately afterwards rail against everything holy—blaspheme against God, against Christ, and against the Bible; express a violent dislike towards all who follow what is good; give vent to the most violent maledictions a thousand times repeated, and furiously rage on perceiving any one engaged in prayer, or merely folding their hands. All this might be considered as symptoms of a foreign influence, even although the voice had not, as it did, betrayed the name of the speaker, calling it a devil. Whenever this demon wished to speak the countenance of the girl immediately and very strikingly changed, and each time presented a truly demoniacal expression, which called to mind the scene in the 'Messiade,' of the devil offering Jesus a stone.

"On the forenoon of the twenty-sixth, January, at eleven o'clock, the very hour which, according to her testimony, she had been told by an angel several days before would be the hour of her deliverance, these attacks ceased. The last thing which was heard was a voice from the mouth of the patient, which said: 'Depart, thou unclean spirit, from this child—knowest thou not that this child is my well-beloved?' Then she came to consciousness.*

"On the thirty-first, January, the same conditions returned with the same symptoms. But gradually several new voices appeared until the

---

* Some one suggests the following comment:
   Between this last voice and the bass voice that repeated the words "I pray earnestly for you," a moral resemblance may be noticed, not shared by the other voice. The patient was a godly child. Upon the hypothesis that the blasphemous voice, which was not properly that of her own spirit, proceeded from an evil spirit why in such an extraordinary providence, should not the bass voice, and that speaking these final words, be referred to the Holy Spirit? Which voice would be the more miraculous, and what, in such a case, may we suppose would the attitude of the Holy Spirit be? See **Romans** viii: 26; also **Luke** xxii: 31, 32; **Hebrews** vii: 25. 1 **John** IV. 4.

number had increased to six, differing from each other partly in their tone, partly in their language and subject; therefore each seemed to be the voice of a special personality, and was considered as such by the voice which had been already so often heard. At this period the violence of the fury, blasphemy and curses reached their highest degree; and the lucid intervals, during which the patient had no recollection of what had occurred in the paroxysm, but quietly and piously read and prayed, were less frequent and shorter in duration.

"On the ninth of February, which, like the twenty-sixth of January, had been announced to her as a day of deliverance, this most lamentable trouble came to an end, and, as on the former date, after there had proceeded from the mouth of the patient the words: 'Depart, thou unclean spirit!' 'This is a sign of the last time!' the girl awoke; and since then has continued well" (*Kerner, Geschichten Besessener Neuerer Zeit, Karlsruhe.* 1834, p. 104.)

Perhaps there are not in the whole range of literature more remarkable cases of phenomena similar in some respects to these given in previous chapters than those which are found in the records of the Wesley Family in England,* and of the Reverend Eliakim Phelps, D. D. † of

* See "Memoirs of the Wesley Family" by Dr. Adam Clark. 4th Ed. vol. I, 245-291. Also the Life of Wesley, by Robert Southey, edited by J. A. Atkinson; pp. 14-18, 552-574.
† See "Spiritual Manifestations" by Rev. Charles Beecher pp. 18-24.

Stratford, Connecticut. These cases are specially worthy of examination, because of the character of the individuals connected with them, the minuteness and circumstantiality of their details and the abundance and reliability of corroborating testimony.

Dr. Austin Phelps, referring to these "spiritual manifestations" in his father's house, says:* "It was after his retirement from public life that he became interested in spiritualism. It would be more truthful to say that it became interested in him; for it came upon him without his seeking, suddenly invading his household, and making a pandemonium of it for seven months, and then departing as suddenly as it came. The phenomena resembled those which for many years afflicted the Wesley family and, those which at one time attended the person of Oberlin. They were an almost literal repetition of some of the records left by Cotton Mather. Had my father lived in 1650, instead of 1850, he and his family would have lived in history with the victims on Tower Hill in Salem. That the facts were real, a thousand witnesses testified. An eminent judge in the state of New York said that he had pronounced sentence of death on many a criminal on a tithe of the evidence which supported those facts. That they were inexplicable by any known principles of

* "My Portfolio," p. 35. For the details our readers must be referred to these various sources of information.

science was equally clear to all who saw and heard them who were qualified to judge. Experts in science went to Stratford in triumphant expectation, and came away in dogged silence, convinced of nothing, yet solving nothing. If modern science had nothing to show more worthy of respect than its solution of spiritualism, alchemy would be its equal, and astrology infinitely its superior. It will never do to confine a delusion so seductive to the ignorant, and so welcome to the sceptic to the limbo of 'an if,' and leave it there."* (See note on page 133.)

Testimony of the Early Christian Fathers.

The presentation of this subject of demon-possession would be incomplete without some reference to the Early Fathers of the Christian church. Their testimony is of special interest in this inquiry because it relates to a period when Christianity first came in conflict with the heathenism of the Roman Empire, just as the facts collected from China in this volume, belong to the first period of evangelization in that empire.

The testimony of the Early Fathers is minute and specific. They give us not only the beliefs and idolatrous practices of heathen Rome in their time, but also the views held and taught by the leaders in the early church respecting the character of demons; the sphere and limits of demon agency; and the manner in which they

---

* See lectures by Joseph Cook on "Spiritualism an If," in The Independent, N. York; Feb. and March, 1880.

deceive men, referring at the same time to the facts of demon-possession and demon expulsion as familiarly known and universally acknowledged both by heathen and Christians.

Tertullian says in his Apology addressed to the Rulers of the Roman Empire:*

"The skill with which these responses are shaped to meet events, your Croesi and Pyrshi know too well. On the one hand it was in that way we have explained, the Pythian was able to declare that they were cooking a tortoise with the flesh of a lamb—in a moment he had been to Lydia. From dwelling in the air, and their nearness to the stars, and their commerce with the clouds, they have means of knowing the preparatory processes going on in these upper regions, and thus can give promise of the rains which they already feel. Very kind, too, no doubt, they are in regard to the healing of diseases. For, first of all, they make you ill, then to get a miracle out of it, they command the application of remedies, either altogether new, or contrary to those in use, and straightway withdrawing hurtful influences, they are supposed to have wrought a cure. What need then to speak of their other artifices, or yet further of their deceptive power which they have as spirits—of these Castor apparitions, of water carried by a sieve, and a ship drawn along by a

*"The Antenicene Fathers." The Christian Literature Publishing Co., Buffalo, 1885.

girdle, and a beard reddened by a touch, all done with the one object of showing that men should believe in the deity of stones, and not seek after the only true God.

. . . "Moreover, if sorcerers call forth ghosts, and even make what seem the souls of the dead, to appear, if with these juggling illusions they make a pretense of doing various miracles; if they put dreams into people's minds by the power of the angels and demons whose aid they have invited, by whose influence, too, goats and tables are made to divine, how much more likely is this power of evil to be zealous in doing with all its might, of its own inclination, and for its own objects, what it does to serve the ends of others! Or if both angels and demons do just what your gods do, where in that case is the pre-eminence of deity, which we must surely think to be above all in might?

. . . "But thus far we have been dealing only in words: we now proceed to a proof of facts in which we shall show that under different names we have real identity. Let a person be brought before your tribunals who is plainly under demoniacal possession. The wicked spirit, bidden to speak by a follower of Christ (*) will as readily make the truthful confession that he is a demon as elsewhere he has falsely asserted that

*This testimony must be noted as something of which Tertullian confidently challenges denial. For modern confirmation of it see "Primitive Christianity and Modern Spiritualism." By H. L. Hastings. pp. 246-250.

9 *Demon*

he is a god.   Or, if you will, let there be produced one of the god-possessed, as they are supposed:—if they do not confess, in their fear of
lying to a Christian that they are demons, then
and there shed the blood of that most impudent
follower of Christ.

"All the authority and power we have over
them is from our naming the name of Christ,
and recalling to their memory the woes with
which God threatens them at the hand of Christ
their judge, and which they expect one day to
overtake them.   Fearing Christ in God and God
in Christ, they become subject to the servants
of God and Christ.   So at one touch and breath-
ing, overwhelmed by the thought and realization
of those judgment fires, they leave at our command the bodies they have entered, unwilling
and distressed and, before your very eyes, put to
an open shame.   You believe them when they
lie, give credit to them when they speak the
truth about themselves.   No one plays the liar
to bring disgrace upon his own head but for the
sake of honor rather.   You give a readier confidence to people making confessions against
themselves than denials in their own behalf.   It
has not been an unusual thing accordingly for
those testimonies of your deities to convert men
to Christianity, for in giving full belief to them
we are led to believe in Christ.   Yes, your very
gods kindle up faith in our Scriptures; they build
up the confidence of our hope."

Justin Martyr, in his second Apology addressed to the Roman Senate, says: (*) "Numberless demoniacs throughout the whole world and in your city, many of our Christian men—exorcising them in the name of Jesus Christ who was crucified under Pontius Pilate—have healed and do heal, rendering helpless, and driving the possessing demon out of the men, though they could not be cured by all other exorcists, and those who use incantations and drugs."

Cyprian (†) expressed himself with equal confidence. After having said that they are evil spirits that inspire the false prophets of the gentiles, that stir up the filth of the entrails of victims, govern the flight of birds, dispose lots, and deliver oracles by always mixing truth with falsehood to prove what they say, he adds: "Nevertheless these evil spirits adjured by the living God immediately obey us, submit to us, own our power, and are forced to come out of the bodies they possess."

Athanasius asserts that the bare sign of the cross made the cheats and illusions of the devils to vanish; and then adds: (‡) "Let him that would make trial of this come, and amidst all the delusions of devils, the impostures of oracles, and the prodigies of magic, let him use the sign of the cross, which the heathen laugh at, and

*Chapter 6.
†Scott on "Existence of Evil Spirits."
‡Ibid, p, 290.

they shall see how the devils fly away affrighted how the oracles immediately cease, and all the enchantments of magic remain destitute of their usual force."

Lactantius asserts that when the heathen sacrifice to their gods, if there be any one present whose forehead is marked with the sign of the cross the sacrifices do not succeed, nor the false prophets give answer. This has given frequent occasion to bad princes to persecute the Christians, etc., etc.

The prevalence of demon-possession in the Roman Empire during the period of the Early Fathers is further evidenced by the use in the church of a special class of laborers called exorcists, whose duty it was to heal, instruct, and prepare for admission to the church candidates for baptism who had been afflicted by evil spirits.*

The testimony of the Fathers proves conclusively that cases of demon-possession were not confined to Judea in the times of our Saviour and the Apostles, but that they were met with in the Roman Empire centuries afterward. Their testimony like that of the Chinese and other nations shows that these cases were distinct from mania, epilepsy, and other diseases, and characterized by a new personality quite

*See Dr. Lyman Coleman's "Ancient Christianity Exemplified," p.124, 191-3. Also, Whately's ''Good and Evil Angels.''

different and distinct from the subject "possessed."   *

*The testimony of the Greek and Latin classical authors is collated and compared with modern phenomena in a most able manner in a book called *The Apocatastasis, or Progress Backwards*. This was written by Leonard Marsh, M. D., for many years a professor in the University of Vermont, and published anonymously in Burlington, in 1854. It was prepared in view of the new tide of so-called spiritualism, then rising in the United States and Europe. It is at once a brilliant satire, and a serious. profound, unique discussion. Though perhaps too learned, and its style somewhat too involved, for popular reading, its intrinsic value is great. It is more needed now than when first issued, and ought to be republished. See Bibliographical Index.

The testimony of the Christian Fathers upon this subject may be found at some length in a valuable series of pamphlets by Wm. Ramsey, D. D., and H. L. Hastings; especially in the three entitled   *The Mystery Solved; Ancient Heathenism and Modern Spiritualism; Primitive Christianity and Modern Spiritualism.*

(See pp. 126, 453.)

The *Stratford Phenomena*, which extended through a period of seven months, were minutely recorded from day to day in the journal of the Rev. Eliakim Phelps. This record was given to his granddaughter, Mrs. Elizabeth Stuart Phelps Ward; and, although now withheld from publication, it may be hoped that it will sometime be made accessible to students. See Autobiographic Paper, by Mrs. Ward, in *McClure's Magazine*, Dec., 1895, p. 50.

CHAPTER X.

CHARACTER OF THE EVIDENCE PRESENTED, AND THE FACTS ESTABLISHED BY IT.

As regards the trustworthiness of the foreign missionaries whose testimony and opinions have been presented in the preceding chapters, nothing need be said. Something may be learned of their views from the communications which have already been given, but more is required to show the attitude of the missionary body as a whole.

It is important to premise that most missionaries come to China with a strong prejudgment of the matter, holding the opinion generally prevalent in Christian countries that demon-possessions were providentially permitted in Apostolic times, and made to subserve important ends in the establishment of the Christian church; but that they are events only of the past. This prejudgment is so strong in some persons that the possibility of such cases at present is not for a moment entertained. A young missionary recently arrived in China, on learning that this subject was being examined into, expressed with great warmth, and in very

134

positive terms, his "surprise that missionaries should spend their time in such an enquiry or allow native Christians connected with them to talk about or believe in 'possessions' as an existing fact."

It is my impression from a large correspondence with missionaries in China, and from personal acquaintance with many of them, that they do not, as a rule, hold the positive and extreme view above expressed. Some whose time is mostly spent in the open ports, and in literary work in the study, have not had their attention specially called to this subject, and have not come into possession of facts upon which to form a judgment. I have only known two who have expressed positive unbelief in the reality of these "possessions."

On the other hand there are Protestant missionaries who have no doubt that numerous cases may be found in China of "demon-possession," similar to those which were met with in the early history of the church. Missionaries who have personal and familiar intercourse with infant churches in the interior of China will I think agree in the statement that supposed cases of this kind are very numerous; and I believe also that it is the growing opinion that the natives are right in attributing them to demons.

The attitude of missionaries generally may, I think, be correctly stated by saying that a few believe that the so-called demon-possessions, are not really such, but only a delusion; a larger number believe them to be real; while a still larger proportion of the whole missionary body are in a state of uncertainty, unprepared to express a positive opinion on one side or the other.

The question is sometimes asked: If these cases are so numerous, why are they not seen by the foreigner; thus giving the public, so far as it is interested in this subject, the advantage of his personal examinations and testimony, instead of leaving it to depend almost exclusively on Chinese evidence?   The reasons for this are not difficult to find.

It should be borne in mind that the foreign missionary is only occasionally and temporarily at these country out-stations, perhaps, on an average, only two or three days in any one village in a year; and these phenomena occurring generally in his absence, are, when the aid of Christians is sought, naturally taken to the resident native Christians or preachers.

Again, race prejudices, and the customary restrictions upon social intercourse, and especially the dread of malicious and scandalous reports which would almost certainly result from inviting a stranger of another race to visit a native family, act as a strong deterrent to prevent natives from bringing these cases to a foreigner.

In a foreign missionary's first visits to a new field of labor (the time during which, for reasons hereafter stated, most of these cases occur), not only the Chinese generally, but many Christian families would instinctively avoid if possible a personal visit from him. His coming to their houses would almost inevitably attract a rabble made up of street loungers, village roughs, and boisterous children, and it is more than probable that suspicious neighbors, and curious strangers influenced by the excitement, and taking advantage of the general confusion, would disregard the ordinary rules of propriety and mingle with the crowd; altogether occasioning no little inconvenience for the time, and a great deal of offensive talk, and perhaps insults and annoyances afterwards.

While the visit of a foreigner at the first stage of intercourse with the Chinese would be attended by the above mentioned inconveniences, a native Christian can enter a Chinese family almost unobserved. Considering all the circumstances it is but natural that these cases should in almost every instance be brought to the notice of the native Christian, rather than the foreign missionary.

There is another reason, perhaps still stronger than those given above, which tends to the same result. Most missionaries—all of them so far as is known to the writer—have an instinctive shrinking from encountering, or even encouraging these manifestations. The feelings of the foreign missionary on this subject are understood by the natives, and consequently they naturally apply to their own people rather than to us. It is interesting to notice that in the instance given from the Roman church in a previous chapter, the case of supposed demon-posssesion was also brought to a native Christian, and not to the foreign teacher.

Missionaries are however sometimes applied to, as I was once myself when in company with Rev. C. P. Scott, now Bishop of the Church of England in North China. We were invited and urged by our muleteer, in whose village we were passing a night, to visit his home and cast an evil-spirit out of his sister-in-law. Our ability to do this was not, however, put to the test; as the member of the family, when she was consulted about the matter, refused to have us enter the house.

The fact of our hearing through native Christians of many more of these cases now, than some years ago, is due to the following reasons: At first Christian teachers, natives as well as foreigners, were viewed with suspicion and distrust, and there was great difficulty in gaining free access to the people. You might be in a village where there were numbers of these "possessed" persons, but the inhabitants would stoutly deny their existence. A variety of reasons combine to produce this reticence, the chief of which are the sense of disgrace on the part of a family so unfortunate as to have such a case; the fear shared by all the villagers of offending and incurring the revenge of the demon; and also the fear of putting a stranger in possession of information which might lead to serious difficulties and complications.

When, however, an individual or a family in an isolated village embraces Christianity, and reads the instances of demon-possession related in the New Testament, he naturally recommends his neighbors who are similarly afflicted to apply to Jesus for relief. When relief has been obtained the fact is soon generally known, and others who are suffering from the same malady are led to apply to Christians for help. After converts have been made, and mutual sympathy and confidence are established among them, and between them and their foreign teachers, then these experiences are freely disclosed.

The above considerations will explain why it is that we must for circumstantial facts in evidence, so far as China is concerned, depend principally upon the native Christians. Their belief, in common with the great mass of their countrymen in the reality of these manifestations is almost universal. It would be useless to argue with them on the subject. You might as well

try to raise doubts in their minds as to their
own personal identity, or the trustworthiness of
their senses. In many cases the only effect of
a missionary's dogmatically denying the reality
of demon-possessions would be to produce in
them the impression that he had a limited experience, narrow views, and was not wholly to
be relied upon as a religious teacher.

Now with regard to the testimony of the
native Christians, which has been presented in
the previous chapters, I would remark:

1.   I have endeavored to give no evidence except that of Christian men and women of intelligence and worth.

2.   They testify to facts of which they have
been eye and ear witnesses; and which are for
the most part of recent occurrence.

3.   The events to which they testify have not
taken place in private, known to themselves
only, or to a few others, but are of general notoriety, the witnesses to which could be indefinitely multiplied.

4.   No conceivable motive can be adduced for
fabrication or misrepresentation. These "demon-possessions" are, even in the view of the
natives, repulsive and disreputable, and they know
that they are still more distasteful to their
foreign teachers.

This is not a hobby, or a subject which is to
them of special interest or concern; as spiritual-

ism, for instance, is to its adherents. On the contrary it is associated with disagreeable experiences which they would gladly forget, and which under ordinary circumstances they seldom allude to.

6.   Belief in the reality of possessions by invisible spirits is not necessarily connected with a superstitious habit of mind. Chinese Christians generally are gradually disenthralled from their old heathenish superstitions such as "fung-shui," the worship of the dragon, of the kitchen god, and the earth god, and their almost innumerable deities of the Buddhist and Taoist religions; but as a rule, they remain unshaken in their belief in the reality of demon-possessions.

7.   They do not regard this subject as belonging to the domain of the marvelous. They do not consider man with his material body, the exclusive rational occupant of the earth. They believe in spirits, and in their view it is no more unnatural for an evil spirit to exist, and to act like an evil spirit, than for a man to be a man.

8.   The opinions held by them are not taught or suggested to them by their foreign teachers. On the contrary these beliefs have generally been discouraged.

9.   There could be no collusion between these witnesses. They belong to sections of country widely separated, which have little or no com-

munication with each other, and in which different dialects are spoken.

10.   These cases are not associated together as the result of a general psychic epidemic, or craze, in which delusion or imposture is sympathetically communicated from one person to another.   They are isolated and independent, both as regards time and locality, and are generally attended with but little excitement.

The question as to the explanation and the actual cause of the phenomena which we are considering is by no means to be determined by the opinions of the Chinese or of any other race.   We have only appealed to the Chinese for facts which have come under their own observation, and of which they are competent witnesses.*   The ques-

*Prof. Langlev in an article entitled "Comets and Meteors" in *The Century*, January, 1887, thus treats of the assumptions of modern thought, and the summary way in which it sets aside credible evidence:—

"Among the many superstitions of the early world, and credulous fancies of the middle ages, was the belief that great stones sometimes fell down out of heaven on to the earth.

"Pliny has a story of such a black stone big enough to load a chariot; the Mussulman still adores one at Mecca; and a mediæval emperor of Germany had a sword which was said to have been forged from one of these bolts shot out of the blue.   But. with the revival of learning, people came to know better!   That stones should fall down from the sky was clearly, they thought, an absurdity; indeed, according to the learned opinion of that time, one would hardly ask a better instance of the difference between the realities which science recognized and the absurdities which it condemned than the fancy that such a thing could be.   So at least the matter looked to the philosophers of the last century, who treated it much as they might treat certain alleged mental phenomena, for instance, if they were alive to-day, and at first refused to take any notice of these stories, when from time to time they still came to hand.   When induced to give the matter consideration they observed that all the conditions for scientific observation were violated by these bodies, since the wonder always happened at some far-off place, or at some past time, and (suspicious circumstance) the stones only fell in the presence of ignorant and unscientific witnesses, and never when scientific men were at hand to examine the facts.   That there were many worthy, if ignorant, men who asserted that they had seen such stones fall, seen them with their own eyes, and held them in their own hands, was accounted for by the general love of the marvelous, and by the ignorance of the common mind, unlearned in the conditions of scientific observation, and unguided by the great principle of the uniformity of the laws of nature."

See also on The Dogmatism of Science, an able and admirable article by R. Heber Newton, D. D., in *The Arena* (Mag.) May, 1890.

tions, what are the facts established, and how are these facts to be accounted for, will be considered hereafter.

It is a confirmation of the truth of the evidence of these Chinese witnesses that it agrees in every important particular with that of other nations ancient and modern. The importance claimed for the evidence of these Chinese witnesses is, that it shows the persistence of these phenomena up to the present time, and furnishes details not to be expected when this subject is not specifically treated, but only referred to incidentally and fragmentarily.

The facts established in the previous chapters may be summarized as follows:

1. Certain abnormal physical and mental phenomena such as have been witnessed in all ages, and among all nations, and attributed to possession by demons, are of frequent occurrence in China and other nations at this day, aud have been generally referred to the same cause.

2. The supposed demoniac at the time of "possession" passes into an abnormal state, the character of which varies indefinitely, being marked by depression and melancholy; or vacancy and stupidity amounting sometimes almost to idiocy, or it may be that he becomes ecstatic, or ferocious and malignant.

3. During transition from the normal to the abnormal state, the subject is often thrown into

paroxysms, more or less violent, during which he sometimes falls on the ground senseless, or foams at the mouth presenting symptoms similar to those of epilepsy or hysteria.

4, The intervals between these attacks vary indefinitely from hours to months, and during these intervals the physical and mental condition of the subject may be in every respect healthy and normal. The duration of the abnormal states varies from a few minutes to several days. The attacks are sometimes mild, and sometimes violent. If frequent and violent the physical health suffers.

5. During the transition period the subject often retains more or less of his normal consciousness. The violence of the paroxysms is increased if the subject struggles against, and endeavors to repress the abnormal symptoms. When he yields himself to them the violence of the paroxysms abates, or ceases altogether.

6. When normal consciousness is restored after one of these attacks the subject is entirely ignorant of everything which has passed during that state.

7. The most striking characteristic of these cases is that the subject evidences another personality, and the normal personality for the time being is partially or wholly dormant.

8. The new personality presents traits of character utterly different from those which really

belong to the subject in his normal state, and this change of character is with rare exceptions in the direction of moral obliquity and impurity.

9. Many persons while "demon-possessed" give evidence of knowledge which cannot be accounted for in ordinary ways They often appear to know of the Lord Jesus Christ as a Divine Person, and show an aversion to, and fear of Him. They sometimes converse in foreign languages of which in their normal states they are entirely ignorant.

10. There are often heard, in connection with "demon-possessions," rappings and noises in places where no physical cause for them can be found; and tables, chairs, crockery and the like are moved about without, so far as can be discovered, any application of physical force, exactly as we are told is the case among spiritualists.

11. Many cases of "demon-possession" have been cured by prayer to Christ, or in his name, some very readily, some with difficulty. So far as we have been able to discover, this method of cure has not failed in any case, however stubborn and long continued, in which it has been tried. And in no instance, so far as appears, has the malady returned, if the subject has become a Christian, and continued to lead a Christian life.

CHAPTER XI.

EXPLANATIONS: EVOLUTION AND OTHER THEORIES.

The phenomena accompanying supposed "demon-possession" are accounted for by different hypotheses in accordance with the views and proclivities of different individuals.

1. Many will doubtless refer them to delusion and imposture, and regard the subjects of these manifestations as either deceivers or deceived.

2. Others will regard them as the result of some occult force, physical or odic, not yet clearly understood.

3. The Development or Evolution school will refer them to a law inherent in man's nature, by which certain beliefs and accompanying phenomena manifest themselves in progressive stages of the development of the race.

4. The great majority of thinkers of the present day will no doubt prefer the pathological theory, and regard these manifestations as the natural results of diseased states of the nervous system.

5. Psychological Theories.

6. Others will refer them, as most nations of the past have done, to the agency of spirits or demons.

We shall consider these different hypotheses in this and the following chapters, in the above order.

1. *Explanation by Imposture.*

There can be no doubt that, in connection with the phenomena we have been considering, there is much deception, both wilful and unintentional. Still this fact should not be regarded as disproving the reality of the phenomena in all cases. To whatever cause they may be attributed, even if referable to, or accompanied by well-known symptoms of disease, simulated manifestations, as well as automatic, may naturally be expected.

Dr. Hecker speaking of cases of hysteria remarks: "This numerous class of patients certainly contributed not a little to the maintenance of the evil, for these fantastic sufferings in which dissimulation and reality could scarcely be distinguished by themselves, much less by their physicians, were imitated in the same way as the distortions of St. Vitus dancers by the impostors of that period." (*)

The same author remarks further in the same connection that "the dancing mania arising, as

*See "Hecker's Epidemics of the Middle Ages," London Edition, 1844, p. 128.

was supposed, from the bite of the tarantula, continued with all these additions of self-deception, and of the dissimulation which is such a constant attendant on nervous disorders of this kind, through the whole course of the seventeenth century."

So in China, in the case of persons subject to these abnormal conditions, voluntary symptoms are often mixed with involuntary, and doubtless many cases of alleged possession are to be referred wholly to imposture. Some persons from love of notoriety, and more often from love of gain, simulate the symptoms of the "possessed", and assume the character of fortune tellers, or healers of diseases, professing to do so by communication with spirits. Missionaries have met with some of this latter class who have acknowledge that they feigned "possession", and thus carried on a deliberate course of deception. It would be unreasonable, however, to infer from such individual cases of simulation that all the phenomena we have been considering are the result of deception and imposture. Simulation generally presupposes a reality simulated.

On the other hand converts to Christianity have declared that they were formerly mediums of demons, during which time these abnormal manifestations were not the result of deception, but of influences operating on them which they could not control. Dr. Tylor gives us the following case of this kind in his "Primitive Culture". When Dr. Mason was preaching near a village of heathen Pwo a man fell down in an epileptic fit, his familiar spirit having come over him to forbid the people to listen to the missionary, and he sang out denunciations like one frantic. This man was afterwards converted, and told the missionary that "he could not account for his former exercises, but that it certainly appeared to him as though a spirit spoke, and he must tell what was communicated."*

Strikingly similar testimony is given by one of Brainerd's Indian converts who was before his conversion a "diviner."†

Two cases similar to the above have occurred in connection with our mission station in Chi-mi, Shan-tung, China. They were described to me in detail by a theological student whose home was in that neighborhood, and who was familiarly acquainted with the subjects of both cases, one being a near relative. Both of them were well-known as sincere and consistent Christians until their deaths. They declared that for many years, before they became Christians, they submitted to, and obeyed the behests of the possessing demons from necessity, being constrained and intimidated by severe physical and mental inflictions and torments; that they believed that

* Primitive Culture: Researches into the Development of Mythology, Philosophy, Religion, Language, Art and Custom. By Edward B. Tylor, LL. D., F. R. S., Vol. 2, p, 131.

† Memoir of David Brainerd, p. 562. Also p.p. 348-351.

the actions purporting to be perfomed by the demons through them as their agents or instruments were in fact so performed; that they had no means to rid themselves of the dominion of the demons until they heard of Christianity. One of these persons, an aunt of the theological student, is said to have had, when in the abnormal state, remarkable clairvoyant powers.

The question is not, are any of these phenomena to be referred to imposture, but are they all to be so referred. I believe that the facts proved render this hypothesis entirely untenable. The subjects of these manifestations are, while in the abnormal state, apparently without their normal consciousness, and incapable either of deceiving or being deceived. If it be assumed that this supposed absence of normal consciousness is itself only deception and imposture, this assumption presupposes a degree of susceptibility to imposture in all nations and ages which passes credence, to say nothing of the evidence, which is, in a large number of cases, full and conclusive that the subject so far from trying to deceive others by inducing them to believe that he is "possessed," is using all his powers of body and mind to free himself from an infliction which he bemoans and abhors.

2. *Explanation by Odic Force.*

There is a class of writers who admit the existence of the alleged facts connected with mesmerism, spiritualism, etc., similar in many respects to these attributed to demon-possession, but believe these facts are not explainable by any natural laws or forces yet discovered; and refer them to some subtle force connected with our physical organization, similar to magnetism, which, though as yet not well understood, is an integral part of our constitution, and under the control of fixed laws. This theory is ably advocated by Rev. G. W. Samson, D.D., formerly president of Columbia University (D. C.), in a book entitled "Physical Media in Spiritual Manifestations". Without attempting an analysis of the arguments upon which Dr. Samson bases his theory, I would merely say that, admitting its probability, it does not necessarily affect the subject of demon-possession. It may perhaps give some hint or suggestion of the mode by which spiritual beings act upon human organizations. It certainly cannot prove the non-existence of supermundane beings, or that they do not at times influence men. In fact the two theories do not conflict; but Dr. Samson's theory does not explain the facts which principally require explanation, to which special reference will be made in this and the following chapters.

3. *Explanation by Evolution.*

The Development, or Evolution, theory of "possessions" is clearly presented by Rushton M. Dorman in his work entitled "Origin of Primitive Superstitions," and also by Dr. Tylor in his "Primitive Culture." The former writer says: "Too much effort has hitherto been directed to tracing a derivation of one mythological belief from another by contact or migrations of myths; the growth of mythologies among all peoples has taken place according to the laws of men's spiritual being. There is therefore a great similarity of religious belief among all peoples in the same progressive stages." He says again, "The laws of evolution in the spiritual world may be traced with as much precision as in the natural."[*]

Dr. Tylor in the introduction to his work deprecates the unwillingness of modern investigators to apply the laws of evolution to the 'higher processes of human feeling and action, of thought and language, etc." He says, "The world at large is scarcely prepared to accept the general study of human life as a branch of natural science nor to carry out in a large sense the poet's injunction to 'account for moral as for natural things.' To many educated minds there seems something presumptuous and repulsive in the view that the history of mankind is part and parcel of the history of nature, that our thoughts, wills, and actions accord with laws as definite as those which govern the motion of waves, the combination of acids and bases, and the growth of plants and animals."[†]

[*] Origin of Primitive Superstitions, Introduction, p. 13.
[†] "Primitive Culture." vol. 2, p. 132.

A few quotations from Dr. Tylor's elaborate and interesting work will show the remarkable correspondence between facts which he has collected from different sources, and those presented in the previous chapters of this work, and will also give us some idea of his way of accounting for these facts. We cannot do justice to this author without giving these quotations at some length.

Dr. Tylor says: "Morbid oracular manifestations are habitually excited on purpose, and moreover the professional sorcerer commonly exaggerates or wholly feigns them. In the more genuine manifestations the medium may be so intensely wrought upon by the idea that a possessing spirit is speaking from within him, that he may not only give this spirit's name, and speak in its character, but possibly may in good faith alter his voice to suit the spiritual utterance. The gift of spirit utterance which belongs to 'ventriloquism' in the ancient and proper sense of the term, of course lapses into sheer trickery. But that the phenomena should be thus artificially excited or dishonestly counterfeited, rather confirms than alters the present argument. Real or simulated, the details of oracle possession alike illustrate popular belief. The Patagonian wizard begins his performance with drumming and rattling till the real or pretended epileptic fit comes on by the demon entering him, who then answers questions within him with a faint and mournful voice."*

Among the wild Veddas of Ceylon, the "devil-dancers" have to work themselves into paroxysms, to gain the inspiration whereby they profess to cure their patients.† So with furious dancing to the music and chanting of the attendants, the Bodo priest brings on the fit of maniacal inspiration in which the deity fills him and gives oracles through him.‡ In Kamtchatka the female shamans, when Billukai came down into them in a thunder-storm would prophesy; or, receiving spirits with a cry of "hush;" their teeth chattered as in fever, and they were ready to divine. Among the Singpho of Southeast Asia, when the "natzo" or conjuror is sent for to see a sick patient, he calls on his "nat" or demon, the soul of a deceased foreign prince, who descends into him and gives the required answers‖. In the Pacific Islands spirits of the dead would enter for a time the body of a living man, inspiring him to declare future events or to execute some commission from the higher deities. The symptoms of oracular possession among savages have been especially well described in this region of the world. The Fijian priest sits looking steadfastly at a whale's tooth

* "Primitive Culture," vol. 2, p. 133.
† Ibid, vol 2, p. 133.
‡ Ibid, p. 133.
‖ Ibid, p. 133.

ornament amid dead silence. In a few minutes he trembles, slight twitchings of face and limbs come on which increase to strong convulsions with swelling of the veins, murmurs and sobs. Now the god has entered him; with eyes rolling and protruding, unnatural voice, pale face and livid lips, sweat streaming from every pore, and the whole aspect of a furious madman, he gives the divine answer, and then the symptoms subsiding, he looks round with a vacant stare, and the deity returns to the land of spirits. In the Sandwich Islands where the God Oro thus gave his oracles, his priest ceased to act or speak as a voluntary agent, but with his limbs convulsed, his features distorted and terrific, his eyes wild and strained he would roll on the ground foaming at the mouth, and reveal the will of the possessing god in shrill cries and sounds violent and indistinct, which the attending priest duly interpreted to the people. In Tahiti it was often noticed that men who in the natural state showed neither ability nor eloquence, would in such convulsive delirium burst forth into earnest lofty declamation, declaring the will and answers of the god, and prophesying future events in well-knit harangues full of the poetic figure and metaphor of the professional orator. But when the fit was over, and sober reason returned, the prophet's gifts were gone.[*]

* Tylor's "Primitive Culture," p. 133,

"Lastly the accounts of oracular possession in Africa show the primitive ventriloquist in perfect types of morbid knavery. In Sofola, after a king's funeral, his soul would enter into a sorcerer, and speaking in the familiar tones that all the bystanders recognized, would give counsel to the new monarch how to govern his people."

"About a century ago a negro fetish woman of Guinea is thus described in the act of answering an enquirer who has come to consult her. She is crouching on the earth, with her head between her knees, and her hands up to her face, till becoming inspired by the fetish, she snorts and foams and gasps. Then the suppliant may put his question, 'Will my friend or brother get well of this sickness?' 'What shall I give thee to set him free from his sickness?' and so forth. Then the fetish woman answers in a thin whistling voice, and with the old-fashioned idioms of generations past; and thus the suppliant receives his command, perhaps to kill a white cock, and put him at a four-cross-way, or tie him up for the fetish to come and fetch him, or perhaps merely to drive a dozen wooden pegs into the ground, so to bury his friend's disease with them."*

"The details of demoniacal possession among barbaric and civilized nations need no elaborate description, so simply do they continue

* Tylor's "Primitive Culture," Vol 2, 135.

the savage cases. But the state of things we notice here agrees with the conclusion that the possession theory belongs originally to the lower culture, and is gradually superseded by higher medical knowledge. Surveying its course through the middle and higher civilization we shall notice first a tendency to limit it to certain peculiar and severe affections, especially connected with mental disorder, such as epilepsy, hysteria, delirium, idiocy, madness; and after this a tendency to abandon it altogether in consequence of the persistent opposition of the medical faculty.

"Among the natives of South East Asia, obsession and possession by demons is strong at least in popular belief.*

"In Birma the fever-demon of the jungle seizes trespassers on his domain, and shakes them in ague till he is exorcised; while falls and apoplectic fits are the work of other spirits. The dancing of women in demoniacal possession is treated by the doctor covering their heads with a garment, and thrashing them soundly with a stick, the demon and not the patient being considered to feel the blows; the possessing spirit may be prevented from escaping by a knotted and charmed cord hung around the bewitched person's neck, and when a sufficient beating has induced it to speak by the patient's voice and declare its

* "Primitive Culture," vol. 2, pp. 135, 136.

name and business, it may either be allowed to depart, or the doctor tramples on the patient's stomach till the demon is stamped to death. For an example of invocations and offerings one characteristic story, told by Dr. Bastien, will suffice. A Bengali cook was seized with an apoplectic fit, which his Birmese wife declared was but a just retribution, for the godless fellow had gone day after day to market to buy pounds, and pounds of meat, yet in spite of her remonstrances would never give a morsel to the patron-spirit of the town; as a good wife, however, she now did her best for her suffering husband, placing near him little heaps of colored rice for the "nat!" "Ah, let him go!" "Grip not so hard!" "Oh, ride him not!" "Thou shalt have rice!" "Ah, how good that tastes!" How explicitly Buddhism recognizes such ideas, may be judged from one of the questions officially put to candidates for admission as monks or talapoins:"Art thou afflicted by madness, or with the ills caused by giants, witches, or evil-demons of the forest and mountain?"*

"Within our own domain of British India, the possession-theory and the rite of exorcism belonging to it may be perfectly studied to this day. There the doctrine of sudden ailment or nervous disease being due to a blast or possession of a "buht" or being, that is, a demon, is recognized

* "Primitive Culture," vol. 2, p. 136.

as of old; there the old witch who has possessed a man and made him sick or deranged will answer spiritually out of his body and say who she is and where she lives; there the frenzied demoniac may be seen raving, writhing, tearing, bursting his bonds, till subdued by the exorcist; his fury subsides, he stares and sighs, falls helpless to the ground, and comes to himself; and there the deities, caused by excitement, singing, and incense to enter into men's bodies, manifest their presence with the usual hysterical or epileptic symptoms, or, speaking in their own divine name and personality, deliver oracles by the vocal organs of the inspired medium." *

After tracing the history of the doctrine of demon-possession as held by the philosophers of Greece and Rome; by the Jews at the opening of the Christian era, by the early Fathers of the Christian church, and subsequently by the existing nations of Europe, Dr. Tylor adds: "It is not too much to assert that the doctrine of demoniacal possession is kept up, substantially the same theory to account for substantially the same facts, by half the human race who thus stand as consistent representatives of their forefathers back into primitive antiquity. It is in the civilized world under the influence of the medical doctrines which have been developing since classic times that the early animistic theory

* "Primitive Culture," Vol 2, pp. 136, 137.

of these morbid phenomena has been gradually superseded by views more in accordance with modern science, to the great gain of our health and happiness."*

It appears from these quotations, and other portions of the books of the two authors above referred to, that in their opinion the remarkable correspondence between the religious beliefs and superstitions of nations in different parts of the world, and in different periods of the world's history, are not due to *ab extra* causes, but are merely the natural outcome of inherent principles or tendencies in man's spiritual nature, always producing, in the same stage of development, the same outward manifestations, and the same theories respecting these manifestations; the causes of which they regard as subjective rather than objective.

In Dr. Tylor's thorough and exhaustive treatise it is but natural to expect that the doctrine of demon-possession which forms such a striking feature of "Primitive Culture" would be specially considered. In this expectation we are not disappointed. His conclusions may be summarized as follows:

I. *The facts of which the "possession" theory is the interpretation and explanation are the same in kind now that they were in the early times.* Says Dr. Tylor, "It has to be thoroughly

* "Primitive Culture." vol 2, pp. 142, 143.

understood that the changed aspect of the subject in modern opinion is not due to disappearance of the actual manifestations which early
philosophy attributed to demoniacal influence."
To repeat a statement of Dr. Tylor's already
quoted: "It is not too much to assert that the
doctrine of demoniacal possession is kept up,
substantially the same theory to account for substantially the same facts, by half the human
race, who thus stand as consistent representatives of their forefathers back into primitve antiquity."*

II. *The "possession" theory has been the
dominant one in all ages, and according to Dr.
Tylor, is rational and philosophical in its place
in man's history.* He says: "This is the savage
theory of demoniacal possession and obsession,
which has been for ages, and still remains, the
dominant theory of disease and inspiration
among the lower races. It is obviously based
on an animistic interpretation, most genuine and
rational in its proper place in man's intellectual history of the actual symptoms of the cases."
Again: "As belonging to the lower culture it is a
perfectly rational philosophical theory to account
for certain pathological facts. The general doctrine of disease-spirits and oracle-spirits appears
to have its earliest, broadest, and most consistent position within the limits of savagery. When

* "Primitive Culture" Vol. 2, p, 142.

10 *Demon*

we have gained a clear idea of it in this, its original home, we shall be able to trace it along from grade to grade of civilization, breaking away piecemeal under the influence of new medical theories, yet sometimes expanding in revival, and, at least in lingering survival, holding its place into the midst of our modern life."*

III. *Dr. Tylor traces demon possession to its supposed cause and presents his view of the philosophy which underlies it.* He says: "As in normal conditions the man's soul inhabitating his body, is held to give it life, to think, speak and act through it, so an adaptation of the self-same principle explains abnormal conditions of body or mind, by considering the new symptoms as due to the operation of a second soul-like being, a strange spirit. The possessed man, tossed and shaken in fever, pained and wrenched as' though some live creature were tearing or twisting him within, pining as though it were devouring his vitals day by day, rationally finds a personal spiritual cause for his sufferings. In hideous dreams he may even sometimes see the very ghost or nightmare fiend that plagues him. Especially when the mysterious unseen power throws him helpless on the ground, jerks and writhes him in convulsions, makes him leap upon the by-standers with a giant's strength and wild beast's ferocity; impels him with distorted

* "Primitive Culture," vol. 2, pp, 124, 125.

face and frantic gesture, and voice not his own, nor seemingly even human, to pour forth wild incoherent raving, or with thought and eloquence beyond his sober faculties to command, to foretell—such an one seems to those who watch him, and even to himself, to have become the mere instrument of a spirit which has seized him or entered into him, a possessing demon in whose personality the patient believes so implicitly that he often imagines a personal name for it which it can declare when it speaks in its own voice and character through his organs of speech; at last quitting the medium's spent and jaded body the intruding spirit departs as it came. This is the savage theory of demonical possession."* Again: "The soul's place in modern thought is in the metaphysics of religion, and its especial office there is that of furnishing an intellectual side to the religious doctrine of the future life. Such are the alternations which have differenced the fundamental animistic belief in its course through successive periods of the world's culture. Yet it is evident that, notwithstanding all this profound change, the conception of the human soul is, as to its most essential nature, continuous from the philosophy of the savage thinker, to that of the modern professor of theology. Its definition has remained from the first that of an animating, separable, surviving entity, the

* "Primitive Culture," Vol. 2, p. 124.

vehicle of individual personal existence. The theory of the soul is one principal part of a system of religious philosophy which unites in an unbroken line of mental connection, the savage fetish worshiper and the civilized Christian. The divisions which have separated the great religions of the world into intolerant and hostile sects are for the most part superficial in comparison with the deepest of all religious schisms, that which divides animism from materialism."* Many questions are here suggested of the deepest interest and the highest importance upon the consideration of which we may not now enter. In our present inquiries we are specially interested in knowing how Dr. Tylor accounts for the origin of this theory of possession, and why he regards it as rational and philosophical in its place.

About 450 pages, (or nearly one half of Dr. Tylor's two large volumes) are taken up with the classification of a wide array of facts under the general head of Animism. Demon-possession is a subordinate head, including a certain class of these facts which are supposed by Dr. Tylor to be accounted for by the same theory.

Dr. Tylor regards the theory of demon-possession in the same light as the generally received theory of the human soul. As the outward normal manifestations of human life, such as think-

* "Primitive Culture." Vol. 1, pp. 501, 502.

ing, speaking, acting, are accounted for by the supposition of a soul—a distinct, separate, surviving entity, in which man's personality inheres, so the abnormal states which we have been considering are explained by the supposition that during these states the body is possessed by another soul, which also has a distinct entity—a new personality.

We suppose Dr. Tylor accepts this theory as rational, genuine, and philosophical, because it covers the whole field which we are investigating, and clearly explains all the facts; not only the central fact of a new personality, but also those relating to the acquisition of new powers, physical and intellectual, such as superhuman strength, gifts of oratory, prophecy, and ventriloquism, and the ability to speak languages before unknown, etc.

IV. *After thus fully presenting and accounting for the doctrine of demon-possession as a hypothesis genuine, rational and philosophical in its proper place in man's intellectual history, Dr. Tylor summarily repudiates and rejects it, on grounds both vague and inconclusive.*

The principal reason which he gives for rejecting the theory of demon-possession is that it belongs to a state of savagery. He says: "Now in dealing with hurtful superstitions the proof that they are things which it is the tendency of savagery to produce, and of higher culture to destroy is accepted as a fair controversial argument. The mere historical position of a belief or custom may raise a presumption as to its origin which becomes a presumption as to its authenticity." This is certainly an easy way of disposing of the question. It is not to be supposed, however, that this assumption that the doctrine of demon-possession belongs characteristically to savages, will command unquestioned assent. On the other hand its general acceptance in all ages and by all races, including those ages and races which have had most to do in moulding the thought and civilization of the world for twenty centuries, establishes a strong presumption of its authenticity. The supposition that the Greeks, and Romans, and Jews were less qualified to form a correct judgment on matters of this kind than we are is gratifying to our self-conceit, but it is still quite possible that they may have been better qualified to weigh the evidence and determine the causes of these phenomena than men who approach the subject with the prejudgment that physical laws are competent to account for all the facts of psychology, as well as physics.

There can be no doubt that there were in former ages many "hurtful superstitions" connected not only with demonology but also with the sciences of astronomy, chemistry, geography, and medicine, which "it is the tendency of savagery to produce, and of higher culture to destroy," but these sciences, modified by higher culture, still survive, and will probably continue to do so until the end of time. It is possible that the same may be true of the long surviving doctrine of demon-posssesion.

V. *What hypothesis does Dr. Tylor adopt in the place of that of "possession" which he rejects?* The answer to this he has not given clearly and categorically, but it may be inferred from incidental statements such as the following: "It has to be thoroughly understood that the changed aspect of the subject in modern opinion is not due to disappearance of the actual manifestations which early philosophy attributed to demoniacal influence. Hysteria and epilepsy, delirium and mania, and such like bodily and mental derangements still exist." . . . "It is in the civilized world under the influence of the medical doctrines which have been developing since classic times, that the early animistic theory of these morbid phenomena has been gradually superseded by views more in accordance with modern science, to the great gain of our health and happiness." . . "Yet whenever in times old or new, we find demoniacal influences brought forward to account for affections which scientific physicians now explain on a different principle, we must be careful not to misjudge the ancient doctrine and its place in history. Just as mechanical astronomy gradually superseded the animistic astronomy of the lower races, so biological pathology gradually superseded animistic pathology, the immediate operation of personal spiritual beings in both cases giving place to the operation of natural processes." * "Jews and Christians at that time held the doctrine which had prevailed for ages before, and continued to prevail for ages after, referring to possession and obsession by spirits the symptoms of mania, epilepsy, dumbness, delirious and oracular utterances, and other morbid conditions mental and bodily." †

There can be no doubt that modern medical science has modified the "possession" theory as held by savages; rendered the belief in many superstitions impossible, and very much circumscribed the sphere of its beliefs. The same is true, as has been noted above, of other sciences, and so that argument, if it proves anything, proves too much, unless we are prepared to relegate all these sciences to the domain of savages and superstition.

Dr. Tylor intimates that all cases of supposed demon-possession are identical with "hysteria, epilepsy, delirium, and mania, and such like bodily and mental derangements;" but this is a pure assumption which is disproved by facts,

* "Primitive Culture," Vol. 2, pp. 142, 143.

† Ibid, Vol. 2. d. 138

as will be shown in the following chapter. He says that the old theory of "possession" "has been gradually superseded by views more in accordance with modern science;" but does not tell us what these views are. He states that "scientific physicians now explain on a different principle" the facts formerly explained by demon-possession, but we search in vain to find what this explanation is. The phenomena in question are referred to "natural processes" rather than "personal spiritual beings," but we are not told how "natural processes" produce or account for these phenomena.

Dr. Tylor seems to think that he has little to do in accounting for the phenomena under consideration, but to assign them their "proper place" in the process of "evolution in the spiritual world." This, however—even if the place assigned be the correct one—could not reasonably be regarded as a full and satisfactory treatment of the subject. Merely assigning a place explains nothing, accounts for nothing. What would we say of a medical work which disposed of such diseases as whooping-cough, measles, gout, and paralysis, by saying that the "proper place" for the former is in childhood, and for the latter in old age?

But we may further inquire, what is meant in Dr. Tylor's treatise, by the "proper place" of the theory of demon-possession? It is simply

the place which Dr. Tylor assigns to it in his
hypothesis of evolution in the spiritual world.
This evolution is supposed to be from the lower
forms of fetishism through polytheism and
pantheism up to monotheism, the process of
evolution to culminate (if we understand Dr.
Tylor) in the negation of a personal God,
and also of a personal soul as a separate
existing entity. This theory which is the
basis of Dr. Tylor's whole treatise is disproved
by the concurrent testimony of the prominent
nations of antiquity. The history and literature of India show us in the earliest period
a close approximation to monotheism, followed
by pantheism and polytheism. The Chinese
race invariably characterize the earliest period of
their history as pre-eminent above all others
for its theoretical and practical ethics and religion. The ancient classics of China, like those
of India, point to a monotheistic period antecedent to pantheism and polytheism. The elaborate languages of some of the tribes of interior
Africa suggest, if they do not prove, that the
races speaking these languages have degenerated
from a higher type. In opposition then to the
theory adopted by Dr. Tylor, the testimony of
antiquity goes to confirm the general teachings
of Scripture, concisely stated in the first chapter of the Epistle to the Romans, that "evolution
in the spiritual world," when it has not been

counteracted by the influences of the truth as revealed in the Old and New Testaments has been downward from primeval monotheism, tending to polytheism and fetishism.

Speaking of this theory of evolution, Rev. W. A. P. Martin, LL. D. President of the Peking University, says:*

"A wide survey of civilized nations (and the history of others is beyond reach) shows that the actual process undergone by the human mind in its religious development is precisely opposite to that which this theory supposes; in a word that man was not left to construct his own creed, but that his blundering logic has always been active in its attempts to corrupt and obscure a divine original. The connection subsisting between the religious systems of ancient and distant countries presents many a problem difficult of solution. Indeed their mythologies and religious rites are generally so distinct as to admit the hypothesis of an independent origin; but the simplicity of their earliest beliefs exhibits an unmistakable resemblance suggestive of a common source.

"China, India, Egypt, and Greece all agree in the monotheistic type of their early religion. The Orphic hymns long before the advent of the popular divinities celebrated the *Pantheos*, the Universal God. The odes compiled by Con-

* "The Chinese," pp. 163, 164.

fucius testify to the early worship of *Shangte*, the Supreme Ruler. The Vedas speak of 'one unknown true Being, all-present, all-powerful; the Creator, Preserver and Destroyer of the universe.' And in Egypt as late as the time of Plutarch, there were still vestiges of a monotheistic worship. 'The other Egyptians,' he says, 'all made offerings at the tomb of the sacred beasts; but the inhabitants of the Thebaid stood alone in making no such offerings, not regarding as a God anything that can die, and acknowledge no God but one that they call Kneph, who had no birth and can have no death.' Abraham in his wanderings found the God of his fathers known and honored in Salem, in Gerar, and in Memphis; while at a latter day, Jethro in Midian, and Balaam in Mesopotamia, were witnesses that the knowledge of Jehovah was not yet extinct in those countries."*

It is too often assumed that we may justly infer a low stage of religious development from a low state of development in the arts and sciences. We may, however, freely admit that civilization was evolved by a slow and gradual progress from the rudest beginnings, without at all invalidating the teachings of Scripture and of history, that, in the knowledge and worship of God, man's progress, when left alone, has been

---

* Similar testimony is given at length from various sources by Rev. F. F. Ellenwood, D. D. in his "Oriental Religions and Christianity," p. 222; also by Chas. Loring Brace in "The Unknown God."

downwards instead of upwards. Men may dwell in caves, use stone implements and be clothed in skins, and still be pious monotheists, free from fetishism or polytheism; and men may be advanced to the highest stage of civilization, with their religious instincts almost obliterated, and worshipers of no God.

Dr. Tylor not only fails to give us a new theory in the place of the "Animistic Theory" which he discards, but in the course of his investigations presents many a fact of which he gives no explanation, and raises new questions to which he gives no satisfactory answers. Having in the introduction to his book quoted with approbation the axiom of Leibnitz that "nothing happens without its sufficient reason" it is but natural to suppose that he would have considered and solved questions constantly arising in connection with the cases which he adduces, such as the following: What is the reason why persons in these abnormal states invariably assume a new personality, and act out that personality with uniform consistency? How do they suddenly acquire the "gift of ventriloquism," "the ability to command, to counsel, and to foretell?" How is it that men who in the natural state show neither ability nor eloquence, in such "convulsive deliverances burst forth into earnest, lofty declamation, prophesying future events in well-knit harangues full of the poetic

figure and metaphor of the professional orator?"
How is it that they are able to speak accurately
and fluently languages which they have never
learned?   These questions call for answers,
but I have not been able to find answers to
them in the two interesting and valuable volumes
for which I gladly acknowledge my indebtedness.
Yet as it is hinted or implied that the desired
answers have been already furnished by the medical profession, a further consideration of this
subject must be reserved for the following chapter in which the Pathological Theory is examined.

CHAPTER XII.

THE PATHOLOGICAL THEORY.

In accounting for the phenomena of so-called "demon-possession" the Medical or Pathological Theory is no doubt the one most generally adopted.

A book entitled "Nervous Derangement" * by William A. Hammond, M. D., Surgeon General U. S. Army; Professor of Diseases of the Mind and Nervous system in the Medical Department of the University of the City of New York, etc., contains the fullest presentation of the Pathological Theory which I have been able to find, and embodies views which so far as my observation goes, are largely adopted by the medical profession.

Dr. Hammond claims to have adopted the purely philosophical or inductive method; and in defining his principles and modes of procedure, excites high expectations that he will be able to throw a flood of scientific and philosophical light on the subject before us. He says: "There is an

* "Nervous Derangement, Somnambulism, Hypnotism, Hysteria, Hysteroid Affections," etc., New York, G. P. Putnam & Sons, 1881.

inherent tendency in the mind of man to ascribe to supernatural agencies those events the causes of which are beyond his knowledge; and this is especially the case with the abnormal and morbid phenomena which are manifested in his own person. But as his intellect becomes more thoroughly trained, and as science advances in its developments, the range of his credulity becomes more and more circumscribed, his doubts are multiplied, and he at length reaches that condition of healthy skepticism which allows of no belief without the proof". . . "He has learned to doubt, and, therefore, to reason better; he makes experiments, collects facts, does not begin to theorize until his data are sufficient, and then is careful that his theories do not extend beyond the foundation of certainty, or at least of probability, upon which he builds."*

"But there have always been, and probably always will be, individuals whose love for the marvelous is so great, and whose logical powers are so small, as to render them susceptible of entertaining any belief, no matter how preposterous it may be; others more numerous, who, staggered by facts which they cannot understand, accept any hypothesis which may be offered as an explanation, rather than confess their ignorance; and others again—and these the most dangerous to the community—whose education, full

* Page 229, 230.

though it may have been in certain directions, is yet narrow, and of such a character as to warp their judgments in all matters affecting the preconceived ideas by which their whole lives are ostensibly governed.

"The real and fraudulent phenomena of what is called spiritualism, and of miraculous cases, are of a character to make a profound impression upon the credulous and the ignorant; and both these classes have accordingly been active in spreading the most exaggerated ideas relative to matters which are either absurdly false, or not so very astonishing, when viewed by the cold light of science."*

As Dr. Hammond proceeds in his investigations he seems much less confident of reaching clear and definite results, and his language assumes a different tone.

"Now after this survey of some of the principal phenomena of natural and artificial somnambulism, are we able to determine in what their condition essentially consists? I am afraid we shall be obliged to answer this question in the negative, and mainly for the reason, that with all the study that has been given to the subject, we are not yet sufficiently well acquainted with the normal functions of the nervous system to be in a position to pronounce with definiteness on their aberrations. Nevertheless, the mat-

* Page 30.

13 Demon

ter is not one of which we are wholly ignorant. We have some important data upon which to base our investigations into the philosophy of the conditions in question, and inquiry, even if leading to erroneous results, at least promotes reflection and discussion, and may in time carry us to absolute truth." * These remarks are most just and reasonable. They are, however, by no means reassuring as to the adequacy of the Pathological Theory to account for the facts in question, and hardly consistent with the authoritative tone, and dogmatic statements which appear in other extracts from his work.

Avowed beliefs and theories on the subject of psychology incapacitate Dr. Hammond for considering this subject without a strong bias almost amounting to prejudgment.

He says: "Science has for ages been fettered by theological and metaphysical dogmas, which give the mind an existence independent of the nervous system, and which teach that it is an entity which sets all the functions of the body in action, and of which the brain is the seat. There can be no scientific enquiry relative to matters of faith, facts alone admit of investigation; and hence so long as psychology was expounded by teachers who had never even seen a human brain, much less a spinal cord, or sympathetic nerve, who knew absolutely nothing of nervous physi-

* Page 30

ology, and who, therefore, taught from a standpoint which had not a single fact to rest upon, it was not to be expected that the true science of mind could make much progress."

The author defines "mind" * to be "the force developed by nervous action." Again † "The mind may be regarded as a force, the result of nervous action, and the elements of which are perception, intellect, the emotions, and the will."

When Dr. Hammond comes to consider directly the subject of demon-possession his statements are characterized by great inaccuracy and misapprehension. Indeed he abandons his purely philosophical method, and assumption and dogmatism take the place of evidence. He ascribes to believers in demon-possession views and theories which they do not hold; points out grounds or reasons on which they base their beliefs which are not so regarded by them, and disregards altogether the real evidence on which their belief rests.

In speaking of the modern scientist he says: "Thus he does not now believe the bodies of lunatics, epileptics, and hysterical women, are inhabited by devils and demons, for he has ascertained by observation that the abnormal conditions present in such persons can be accounted for by material derangments of the organs or functions of the system."

* Page 30.
† Page 243.

The argument here is, or rather the inference suggested to the reader is, that nations who hold the theory of demon-possession believe that the bodies of lunatics, epileptics, and hysterical women are inhabited by devils and demons, and that cases of lunacy, epilepsy, and hysteria, are regarded by these nations as cases of possession. These intimations, however, are not justified by facts and are very misleading That there may have been individuals in some nations and ages who have held such views is quite probable.   What is insisted on is that such are by no means general or typical.   Nations who hold the doctrine of demon-possession, distinguish between it and nervous diseases.   The Chinese of the present day have separate and distinct names for idiocy, insanity, epilepsy and hysteria, which they ascribe to physical derangment as their immediate cause, regarding them as quite distinct from demon-possession.   They not unfrequently ascribe diseases of various kinds to evil spirits, as their originating causes, considering them, however, as differing from the same diseases originating without the agency of spirits, only in origin and not in nature, and, as quite distinct from the abnormal conditions of "possession."

The assertion that instances of so-called "possession" are only cases of physical disease originating in abnormal conditions of the nervous

system is of such general acceptance that it is
met with in our current periodical and book literature; in our standard encyclopedias, and some
times, (by implication at least) in Christain
treatises. The instances given in Scripture are
accounted for in the same way. I believe however, that this assertion must be rejected.
It is not true, as we have seen in the cases
from China, and a little consideration will show
that it is not true with regard to the cases
in the New Testament.

First. The Scriptures do not confound demon-possession with diseases, but uniformly
make a clear distinction between them. We
read: "He cast out spirits with a word, and
healed all that were sick" Matt. viii. 16. "They
brought unto him all that were sick, holden with
divers diseases and torments, possessed with
demons; and epileptic and palsied, and he healed them." Matt. iv:24. "They brought unto him
all that were sick, and those that were possessed
of demons." Mark i. 32. In the above passages
demon-possession is differentiated from all sickness or disease; also from divers diseases and
torments, and specifically from epilepsy and paralysis. This is the uniform testimony of the
New Testament. *

Second. But it may be said that, though it
be true that the Scripture writers make a dis-

* Compare Matt. ix: 32, 33; Matt. x: 1; Luke vi: 17, 18 and ix: 1;Mrk.iii:
15. vii. 12.

tinction between demon-possession and disease, there is really no such distinction; cases of "possession" being in fact only cases of physical disease. * In opposition to this view it will be shown in the latter part of this chapter, and the following chapter, that there is now a tendency among prominent scientific writers to relegate these cases of "possession" to the domain of Psychology rather than Pathology, and to refer these phenomena to causes not yet understood. The presumption seems to be very strong that the unscientific Chinese, and Jews, (to say nothing of other nations) were, so far as this subject is concerned more careful observers of facts, and more correct in their deductions and conclusions than many who have been leaders of public opinion in our times.

Dr. Hammond depreciates the doctrine of "possession" by representing it as belonging to races of a low type of culture, incapable by reason of ignorance and superstition of forming an intelligent opinion on this subject. In this respect his position is similar to that taken by Dr. Tylor. He says of "persons who ascribe occurrences which do not accord with their experiences to the agency of disembodied individ-

---

* In recent times "Epilepsy" has with some medical writers acquired a wider range of meaning than it formerly had. Having assumed that "possession" is a form of "epilepsy" the distinguishing characteristics of "possession" are attributed to it. By this process "possession" *is* "epilepsy" because "epilepsy" is made the same as "possession." The difficulty, however, of accounting for the phenomena in question on the hypothesis of their being the result of disease still remains.

uals whom they imagine to be circulating through the world:" " in this respect they resemble those savages who regard the burning lens, the mirror, and other things which produce unfamiliar effects, as animated by deities. Their minds are decidedly fetish worshiping in character, and are scarcely in this respect of a more elevated type than the Congo negro who endows the rocks and trees with higher attributes than he claims for himself."* It would be more in accordance with fact to say that the doctrine of demon-possession has been held by almost all the nations of the world, including those most highly cultivated, such as Egypt, Greece, Rome and India, nations to whom we owe a large portion of what is highest and noblest in the civilization of this 19th century. It is quite true that they were ignorant respecting the "human brain," "the spinal cord," "the sympathetic nerves," and "nervous physiology" generally, but they were favored with the teachings of men who were close observers of nature, who were accustomed to weigh evidence accurately and impartially, who were philosophers and men of genius of the highest type, and who came to the consideration of this subject free from bias and preconception. Is it not quite possible that it was an advantage rather than a disadvantage that they had not formed the prejudgment that possession is im-

* Page 230.

possible and absurd, and that mind is not a separate entity, but only the force developed by nervous action? So far as the historical argument is worth anything it goes to establish a presumption that the possession theory is the true one. This question is to be decided, however, not by individual authority, but by well ascertained facts, in gaining a knowledge of which it is our privilege to avail ourselves of all the light which modern science can give us.

After Dr. Hammond's confident assurance that modern medical science is able to account for all the abnormal conditions connected with "demon-possession," we had certainly every reason to expect that he would show us clearly and specifically how medical science explains these facts. It is not too much to say that he has hardly even attempted to do this.

He illustrates what he supposes have always been regarded as symptoms of "possession," by reference to a case of "hystero-epilepsy" which he met with in his practice. He says in speaking of it: "Such a case as this would, undoubtedly, at a not very remote anterior period have been regarded almost without a dissentient voice, as one of diabolical or demoniacal possession, and even now there are not wanting learned and pious theologians, Catholic and Protestant, who would certainly thus designate it, for it fulfills in all respects the description given of such cases, both in ancient and modern times."* The fact is, this case only presents pathological symptoms that belong alike to cases of "possession," and diseases or derangements of the nervous system, and is almost entirely wanting in the special symptoms of "possession."

Dr. Hammond goes on to say: "Thus if we go back to the writers of the New Testament we find the phenomena well described. There are convulsive movements, the body is contorted, the patient cries out, he foams at the mouth, falls down and then reposes. The patient is torn, gnashes his teeth. He falls on the ground and wallows foaming. He is contorted (vexed;) falls sometimes into the fire and sometimes into the water."† Here again Dr. Hammond cites only pathological symptoms which are common to cases of "demon-possession" and to ordinary derangements of the nervous system, and strangely fails to notice symptoms which specially characterize cases of "possession" which are not pathological, and do not harmonize with his purely pathological theory. It is readily admitted that Mania, Idiocy, Epilepsy, and Hysteria have symptoms similar to those of "possession." This by no means proves, however, that so-called cases of "possession" are only varied forms of these diseases. The same symptoms may

* Hammond; p. 150.

† Hammond; 150 151.

be due to very different causes, and belong to very different diseases. This familiar fact is the well-known cause of the difficulty which physicians constantly meet with in the diagnosis of diseases, being often obliged to wait until the disease in hand developes some new and pronounced symptoms which at once reveal its true character, and differentiate it from all other diseases with which it has symptoms in common. It is important then to inquire what the symptoms which peculiarly characterize and differentiate demon-possession are, and we will here particularly mention three of them. (Compare pp. 143-5)

FIRST MARK. *The chief differentiating mark of so-called demon-possession is the automatic presentation and the persistent and consistent acting out of a new personality.*

(1) This is shown in categorical assertions of the person speaking declaring that he is a demon, and often giving his name and dwelling place;

(2) Also in the use of pronouns. The first personal pronoun always represents the demon while by-standers are addressed in the second person, and the subject "possessed" is generally spoken of in the third person, and regarded for the time being as in an unconscious state, and practically non-existent.

(3) The same distinction of individuality appears in the use of names or titles. In China the professed demon generally applies to himself

or herself the title *shien* "genius," and speaks of the possessed subject as my *hiang to*, "incense burner," or "medium."

(4) This new personality also manifests itself in sentiments, declarations, facial expressions and physical manifestations, harmonizing with the above assumption.

The appropriate and consistent use of these pronouns, epithets, and sentiments in rapid conversations with numerous by-standers, would, on the supposition of deception or imposture, be exceedingly difficult, if not quite impossible, even in the case of adepts in the art of simulation; to say nothing of the same phenomena (occurring apparently with perfect spontaneity) in the case of children, who pass into this state suddenly and unexpectedly, and have no recollection or consciousness of what happens while in it.

This matter of the assumption of a new personality throws an important light on the origin of the theory of demon-possession. Most writers regard it as having been devised by the observers of these phenomena, and it is, as we have seen, ascribed to savages. In point of fact, however, it probably should be referred rather to the "demoniac." It is he who asserts this theory, and the minds of observers are simply exercised in determining whether this declaration is true or false.

This new personality may seem at first analogous to or identical with the assumption and apparent belief in a different personality not uncommonly met with in insane persons. A man imagines himself to be the Duke of Wellington, or Bonaparte, or George Washington, or some other distinguished personage. A closer comparison of these cases, however, will show that they are quite different. (1). In cases of demonomania there is a clear and constant recognition by the new personality of the continued and distinct existence and individuality of the subject "possessed", the new personality speaking of the possessed subject in the third person, which peculiarity, so far as my knowledge goes, is entirely wanting in insane persons. (2). The demoniac when in the abnormal state characterized by the new personality really seems and acts in all respects like an entirely different person, while the insane person is his diseased self, and the assumed personality is a transparent unreality.

Frederick W. H. Myers, in a paper which appeared in the Nineteenth Century, Nov. 1886, gives a very interesting account of what he designates "Multiplex Personality." A patient in consequence of an injury received by the brain in childhood had different stages of his life dissevered, so that he lived in only one stage at a time, without any consciousness or memory of any other stage. Mr. Myers gives a full account of these different states of consciousness, and the means by which they might be artificially induced. It is evident that the various exhibitions of personality in this case all belong distinctly to the same subject.

Mr. Myers says further in this article: "Instances of self severance profound as Louis V's are naturally to be sought mainly in the lunatic asylum. There indeed we find duplicated individuality in its grotesque forms. We have the man who has always lost himself, and insists on looking for himself under the bed. We have the man who maintains that there are two of him, and sends his plate the second time, saying: 'I have had plenty but the other fellow has not.' We have the man who maintains that he is himself and his brother too; and when asked how he can possibly be both at once he replied; 'Oh, by a different mother.'"

In all cases of this kind the personality presented is that of the diseased subject. The pronoun "I" always refers to the diseased subject; in cases of demonomania never.

This topic of changes in personality is elaborately treated in a recent work entitled: "The Diseases of Personality" by M. Ribot. The illustrative cases which this author presents are simply, to use an expression borrowed by him from another author, "successive attitudes of the Me." Many of them appear to be cases of mania, and some of them show symptoms similar to those we have been considering; but in no case is the original normal personality lost sight of, and referred to by the new personality in the third person. Nor do we ever find in this ably written book any hypothesis which accounts for the facts in question.

A further consideration of the changes of personality will be found in the following chapter.

SECOND MARK. *Another differentiating mark of demon-possession is the evidence it gives of knowledge and intellectual power not possessed by the subject; nor explainable on the pathological hypothesis.* We have had proof in the previous chapter in extracts from Dr. Tylor's "Primitive Culture" of the sudden acquisition of powers of oratory and poetic expression, and the gift of ventriloquism. In the cases which have come before us, from whatever source they have been derived, the possession of knowledge and information which could not be acquired in any ordinary way, is a constantly occurring characteristic. Perhaps the most palpable and striking evidence of this kind is the ability to speak languages unknown by the subject. This ability is frequently referred to by Chinese witnesses.

In one of the cases from Germany, given on page 115, we are told: "The demons spoke in all the European languages, and in some which Blumhardt and others did not recognize."

Andrew Dickson White LL. D. in an article in the "Popular Science Monthly" on Diabolism and Hysteria, June, 1889, gives an account of alleged cases of diabolical possession in a French village on the borders of Switzerland, which occurred in 1853. He says: "The afflicted were said to have climbed trees like squirrels, to have shown superhuman strength, and to have experienced the gift of tongues, speaking in German and Latin, and even in Arabic."

Not long after this, Prof. Tissot an eminent member of the medical faculty at Dijon visited the spot, and began a series of researches of which he afterwards published a full account.

Dr. White further states: "Dr. Tissot also examined into the gift of tongues exercised by the possessed. As to German and Latin no great difficulty was presented; it was by no means hard to suppose that some of the girls might have learned some words of the former language in the neighboring Swiss Canton, where German was spoken, or even in Germany itself; and as to Latin, considering that they had heard it from childhood in the church, there seemed nothing very wonderful in their uttering some words in that language also."

The following is from "Ten years with Spiritual Mediums." "In certain abnormal and highly excited states of the nervous system, as is proved by abundant facts, matters impressed deep on the memory of a father present themselves to the consciousness of his posterity.   I have no doubt, for instance that the daughter of Judge Edmonds derives her capacity to speak, in the trance state, in languages unfamiliar to her in the ordinary moods of consciousness, from her father's studies in that direction, or rather, from the nervous habit engendered by those studies."

The above quotations are given as furnishing other instances of the "gift of tongues,"   What is worthy of notice is—First, that the fact is acknowledged; Second, the extreme improbability, not to say absurdity, of the hypotheses proposed to account for it.

Further references to this subject may be found in the writings of the early Fathers of the Christian church.   Clemens Alexandrinus says: "Plato attributes a peculiar dialect to the gods, infering this from dreams and oracles, and especially from demoniacs, who do not speak their own language or dialect, but that of the demons who are entered into them." *

Lucian, who died about A. D. 181, speaks of some in his day who "delivered the demoniacs from their tortures."   He then alludes to our Lord as "that Syrian of Palestine who cured the sick man," saying "The man is silent but the

* Miscellanies, Bk I, p. 443.

demon answers either in the language of the Greek, or Barbarians, or whatever country he be."*

Dr. Hammond in his book, repeatedly refers to the fact that his bromide prescriptions form the best formulas for exorcising spirits, as conclusive evidence that these symptoms are only pathological. The proof is not, however, so conclusive as might at first appear. If bromides have the effect of giving tone to the nervous system and strengthening the will so as to emancipate it from "ab extra" control, the use would be just as appropriate and consistent on the supposition of the possession theory as of the pathological.

In a manner somewhat similar, it is inferred by some writers that, as patients in India supposed to be possessed by spirits are cured by a good flagellation, it is evident that the supposed "possessed" persons are pretenders and impostors. Whatever we may think about it, it should be remembered, that flaggelation, and other modes of inflicting pain, are common means of exorcising spirits by those who are believers in spirit-posssesion and they regard this method as perfectly consistent with their belief, and most rational. Their theory is this: Spirits seek to inhabit the bodies of men and animals for the sake of finding a resting place, and, in some way

* Lucian, in Philopsend, p. 833 Quoted by Wm. Ramsey.

13 Demon

not understood by us, getting physical gratification. It is supposed that while the person "possessed" is in a state of unconsciousness, physical pain and pleasure are transferred to the possessing spirit, and he may be driven out by making him so uncomfortable in his new abode that he is glad to leave and go elsewhere. The crying out from pain with the strange abnormal voice, the promising to leave, and the immediate fulfillment of the promise, are regarded as obvious confirmations of the truth of this theory. (Compare p. 103, in this vol.)

THIRD MARK. *Another differentiating mark of demonomania, intimately connected with the assumption of the new personality is, that with the change of personality there is a complete change of moral character.*

The character presented is debased and malicious, having an extreme aversion and hatred to God, and especially to the Lord Jesus Christ and the Christian religion. Prayer, or even the reading of the Bible or some Christian book, throws the patient into a paroxysm of opposition and rage; and persistence in these exercises is almost invariably followed by the return of the subject to the normal state. These peculiarities, appear frequently in the previous chapters. (See note, p. 206.)

It is needless for us to extend our inquiries

respecting Dr. Hammond's treatment of demon-possession. We have already presented all the light which his book affords on the subject. The result is certainly meagre, superficial, and disappointing. The author of a *quasi* medical work,* who holds to the theory that the abnormal conditions, and the psychological phenomena of spiritualism are referable to, and demonstrably produced by diseased states of the nervous system, endeavors to furnish a more philosophical basis for the theory. He treats specifically of the phenomena of spiritualism some of which are, as will be shown in a subsequent chapter, very similar to, if not identical with, those of demon-possession.

He says, "I was reluctantly forced to dismiss one scientific explanation after another, as inadequate to the facts, and either to suspend opinion, or to cast about for explanation, both adequate to the phenomena and rigidly scientific in its terms."

The phenomena, which he regards as actual objective realities, and not hallucinations or illusions, he describes as follows: "The phenomena appear to me to present two very distinct series, seldom present in the same person, which I shall style respectively nervo-psychic and nervo-dynamic—meaning, under the former, to include

* "Ten years with Spiritual Mediums," by Francis Gerry Fairfield. D. Appleton & Co. N. Y. 1875.

clairvoyance in its ordinary aspects, trance prevision, presentiment, and the like; under the latter, table-tipping, rappings, elevation of bodies, writing with phantom-hands, production of visible phantoms from luminous clouds, and other feats involving the presumption of an invisible dynamic agency."

His theory for accounting for this may be briefly stated as follows:

Mediums, or those capable of producing these phenomena, are persons whose nervous condition is ~~diseased or~~ abnormal, who have some "nervous or cerebral lesion." Mediums of "cephalic" temperament are clairvoyants; and those of vital temperaments produce the "nervo-dynamic" feats of table-tipping, rapping and the like. These phenomena of both kinds, he believed to be effected through the means of a "peripheral nervous aura," which is emitted by the medium and surrounds him as a kind of halo, which is even visible to persons of a highly sensitive constitution. The mediums through and within the range of this "peripheral nervous aura," which is more or less extended in different individuals, produce the phenomena of spiritualism both dynamic and psychical, which are merely the natural result of the working of the nervous system, in accordance with laws of our being not yet fully understood. The supposition of **spirit** agency he regards as unnecessary and **unscientific.**

In support of this theory, the author refers to the fact that mediums are characteristically persons of abnormal or sensitive nervous constitutions; and that their performances are attended with unnatural and intense nervous or cerebral action, which taxes to a higher degree the vital powers, and produces premature physical exhaustion and death.

These well known facts are quite as consistent with the old hypothesis that the soul of man in his normal condition is the efficient cause of all his actions dynamic and psychic, and that in cases of "possession" the efficient cause is the demon.

This book is referred to as furnishing another instance of an earnest attempt to formulate and reduce to order and consistency, the hypothesis which would account for abnormal psychical conditions of men by the action of a diseased nervous system. The theory propounded seems to have been as unsatisfactory to the scientific world, as the existing scientific theories at the time it was written were to the author.

We are fortunate in having a further presentation of the Pathological Theory of "demonomania" by no less an authority than Dr. Griesinger of Berlin. He approaches the subject from the standpoint of mental pathology rather than physical. Three illustrative cases from his valuable work on Mental Pathology and Therapeutics have already been given in the ninth chapter of this book.

These cases are represented as having symptoms "evidently analogous to epileptic, or still more frequently to hysterical attacks," but distinguished from these and other abnormal states by the one differentiating mark which has been insisted on in the previous part of this chapter, viz; the persistent assertion of a new and distinct personality. The cases given by this author differ somewhat from those which have been presented to the reader in the previous chapters of this book, in the fact of the consciousness of the subject or patient not being wholly suppressed, the new personality manifesting itself in connection with that of the subject, and addressing the subject in the second person. In one case presented there are six distinct personalities present. This author has the great merit of distinguishing clearly between these cases and others which have symptoms in common with them; of seizing upon the characteristic marks of these cases and endeavoring to account for them. How far he succeeds in doing this the reader must judge for himself. We will give Dr. Griesinger's views in his own words. "That form of melancholia in which the predominant delusion is that the subject of it is possessed by some demon, appears chiefly in females (almost always hysterical women) and in children.

The most easy explanation of this physiological phenomenon is found in those by no means rare cases where the trains of thought are always accompanied by a feeling of inward contradiction, which quite involuntarily attaches itself to them, the result of which is a fatal division or separation in the personality.   In the more developed cases, this circle of ideas, which constantly accompanies and arrays itself in opposition to the actual thought, asserts a perfectly independent existence; it sets in motion the mechanism of speech, exhibits and clothes itself in words, and appears to have no connection with the (ordinary) *ego* of the individual. Of this train of ideas which acts independently on the organs of speech, the individual giving utterance to them has no consciousness before he hears them; the *ego* does not perceive them; they spring from a region of the soul which is in obscurity so far as the *ego* is concerned; they appear to the individual to be utterly foreign, and are felt as intruders exercising a constraint upon his thoughts.   Hence uneducated persons see in these thoughts the presence of a strange being. In some cases we find in the extravagant discourse of these women or children a vein of poetry or irony utterly at variance with the opinions which they formerly most dearly prized; but usually the demon is a very dull and trivial fellow." *

* Griesinger; pp. 169.

Dr. Griesinger regards the above as the "most easy explanation" of these physiological phenomena, but does not say whether he considers it as quite satisfactory or not. Its effect on most minds will probably be to raise new questions and difficulties. Whence arises this "involuntary inward contradiction?" this fatal division or separation of the personality? How is it that this "circle of ideas" or in other words "this train of ideas," supposed to "spring from a region of the soul which is in obscurity so far as the *ego* is concerned," at the same time "appears to have no connecton with the ordinary *ego* of the individual?"

By what process does "this train of ideas," arraying itself against the actual thought, "assert a perfectly independent existence?" becoming in fact an "intruder," an *alter ego*? How is it that this *alter ego*, "acts independently on the organs of speech," and "sets in motion the mechanism of speech," so that the "ordinary *ego*" "has no consciousness of the ideas uttered before he hears them?" As this "train of thought appears to have no connection with the ordinary *ego* of the individual,"whence does it proceed? Why does it happen that out of an indefinite number and variety of "trains of thought", only this one "train of thought" or "circle of ideas," and that such an unusual and extraordinary one, should take possession of and "set in motion the mechanism of speech, exhibit and clothe itself in words, etc?" What is the one cause for this unique class of phenomena, occurring with such remarkable similarity and large degree of uniformity in France, Germany, China, India, Africa, in all ages, and all nations? The phenomena in question cannot be regarded as explained until such obvious questions as the above are satisfactorily answered.

We have still another medical theory for accounting for the facts connected with so-called demonomania, given by Dr. Baelz, of the Imperial University of Japan. A case selected from several others, as occurring in his medical practice in Japan, is given in chapter nine. We will give Dr. Baelz' theory in his own words. He says: "The explanation of the disorder is not so far to seek as might be supposed. Possession is evidently related to hysteria, and to the hypnotic phenomena which physiologists have recently studied with so much care, the cause of all alike being the fact that, whereas in healthy persons one half of the brain alone is actually engaged—in right-handed persons the left half of the brain, and in left-handed persons the right—leaving the other half to contribute only in a general manner to the function of thought, nervous excitement arouses this other half, and the two, one the organ of the usual self, the other the organ of the new pathologically affected self, are set over against each other. The *rationale* of possession is an auto-suggestion, an idea arising either with apparent spontaneity, or else from the subject matter of it being talked about in the patient's presence, and then over-mastering her weak mind exactly as happens in hypnosis. In the same manner the idea of the possibility of the cure will often actually effect the cure. The cure-worker must be a person of strong mind and power of will, and must enjoy the patient's full confidence. For this reason the priests of the Nichiren sect, which is the most superstitious and bigoted of the Japanese Buddhist sects, are the most successful expellers of foxes, occasionally fits and screams accompanying the exit of the fox. In all cases, even when the fox leaves quietly, great prostration remains for a day or two, and sometimes the patient is unconcious of what has happened."

This theory is certainly interesting and plausible. Being in the main identical with that of Dr. Griesinger, representing the machinery of the mind, or at least one-half of it, as set in motion by an "idea," it is liable to the same objections. In its distinguishing feature, that of two halves of the brain acting separately and independently, it is not in harmony with the facts which he himself adduces. According to this theory "the two halves of the brain are set over against each other." Again we are told:*

* p. 105 in this volume.

"there thus results a double entity or double consciousness. The person possessed hears and understands everything that the fox inside says or thinks, and the two often engage in a loud and violent dispute," etc. From this we would naturally infer that the cases of possession in Japan differ from those met with elsewhere, in the co-existence of, and mutual communication between, the original normal personality, and the new or acquired personality connected with the other half of the brain. When we turn, however, to the case given in detail by Dr. Baelz, and to the other case from Japan,* we find no trace of this "double entity" or "double consciousness," and the facts presented correspond throughout with those connected with other cases which have come before us. For instance, Dr. Baelz in giving the details of the case he presents says: "The priest upbraided the fox sternly. The fox, always of course speaking through the girl's mouth, argued on the other side. At last he said, 'I am tired of her. I ask no better than to leave her. What will you give me for doing so?'"

Here no personality appears in connection with the subject, but the new one. There is no conversation between the two sides of the brain, but solely between the priest and the new personality. The normal personality of the subject, as in the other cases which have come to our notice,

* p. 106 in this volume.

is dormant. The new personality uses the first personal pronoun *I* in speaking of himself, and speaks of the subject in the third person as *her*. The theory of Dr. Baelz then finds no support in the facts which he adduces, nor in any other facts which have come to our knowledge from other sources; neither does it attempt to account for the many phenomena connected with cases of "possession" to which the attention of the reader has been called.

As to Dr. Baelz' special theory for accounting for Changed Personality, or Alternating Personality, it does not appear to have borne the test of further investigation, or to be generally adopted by advanced scientists of the present day. Dr. William James, Professor of Psychology in Harvard College, in speaking of Dr. F. W. H. Myers' reference to the two hemispheres of the brain in connection with Automatic Writing, etc. says: * "The crude explanation of two selves by two hemispheres is of course far from Mr. Myers' thought. The selves may be more than two; and the brain systems severally used for each must be conceived as interpenetrating each other in very minute ways."

M. Ribot, in his "Diseases of Personality," in speaking of this theory that duplication of personality is accounted for by the two hemispheres of the brain, says: "Griesinger on encountering

* "The Principles of Psychology, Henry Holt & Co., N.Y. 1890, P. 400.

this theory, for it was put forth timidly in his day,* having cited the facts supposed to make in its favor, concludes in these words: 'As for me I am not in the least disposed to accord any great weight to these facts.' Have they gained in cogency since? It is very doubtful. The ultimate ground of the theory in question is the perfectly gratuitous hypothesis that the contest is always between two states only. This is flatly contradicted by experience." Further reasons are also given by M. Ribot for discrediting this hypothesis.

So far then as we can discern, medical science and medical theories fail to account for the facts which we are considering. Some theories present a possible explanation of some of the facts, but none of them covers the whole ground, or even attempts to explain all the phenomena.

As the "possession" theory is, in the words of Dr. Tylor, "genuine, rational and philosophical in its proper place," we may well retain it in its place, until some other theory is found which explains the facts equally well.

The investigations relating to Multiplex Peronality, Trance States, etc, are gradually being transferred from the domain of pathology to that of experimental psychology The many results which have been published by recent explorers

---

* This theory was elaborated by an English Physician, Dr. Wigan in a book entitled "The Duality of Mind" pub'd in London in 1844. It was dedicated to Sir Henry Holland, a high authority in medical psychology, in whose "Recollections," (Ch. XII. p. 307-8 D. Appleton & Co.1875,) may be found Dr. Holland's comments.

in this new field of research, and the new theories propounded for the explanation of mental or physical phenomena, naturally lead to the enquiry how far these new theories account for the facts we are considering, which enquiry will form the subject of the next chapter.

It may, however, be said here that not all physicians make light of the possession theory. Few, if any, British alienists have won a better right to be heard in the field of medical psychology than the late Dr. Forbes Benignus Winslow, (1810—1874.)*

G. H. Pember (London) states that Dr. Winslow expressed to him the "conviction that a large proportion of the patients in our asylums are cases of possession, and not of madness. He distinguished the demoniac by a strange duality, and by the fact that, when temporarily relieved from the oppression of the demon, he is often able to describe the force which seizes upon his limbs, and compels him to acts or words of shame against his will." †

(Note for page 194.)

In a review of this book printed in the *Illustrated London News*, June 26, 1895, Andrew Lang writes as follows: "To these three marks we might add (a fourth): The reports of extraordinary movements of inanimate objects in the neighborhood of the possessed. These alleged phenomena exactly answer to what is told in the case of the Demon of Spraiton, and in scores of similar narratives, ancient or modern. Patients, as in these European, or American, or Indian stories, are elevated into the air. In fact the Folklorist finds himself in very well known country, *quod semper*, *quod ubique, quod ab omnibus*. But what it is that causes this ubiquitous and uniform belief the Folklorist does not pretend to know."

* On whom consult *Encyc. Brit.* and other Cyclopædias.

† See "Earth's Earliest Ages, and their Connection with Modern 'Spiritualism,' " etc., by G. H. Pember, M.A, Am. Ed. F. H. Revell Co., N.Y. p. 261-2,

CHAPTER XIII.

THE PSYCHOLOGICAL THEORY.

It is the object of this chapter to find what light is thrown on the questions we are considering by the results of recent psychical investigation. In this enquiry we shall review briefly the opinions and theories of well-known and representative writers on Psychology, Hypnotism, Diseases of Personality, and Psychical Research.

The effect of modern materialism on the science of Psychology is obvious. Psychology was originally (as its etymology shows) the science which treated of the soul. At present, many so-called psychological treatises teach or assume that there is no soul as an absolute entity, separable from a material organism. We have been accustomed to regard heathen nations, or rather some of the most uncultured and degraded of them, as objects of commiseration, because they do not know that they have souls. Now we find advanced "scientists" not knowing that they have souls, while they regard with compassion or contempt those who believe or imagine that they have. Are we to regard this change in the view of writers on psychology as in the direction of truth, and indicating a fixed and permanent conclusion, or is it only an eddy in the stream of thought which is destined, after a temporary diversion, to flow on in the old channel?

This prevailing tendency of the age, so far as "scientists" are concerned, together with a strong opposing undercurrent, is seen in an interesting and instructive work entitled: "The Principles of Psychology" by Dr. William James, Professor of Psychology in Harvard college. After treating with great minuteness in fifty octavo pages, of the "Automaton" and "Mind-Stuff" theories of "brain activity," he introduces the "Soul Theory" of brain activity as follows:

"But is this my last word? By no means. Many readers have certainly been saying to themselves for the last few pages:, 'Why on earth doesn't the poor man say *the soul* and have done with it?' Other readers of anti-spiritualistic training and prepossessions, advanced thinkers or popular evolutionists, will perhaps be a little surprised to find this much-despised word now sprung upon them at the end of so physiological a train of thought. But the plain fact is that all the arguments for a 'pontifical cell' or an 'arch monad' are also arguments for that well-known spiritual agent in which scholastic psychology, and common sense have always believed. And my only reason for beating the bush so, and not bringing it in earlier, as a possible solution of our difficulties, has been that by this procedure I might force some of these materialistic minds to feel the more strongly the logical respectability of the spiritualistic position. The fact is that one cannot afford to despise any of these great traditional objects of belief. Whether we realize it or not, there is always a great drift of reasons positive and negative towing us in their direction. If there be such entities as souls in the universe they may possibly be affected by the manifold occurrences that go on in the nervous centers.

"I confess, therefore, that to posit a soul influenced in some mysterious way by the brain-states and responding to them by conscious affections of its own, seems to me the line of least logical resistance so far as we yet have attained. If it does not strictly *explain* anything, it is at any rate less positively objectionable than either mind-stuff or a material monad creed."*

"One great use of the soul has always been to account for, and at the same time, to guarantee the closed individuality of each personal consciousness. The thoughts of one soul must unite into one self, it was supposed, and must be eternally insulated from those of every other soul. But we have already begun to see that, although

* Vol. 1, pp 180, 182.

14 Demon

unity is the rule of each man's consciousness, yet in some individuals, at least, thoughts may split away from the others and form separate selves. As for insulation, it would be rash in view of the phenomena of thought-transference, mesmeric influence, and spirit-control, which are being alleged now-a-days on better authority than ever before, to be too sure about that point either. The definitely closed nature of our personal consciousness is probably an average statistical resultant of many conditions, but not an elementary force or fact; so that, if one wishes to preserve the soul, the less he draws his arguments from that quarter the better. So long as our self, on the whole, makes itself good, and practically maintains itself as a closed individual, why, as Lotze says, is not that enough? And why is the *being*-an-individual in some inaccessible metaphysical way so much prouder an achievement.

"My final conclusion, then, about the substantial soul is that it explains nothing and guarantees nothing. Its successive thoughts are the only intelligible and verifiable things about it, and definitely to ascertain the correlations of these with brain processes is as much as psychology can empirically do. From the metaphysical point of view, it is true that one may claim that the correlations have a rational ground; and if the word soul could be taken to mean merely some such vague problematical ground, it would be unobjectionable. But the trouble is that it professes to give the ground in positive terms of a very dubiously credible sort. I therefore feel entirely free to discard the word soul from the rest of this book. If I ever use it, it will be in the vaguest and most popular way. The reader who finds any comfort in the idea of the soul, is however, perfectly free to continue to believe in it; for our reasonings have not established the non-existence of the soul; they have only proved its superfluity for scientific purposes. "*

"With this, all possible rival formulations have been discussed. The literature of the Self is large, but all its authors may be classed as radical or mitigated representatives of the three schools we have named, substantialism, associationism or transcendentalism. Our own opinion must be classed apart, although it incorporates essential elements from all three schools. There need never have been a quarrel between association-ism and its rivals if the former had admitted the indecomposable unity of every pulse of thought, and the latter been willing to allow that 'perish-ing'pulses of thought might recollect and know.

"We may sum up by saying that personality implies the incessant presence of two elements, an objective person, known by a passing subjec-tive Thought, and recognized as continuing in time.

* Vol. I. pp 349, 350,

Hereafter" (the italics are Prof. James') *"let us use the words Me and I for the empirical person and the judging Thought.''**

This technical distinction between the I and the Me is not Prof. James' alone, but is made use of by other writers, and is worthy of special notice. Prof. James uses Thought as nearly synonymous with soul. The "Thought" then may be regarded as a conscious soul viewing itself objectively, and the Me represents the soul as thus objectively considered. There is an obvious ground for this distinction in every man's conscious experience. We often pass judgment upon ourselves as doing things which we disapprove, and which it is our earnest purpose and effort to avoid doing. The Apostle Paul refers to this internal schism and opposition as "another law in my members, warring against the law of my mind;"† and declares "it is no more I that do it, but sin that dwelleth in me."‡ Here then we have no severance in the personality, but the ordinary condition of it. A different "Me" is perfectly consistent with our normal personality but not a different "I."

That part of Prof. James' book which has special reference to phases of changed personality, and his distinctions and classifications, is of special interest to us. He says: "When we pass beyond alternations of memory to abnormal *al-*

* Vol. 1, pp 370, 371.
† Rom. vii. 23.
‡ Rom. vii, 17.

ternations in the present self we have still graver
disturbances. The alternations are of three main
types from the descriptive point of view. But
certain cases unite features of two or more types;
and our knowledge of the elements and causes
of these changes of personality is so slight that
the division into types must not be regarded as
having any profound significance." The types
are:

(1.) Insane delusions.
(2.) Alternating selves.
(3.) Mediumship or Possessions.*

After giving an illustrative example from
"Krishaber's book, *La Nervopathie Ceribro-car-
diaque, 1873*" which he says "is full of similar
observations," Prof. James says: "In cases similar to this, it is as certain that the I is unal-
tered, as that the "Me" is changed. That is, the
present Thought of the patient is cognitive of
both the old *Me* and the new so long as its
memory holds good."

It is important to notice that in the type of
change of personality called "Insane delusions,"
the cognitive Thought, or I of the patient, represents not a new personality, but the normal personality of the patient.

Under the second head "Alternating personality," Prof. James gives several interesting cases
of persons who virtually lived two distinct lives,

* Vol. 1 p. 375.

in each of which they had no memory or knowledge of the other. Among the most remarkable of these is the case of Mary Reynolds, which is fully described by Dr. Weir Mitchell.* The account of this is here necessarily condensed. In 1811, when she was still a young woman, she woke up one morning without any recollection of her past life. "To all intents and purposes she was as a being for the first time ushered into the world." . . . "She had not the slightest consciousness that she had ever existed previous to the moment when she awoke from that mysterious slumber. In a word, she was an infant just born, yet born in a state of maturity with a capacity for relishing the rich, sublime, luxuriant wonders of created nature."

From this starting point in her new existence she acquired knowledge as children do, though more rapidly.

"Thus it continued for five weeks when one morning after a protracted sleep she woke and was herself again, and immediately went about the performance of duties incumbent upon her, and which she had planned five weeks previously.

"After the lapse of a few weeks she fell into a profound sleep and awoke in her second state, taking up her new life again precisely where she had left it when she before passed from that state."

* Transactions of the College of Physicians of Philadelphia, April 1888.

These alternations from one state to another continued at intervals of varying length for fifteen or sixteen years, but finally ceased when she attained the age of thirty-five or thirty-six, leaving her permanently in her second state. In this she remained without change for the last quarter of a century of her life.*

Prof. James says: † "Of course it is mere guess work to speculate on what may be the cause of the amnesias which lie at the bottom of changes in the self. Changes of blood-supply have naturally been invoked. Alternate action of the two hemispheres was long ago proposed by Dr. Wigan in his book on the "Duality of the Mind."‡ I shall revert to this explanation after considering the third class of alternations of the self, those namely, which I have called "possessions.'

"I have myself become quite recently acquainted with the subject of a case of alternate personality of the 'ambulatory' sort, who has given me permission to name him in these pages." The case is too long to give here in detail, and may be summarized as follows: The Rev. Ansel Bourne of Green, R. I., on Jan. 17th, 1887, suddenly disappeared from his home, and foul

---

* Miss Reynolds lived in Meadville, Penn. The above facts given with many interesting details, are vouched for by Miss Reynolds' nephew, Rev. Dr. John V. Reynolds with whom she lived during a part of the last twenty-five years of her life.

† Page 390.

‡ See note on page 205.

play was suspected. He was advertized for and sought for by the police in vain. "On the morning of March 14th, at Norristown, Penn., a man calling himself A. J. Brown, who had rented a shop six weeks previously, stocked it, and carried on his quiet trade without seeming to any one unnatural or eccentric, woke up in a fright and called on the people of the house to tell him where he was. He said that his name was Ansel Bourne, that he was entirely ignorant of Norristown, that he knew nothing of shop-keeping, and that the last thing he remembered—it seemed only yesterday—was drawing money from the bank, etc, in Providence, R. I. He would not believe that two months had elapsed."

He returned to his home and resumed his old life again.

In June, 1890 Mr. Bourne was induced to submit to hypnotism, and in his hypnotic trance his Brown memory came back. When asked if he knew Ansel Bourne he said he had heard of him, but "didn't know as he had ever met the man." "When confronted with Mrs. Bourne he said he had never seen the woman before," etc. On the other hand he gave all the details of his history between leaving Providence and settling in business in Norristown.

After giving the above and similar cases of "Alternating personality" Dr. James proceeds to the consideration of "possession" as follows:

* "In 'mediumships' or 'possessions' the invasion and the passing away of the secondary state are both relatively abrupt, and the duration of the state is usually short—i. e. from minutes to a few hours. Whenever the secondary state is well developed no memory for aught that happened during it remains after the primary consciousness comes back. The subject during the secondary consciousness speaks, writes, or acts as if animated by a foreign person, and often names this foreign person or gives his history. In old times the foreign 'control' was usually a demon, and is so now in communities which favor that belief."

† "Whether all sub-conscious selves are peculiarly susceptible to a certain stratum of the Zeitgeist (spirit of the times) and get their inspiriation from it I know not; but it is obviously the case with the secondary selves which become developed in spiritualistic circles. There the beginnings of the medium trance are indistinguishable from effects of hypnotic suggestion. The subject assumes the rôle of a medium simply because opinion expects it of him under the conditions which are present; and carries it out with a feebleness or a vivacity proportionate to his histrionic gifts. But the odd thing is that persons unexposed to spiritualist traditions will so often act in the same way when they become

* Ibid. p. 393.
† Ibid. p. 394.

entranced, speak in the name of the departed, go through the motions of their several death-agonies, send messages about their happy home in the summer-land, and describe the ailments of those present. I have no theory to publish of these cases, several of which I have personally seen."

"As an example of the automatic writing performances I will quote from an account of his own case kindly furnished me by Mr. Sidney Dean of Warren, R. I., Member of Congress from Connecticut from 1855 to 1859, who has been all his life a robust and active journalist, author, and man of affairs. He has for many years been a writing subject, and has a large collection of manuscript automatically produced:

'Some of it,' he writes, 'is in hieroglyph or strange compounded arbitrary character, each series possessing a seeming unity in general design or character followed by what purports to be a translation or rendering into mother English. I never attempted the seemingly impossible feat of copying the characters. They were cut with the precision of a graver's tool, and generally with a single rapid stroke of the pencil. Many languages, some obsolete and passed from history, are professedly given. To see these would satisfy you that no one could copy them except by tracing.'

" 'It is an intelligent *ego* who writes, or else the influence assumes individuality, which practically makes of the influence a personality. It is *not* myself; of that I am conscious at every step of the process. I have also traversed the whole field of the claims of unconscious cerebration,* so-called, so far as I am competent to critically examine it, and it fails as a theory in numberless points, when applied to this strange work through me. The easiest and most natural solution to me is to admit the claims made, i. e., that it is a decarnated intelligence who writes. But *who?* that is the question. The names of scholars and thinkers who once lived are affixed to the most ungrammatical and weakest of *bosh.*'"

After further extracts Prof. James proceeds as follows:

† "I am myself persuaded by abundant acquaintance with the trances of one medium that the 'control' may be altogether different from any possible waking self of the person. In the case I have in mind it professes to be a certain departed French doctor; and is, I am convinced, acquainted with facts about the circumstances and the living and dead relatives and acquaintances, of numberless sitters whom the medium never met before, and of whom she has never heard the names. I record my bare opinion here unsupported by the evidence, not, of course, to convert any one to my view, but because I am

* See "Mechanism in Thought and Morals," By Oliver Wendell Holmes. Also W. B. Carpenter's "Mental Physiology."
† Ibid, p, 396.

persuaded that a serious study of these trance-phenomena is one of the greatest needs of psychology, and think that my personal confession may possibly draw a reader or two into a field which the *soidisant* 'scientist' usually refuses to explore.

"Many persons have found evidence conclusive to their minds that in some cases the control is really the departed spirit whom it pretends to be. The phenomena shade off so gradually into cases when this is obviously absurd, that the presumption (quite apart from *a priori* 'scientific' prejudice) is great against its being true. The case of Lurancy Vennum is perhaps as extreme a case of 'possession' of the modern sort as one can find. * Lurancy was a young girl of fourteen living with her parents at Watseka, Ill., who (after various distressing hysterical disorders and spontaneous trances, during which she was possessed by departed spirits of a more or less grotesque sort), finally declared herself to be animated by the spirit of Mary Roff, a neighbor's daughter who had died in an insane asylum twelve years before, and insisted on being sent 'home' to Mr. Roff's house. After a week of 'home-sickness' and importunity on her part, her parents

* The "Watseka Wonder" by E, W. Stevens, Chicago 1887. We only give Prof. James' summary of the case. He says in a foot note: "My friend, Mr. R. Hodgson informs me that he visited Watseka in April 1889, and cross-examined the principal witnesses in the case. His confidence in the original narrative was strengthened by what he learned, and various unpublished facts were ascertained, which increased the plausibility of the spiritualistic interpretation of the phenomena."

agreed, and the Roffs, who pitied her, and were spiritualists in the bargain, took her in. Once there she seems to have convinced the family that their dead Mary had exchanged habitations with Lurancy. Lurancy was said to be temporarily in heaven, and Mary's spirit now controlled her organism, and lived again in her former earthly home. The so-called Mary while at the Roffs' would sometimes 'go back to heaven' and leave the body in a 'quiet trance,' i. e. without the original personality of Lurancy returning. After eight or nine weeks, however, the memory and manner of Lurancy would sometimes partially, but not entirely, return for a few minutes. Once Lurancy seems to have taken full possession for a short time. At last after some fourteen weeks comformably to the prophecy which 'Mary' had made when she first assumed 'control,' she departed definitively, and the Lurancy-consciousness came back for good."

Perhaps there is no source from which such abundant material can be obtained relating to mysterious psychical phenomena, as the reports and Journals of the Society for Psychical Research. This society originated in London. It includes among its members many European names of world-wide reputation as literary men and scientists. It has an American branch, of which Dr. Richard Hodgson, 5 Boylston Place, Boston, is secretary and treasurer. Its origin, character, and objects are stated in its own publications, as follows:

"The Society for Psychical Research was formed at the beginning of 1882, for the purpose of making an organized and systematic attempt to investigate various sorts of debatable phenomena which are *prima facie* inexplicable on any generally recognized hypothesis. From the recorded testimony of many competent witnesses, past and present, including observations recently made by scientific men of eminence in various countries, there appears to be, amidst much illusion and deception, an important body of facts to which this description would apply, and which therefore, if incontestably established, would be of the very highest interest. The task of examining such residual phenomena has often been undertaken by individual effort, but never hitherto by a scientific society organized on a sufficiently broad basis. The following are the principal departments of work which it is proposed to undertake:

1. An examination of the nature and extent of any influence which may be exerted by one mind upon another, otherwise than through the recognized sensory channels.

2. The study of hypnotism and mesmerism; and an inquiry into the alleged phenomena of clairvoyance.

3. An inquiry as to the existence of relations,

hitherto unrecognized by science, between living organisms and magnetic and electric forces, and also between living and inanimate bodies.

4. A careful investigation of any reports, resting on strong testimony, of apparitions occurring at the moment of death or otherwise, and of disturbances in houses reputed to be haunted.

5. An inquiry into various alleged physical phenomena commonly called 'spiritualistic.'

6. The collection and collation of existing materials bearing on the history of these subjects.

"The aim of the society is to approach these various problems without prejudice or prepossession of any kind, and in the same spirit of exact and unimpassioned inquiry, which has enabled science to solve so many problems, once not less obscure nor less hotly debated. The founders of the society have always fully recognized the exceptional difficulties which surround this branch of research; but they nevertheless believe that by patient and systematic effort some results of permanent value may be attained."

A few extracts from the reports of this society will show the present drift of opinion with regard to changes in personality.

In a long article in the Report, May 1885, by Fredrick W. H. Myers, on Automatic Writing, the author says:

*. "*A secondary self*—if I may coin the phrase

* Page 27.

—is thus gradually postulated, a latent capacity, at any rate, in an appreciable fraction of mankind of developing or manifesting a second focus of cerebral energy which is apparently neither fugitive, nor incidental merely—a delirium or a dream, but may possess, for a time at least, a kind of continuous individuality, a purposive activity of its own."

The explanation which Mr. Myers offers to account for what he designates as "certain widespread phenomena, which, while ignored or neglected by the main body of men of science, have been for the most part ascribed by those who have witnessed them to the operation of some external or invading power" is that they are * "partly dependent on telepathic influence, and partly on unconscious cerebration alone, though unconscious cerebration raised, if I may so say, to a higher power than had previously been suspected."

A few extracts from an article by Mr. Myers on Subliminal Consciousness, published in the Report of the society for February, 1892, will show the conclusions, both actual and probable, which he regards as having been reached, and his way of accounting for cases of "Alternating Personality" by different phases of consciousness which are united in one general personality. He says:

* Page 61.

"I hold that both that group of facts which the scientific world has never learned to accept, (as the hypnotic trance, automatic writing, alternations of personality, and the like); and that group of facts for which in these proceedings we are still endeavoring to win scientific acceptance (as telepathy and clairvoyance) ought to be considered in close alliance and correlation, and must be explained, if explicable at all by some hypothesis which does not need constant stretching to meet the emergencies of each fresh case.

"I will ask the reader then to bear in mind that in what follows I am not attacking any recognized, coherent body of scientific doctrine. Rather I am making a first immature attempt to bring some kind of order out of a chaotic collection of strange and apparently disparate observations. My hypothesis—developed here from briefer indications in earlier papers—cannot possibly, considering the novelty of the inquiry, be true in all details. But it may be of use at least in pointing out the nature and the complexity of the problems which any valid hypothesis must recognize and solve.

"I suggest then that the stream of consciousness in which we habitually live, is not the only consciousness which exists in connection with our organism. Our habitual or empirical consciousness may consist of a mere selection of a multitude of thoughts and sensations, of which some

15 *Demon*

at least are equally conscious with those that we empirically know. I accord no primacy to my ordinary waking self except that, among my potential selves, this one has shown itself the fittest to meet the needs of common life. I hold that it has established no further claim, and that it is perfectly possible that other thoughts, feelings, and memories, either isolated or in continuous connection, may now be actively conscious, as we say, "within me" in some kind of co-ordination with my organism, and forming some part of my total individuality. I conceive it possible that at some future time, and under changed conditions, I may recollect all: I may assume these various personalities under one single consciousness, in which ultimate and complete consciousness the empirical consciousnses which at this moment directs my hand, may be only one element out of many." . . . . . .

"Yet it will be well to avoid the use of terms which, like the words *soul* and *spirit* carry with them associations which cannot fairly be imported into the argument.

"Some word, however, we must have for that underlying psychical unity which I postulate as existing beneath all our phenomenal manifestations. Let the word *individuality* serve this purpose; and let us apply the word *personality*. as its etymology suggests, to something more external and transitory, to each of those apparent characters, or chains of memory and desire which may at any time mask at once, and manifest a psychical existence deeper and more perdurable than their own. . . . ."

"The self manifests itself through the organism; but there is always some part of the self unmanifested; and always, as it seems, some power of organic expression in abeyance or reserve. Neither can the player express all his thoughts on the instrument, nor is the instrument so arranged that all its keys can be sounded at once. One melody after another may be played upon it; nay,—as with the messages of duplex or multiplex telegraphy, simultaneously or with imperceptible intermissions, several melodies can be played together; but there are still unexhausted reserves of instrumental capacity, as well as unexpressed treasures of informing thought."

These extracts are important as treating alleged changes in personality as established facts; and presenting Mr. Myers' labored attempt to explain these facts, the difficulties in doing so being much increased by the necessity he has placed himself under of "avoiding the use of the word soul, which," he says, "from the associations connected with it, cannot fairly be imported into the argument."

M. Ribot, like other materialistic evolutionists, regards personality as a development of man's material organism. A few quotations from his "Diseases of Personality" will show what ideas are intended to be conveyed by the word "personality." He says: * "If one is fully imbued with the idea that personality is a con-sensus, one will easily see how the mass of con-scious, sub-conscious and unconscious states which make it up may at a given moment be summed up in a tendency or a predominant state, which for the person himself, and for others, is its expression at that moment. Straightway this same mass of constituent elements is summed up in an opposite state which has become pre-dominant. Such is our dipsomaniac who drinks and who condemns himself. The state of con-sciousness predominant at a given moment is for the individual himself, and for others, his person-ality." Again; † "If in the normal state person-ality is a psycho-physiological co-ordination of the highest degree possible which endures amid perpetual changes and partial and transitory in-co-ordinations, such as sudden impluses, eccentric ideas, etc., then dementia, which is a progressive movement towards physical and mental dissolu-tion, must manifest itself by an ever-increasing incoordination till at last the Me disappears in absolute incoherence, and there remain in the individual only the purely vital co-ordinations— those best organized, the lowest, the simplest,

* Page 37.
† Page 42.

and consequently the most stable, but these in turn disappear also."

Albert Moll, in his treatise on Hypnotism, is disposed to account for changed personality and many of the symptoms connected with it by "auto-hypnotism," and not a few others adopt the same theory. His account of auto-hypnotism, however, shows that it is quite different from "possession." He says: "In auto-hypnosis the idea of the hypnosis is not aroused by another person, but the subject generates the image himself. This can only happen by an act of will. Just as the will is otherwise able to produce particular thoughts, so it can allow the idea of hypnosis to become so powerful that finally hypnosis is introduced; this is, however, rare. Auto-hypnosis generally takes place in consequence of some incident by means of which the idea of hypnosis is produced. This often happens when the subject has been frequently hypnotized." *

In speaking of the effect of hypnotism in quickening and intensifying the power of memory this author, after giving a case in which a subject remembered distinctly what had taken place thirteen years before, says: "Events in the normal life can also be remembered in hypnosis even when they have apparently been long forgotten. . . . An English officer was hypnotized by

* Page 28.

Hansen, and suddenly began to speak a strange language. This turned out to be Welsh, which he had learned as a child but had forgotten."

"Such cases as these recall others which are mentioned in the history of hypnotism, for example the famous one of the servant who suddenly spoke Hebrew." . . . "Many apparently supernatural facts may be explained in the same way. Among these I may mention the carefully constructed religious addresses, sometimes supposed to be inspired, which are delivered by pious but uneducated fanatics in a peculiar physical state of ecstasy; and the eloquence occasionally displayed by some spiritualistic mediums belongs to the same category."*

We can hardly hope, by the use of this hypothesis, to whatever extent it may be pushed, to account for the actual phenomena of so-called demon-possession. Mr. Moll says that auto-hypnotism "can only happen by an act of the will," when the subject "allows the idea of hypnosis to become so powerful that finally hypnosis is introduced;" and that "this is rare." Now it is probably safe to say that in most cases of "possession" the subject has never had the idea of hypnosis, and so far from indicating the abnormal state by an act of his will, he has used the utmost efforts of his will to prevent it. Furthermore, this hypothesis has no way of account-

* Page 126.

ing for this uniformity in the assumption of a personality from another world.

Having endeavored fairly to present the theories, and the conclusions (so far as conclusions have been reached) of prominent representatives of different departments of psychological study, it remains to inquire what help they give in accounting for the phenomena in question. In this inquiry we cannot do better than examine the estimates which these writers put upon their own work.

Prof. James says, "The special natural science of *psychology* must stop with the mere functional formula. If the passing thought be the directly verifiable existent which no school has hitherto doubted it to be, then that thought is itself the thinker, and psychology need not look beyond. The only pathway that I can discern for bringing in a more transcendental thinker would be to deny that we have any direct knowledge of the thought as such. The latter's existence would be reduced to a postulate, an assertion that there must be a *knower* correlative to all this *known*, and the problem *who that knower is* would have become a metaphysical problem. With the question once stated in these terms, the spiritualist and transcendentalist solutions must be considered as *primâ facie* on a par with our own psychological one, and discussed impartially. But that carries us beyond the psychological or naturalistic point of view." *

The following additional quotations from Prof. James will present the acknowledged difficulties connected with the materialistic theory, which, in common with so many modern scientists, he seems to have adopted.

"If we speculate on the brain condition during all these different perversions of personality we see it must be supposed capable of successively changing all its modes of action, and abandoning the use for the time being of whole sets of well organized association paths.   In no other way can we explain the loss of memory in passing from one alternating condition to another.   And not only this, but we must admit that organized systems of paths can be thrown out of gear with others, so that the processes in one system give rise to one consciousness, and those of another system to another simultaneously existing consciousness. Thus only can we understand the facts of automatic writing, etc., whilst the patient is out of trance and the false anaesthesias and amnesias of the hysteric type.   But just what sort of disassociation the phrase 'thrown out of gear' may start from we cannot even conjecture; only I think we ought not to talk of the doubling of the self as if it consisted in the failure to combine on the part of certain systems of *ideas* which usually do so.   It is better to talk of *objects*

* Page 401.

usually combined, and which are now divided between the two 'selves' in the hysteric and automatic cases in question. Each of the selves is due to a system of cerebral paths acting by itself."*

Mr. Myers says: (†) "*Hypotheses non fingo* is an absolutely necessary rule for psychical inquirers at the present time. Our work is to mass facts for some master mind of a future generation to piece together. Most assuredly I shall offer no theory to explain this curious appearance of what looks like the presence of a 'third center of intelligence,' distinct from the *conscious* intelligence and character of either of the two parties engaged in the experiments."

Mr. Myers, in speaking of Automatic Writing, further says: "The phenomena, however, which I have described by no means exhaust those which are alleged to occur in the course of graphic automatism. It is said that the handwriting of dead persons is sometimes reproduced; that sentences are written in languages of which the writer knows nothing; that facts unknown to any one present are contained in the replies, and that these facts are sometimes such as to point to some special person departed this life, as their only conceivable source. If these things be so, they are obviously facts of

* Page 399.

† Proceedings of the Society for Psychical Research. May 1885, p. 22.

the very highest importance. Nor are we entitled to say that they are impossible *a priori*. The spiritualistic hypothesis, though frequently presented in an unacceptable shape, is capable, I believe, of being so formulated as to contradict none of the legitimate assumptions of science. And furthermore, I readily admit that should the agency of departed spirits be established as a *vera causa* , then the explanations here suggested will need revision in a new light."*

In speaking of the various results of Psychical Research thus far, Mr. Myers says:† "There has been evidence which points *prima facie* to the agency of departed personalities, although this evidence has also been interpreted in different ways."

M. Ribot, in referring to hallucinations says: "Certainly these voices and visions emanated from the patient. Why then does he not regard them as his own? It is a difficult question, but I will endeavor to answer it. There must exist anatomical and physiological causes which would solve the problem, but unfortunately they are hidden from us. Being ignorant of these causes, we can view only the surface of the symptoms, the states of the consciousness, with the signs which interpret them."

With regard to the hidden causes which lead

---

* Proceedings of the Society for Psychical Research, May 1885, p. 62.

† Proceedings of the Society for Psychical Research, April 1891, p. 11,

to these "diseases of personality" M. Ribot says: "We can add nothing more without repeating what we have already said, or without heaping up hypotheses. Our ignorance of the causes stops us short. The psychologist is here like the physician who has to deal with a disease in which he can make out only the symptoms. What physiological influences are they which thus alter the general tone of the organism, consequently of the coenaesthesis, consequently too of the memory? Is it some condition of the vascular system? Or some inhibitory action, some arrest of function? We cannot say. So long as this question remains undecided, we are still only at the surface of the matter. Our purpose has simply been to show that memory, though in some respects it may be confounded with personality, is not its ultimate basis."

The researches of the authors above quoted and many others of like spirit and aims cannot be too highly commended. They are collecting facts of universal interest, in a field of inquiry too much neglected. The true interpretations, the relations, and bearings of these facts are not yet disclosed. Our attention must be confined, in the present treatise, to a few points where these investigations touch the subject of so-called demon-possession. The conclusions from what we have learned in this chapter maybe summarized as follows:

1. The authorities we have consulted are not in full accord in their theories, and the theories introduced by them are not regarded even by their authors as final and authoritative but only as tentative and provisional.

2. The tendency of recent psychical research· is to strengthen the presumption of the existence of spiritual intelligences capable of producing effects on material objects and on man's physical and psychical constitution.

3. It is admitted that if the agency of spirits be established as a *vera causa*, then certain proposed theories will need revision in a new light.

4. Recent psychical researches, so far from conflicting with this possession theory, present mysterious facts which are only readily explained by that theory. In treating of changes in personality, the efforts of writers of different schools to account for these changes as the natural outcome of our physical organism are beset with grave difficulties. This change is treated of as "thoughts split from the others, and forming separate selves;" as the "breaking away" of man's consciousness; as "failure to combine on the part of certain systems of ideas;" as "organized systems and paths thrown out of gear so that the processes of one system give rise to one consciousness, and those of another to another consciousness." Mr. Myers' solution of the difficulty is the theory of a "subliminal consciousness."

Now if we consider the changes of personality met within pronounced cases of "demon-possession," in the light of the "possession" theory all these difficulties disappear. The splitting way of oneself from another is a matter of course; because there are in fact two (or more) selves, actual, distinct entities, which have no connection except through the physical organization of the subject. Each personality, separate, persistent, and unchanging, has in the nature of the case its own, and only its own, memory and consciousness. In a word, the phenomena which present themselves are only what might be naturally expected. The difficulties encountered are not to be attributed to the phenomena but to the theories adopted to account for them.

5. The results of psychic studies harmonize with the "possession" theory, and tend to explain and confirm it. We have had frequent occasions in the previous pages of this treatise to notice the remarkable resemblance between cases of "possesssion," and the hypnotic trance. While, so far as we can discern, hypnotism does not furnish any substitute for the theory of "demon-possession," it seems to throw important light on the means and process of "possession."

Here again we may refer to the book of Dr. Hammond to which frequent reference was made in the previous chapter. In the former part of his book Dr. Hammond adheres to the inductive method, and gives us information and suggestions well worthy of consideration.

In pointing out the stages and degrees of the abnormal action of the nervous system he refers first to Somnambulism, where the subject in sleep passes into an abnormal state, during which some of the functions of the mind are suspended, while other functions of the mind and body are performed with remarkable facility and precision. The results of experiments by Dr. Belden on a patient under his care are given as follows, "Though it was found that her sense of sight was greatly increased in acuteness, she had no clairvoyance, properly so called. It was ascertained, too, that while she had no recollection when awake of what she had done during a paroxysm, she remembered in one paroxysm the events of a previous one."

Next in order Dr. Hammond treats of Artificial Somnambulism, which may be induced in the somnambulistic patient by himself or by another person "*ab extra.*" Here we have the familiar phenomena of Mesmerism, or Hypnotism. "Now somnambulism" says the author, "natural or artificial, appears to be a condition in which consciousness is subordinated to automatism. The subject performs actions of which there is no complete consciousness, and often none at all. Consequently there is little or no subsequent recollection." * We learn from these quotations that the outward symptoms of the mesmeric state are similar to those of somnambulism, but have certain peculiarities superadded, the transition from the normal to the abnormal state being characterized by symptoms more pronounced than those which are witnessed in passing from ordinary sleep to somnambulism. The special mark of differentiation is that the subject has to a greater or less degree lost the power of voluntariness, and his acts are determined by the will of the mesmerizing agent. In describing this state as exhibited in a patient under his care, Dr. Hammond says: "It will be readily perceived, therefore, that certain parts of her nervous system were in a state of inaction, were in fact dormant, while others remained capable of receiving sensations and originating nervous influence. Her sleep was therefore incomplete. Images were formed, hallucinations entertained, and she was accordingly in these respects in a condition similar to that of a dreaming person; for the images and hallucinations were either directly connected with thoughts she had previously had, or were immediately suggested to her through her sense of hearing. Some mental faculties were exercised, while others were quiescent. There was no correct judgment and no volition. Imagination, memory, the emotions, and *the ability to*

* p. p. 32-33.

be impressed by suggestions, (the italics are Dr. Hammond's) were present in a high degree." *

Now the resemblance between the symptoms of Hypnosis and "demon-possession" are apparent, viz: The "inaction" or dormant condition of the normal consciousness; susceptibility to impressions from without; marked symptoms of nervous disturbance in passing from the normal to the abnormal state; and an entire want of recollection on the part of the subject of what occurred in the abnormal state. The differentiating marks between natural and artificial somnambulism are both pathological and psychological, and are referable to the *ab extra* influence of the hypnotizing agent as the cause.

Now may not demon-possession be only a different, a more advanced form of hypnotism? On the supposition of the more complete possession and control of man's nervous system by demons, we might, on Dr. Hammond's theory, expect still more violent paroxysms in the transition state, and further new conditions, pathological and psychological, in addition to those common to hypnotism and demon-possession. On the supposition of the existence of spirits and their having access to human beings it is, to say the least, possible that they are familiar with the organism of the nervous system, and are capable of acting upon and influencing mankind in accordance with

* P. 15.

physical and psychological laws. How then can it be regarded as unreasonable or necessarily unscientific to suppose that demons, with perhaps in some respects superior powers, and longer experience, may have penetrated still deeper into the mysteries of man's being, and made further advances than man has in the use of the mechanism of the nervous system?

It may be objected that to infer from the fact that one man can hypnotize another man, therefore spirits can hypnotize men, is unwarranted, inasmuch as the hypnotizing of a man is an act implying a physical agent. This objection is answered by reference to the fact that though the hypnotic trance is induced by a physical agent, and sometimes by the use of physical contact and human speech, it may also be effected without any use of physical organs, by the mere force of will-power, spirit acting upon spirit. Again, it is now confidently asserted that Telepathy, or Thought Transference, independent of bodily organs is an established fact. Mr. Myers. in an article on "Human Personality" written above five years, ago, says:

* "I cannot here enter into the reasons which, as already stated, convince me that this method of experimental psychology, when carried further, will conduct us not to negative but to positive results of the most hopeful kind. . . . .

* Fortnightly Review, Nov. 1885.

16 Demon

One such discovery, that of telepathy, or **the** transference of thought and sensation from mind to mind without the agency of the recognized organs of sense, has, as I hold, been already achieved." The evidence in support of Telepathy has during the past five years increased tenfold, and has gained for it very general credence. Now if we accept the postulate that spirit can act upon spirit without the intervention of physical organs, then, assuming the existence of demons, "demon-possession" may perhaps be accounted for by telepathy and hypnosis, and may be in accord with the most recent deductions of science.

Once more we are brought to the conclusion that modern science furnishes no substitute for the theory of "demon-possession" which still stands as the only "genuine," "rational," "philosophical," and consistent theory for accounting for a certain class of established facts.

CHAPTER XIV

THE BIBLICAL THEORY.

Hitherto, in considering the different theories which have been propounded to account for the facts we are considering, no reference has been made to the Scriptures as having any higher authority than other authentic records. It is evident that the connection of the Scriptures with this subject is close and vital. Actual communication with unseen spirits; their influence on the acts and destinies of individuals and nations; and demon-possession, are taught clearly and unmistakably in both the Old and New Testaments. These teachings are not occasional and incidental, but underlie all Biblical history and Biblical doctrine. The Bible recognizes not only the material world, but a spiritual world intimately connected with it, and spiritual beings both good and bad, who have access to, and influence for good and ill, the world's inhabitants. If the claim of the Bible to be of divine origin is well founded, it is the very guide we need, and the only authoritative guide to answer the questions which have been raised in this inquiry. If the teachings of the Bible on this subject are unreliable and inconclusive, the authority of the Scriptures is shaken to its very foundations, and a wide door is open to doubt and unbelief. The assaults of infidelity against the Bible are often made at this, which is supposed to be, its weakest point. Not a few who have given unreasoning assent to the oft repeated and very generally believed assertion that there is, and in the nature of things can be, no evidence of unseen existences, and that possession by demons is a superstitious delusion of an unscientific age, have in consequence had their confidence in the Scriptures shaken or permanently destroyed.

The testimony of the Scriptures on this subject, and that which we derive from sources outside the Scriptures, are mutually confirmatory. To one in whose mind doubts have risen as to the *possibility* of occurrences which are declared in the Scriptures to have takenplace, the appearance in the present age, and in ordinary life, of facts similar to or identical with those to which the Bible bears witness tends to solve his doubts. The very statements which were the means of shaking his confidence in the Bible become to him convincing evidence of its truth. On the other hand, the testimony of the Bible on this subject confirms and authenticates similar testimony from other sources; and above all gives us authoritative instruction respecting the char-

acter and origin of this class of phenomena.
The importance then of a careful and unprejudiced consideration of what the Bible teaches
on this subject is apparent. Before proceeding
however, to a comparison between the testimony
of Scripture and facts of observation and experience, it is important to consider first some theories of Scripture interpretation which are closely
related to the subject before us.

First, we have the theory that our Saviour and
his disciples, living in a primitive and unscientific
age, simply represented, at least so far as regards
this subject, the thought and intellectual advancement of that age; and like their contemporaries, accepted and believed in the doctrine of
the existence of demons and demon-possession,
though in fact, through ignorance and superstition, they were entirely mistaken. It is evident
that this theory is utterly at variance with the
claim which our blessed Lord made to a knowledge of the unseen world from which he came,
and to the views which have been held by the
church in all ages respecting the authenticity
and divine origin of the Scriptures. As it is far
from the purpose of this treatise to enter upon
the subject of the authenticity and inspiration
of Scripture, both of which are assumed, this
theory may be dismissed without further notice.

Second, there is another theory, which has
been adopted **by** not a few who are regarded as

most intelligent and orthodox Christians, which may be represented as a compromise between theological and scientific orthodoxy. It asserts that our Saviour was free from the ignorance and superstitions of the age in which he lived, but in accordance with the prevailing ideas of his time, and the ordinary use of language, spoke of cases of demon-possession, as his contemporaries did. His mission on earth was not to teach science, or to start curious discussions or controversies on indifferent and unimportant subjects. He came to teach spiritual truths, and did so as he necessarily must, in the language of the people, speaking of phenomena as *they* did, and in language with which *they* were familiar. He recognized in men and women brought to him as possessed by demons only different forms of bodily disease, but as the people spoke of these diseases as demon-possessions, he so spoke of them; as they represented the curing of the diseases as casting out demons, he so represented it; and when he gave power to his disciples to heal these diseases miraculously, he, accommodating his language to the popular belief, called it the power to cast out demons.

This theory is very intelligible and plausible, but, as we believe, open to serious and fatal objections, and scarcely less derogatory to the character of our Saviour than the former.

(1.) It represents him not as instructing but deceiving his disciples, as encouraging superstition rather than inculcating truth.

(2.) The above objection acquires additional force when we consider its intimate relations with other teachings of our Saviour recorded in Scripture.

Our Lord represented demons as connected with, and as the agents and representatives of Satan; and casting out of demons as open war upon his dominion. When the seventy returned saying "Lord even the demons are subject to us in thy name," our Lord replied: "I beheld Satan as lightning falling from heaven."* Can we for a moment regard our Saviour as sanctioning and encouraging the belief that demon-possession was to be referred to Santanic agency when in fact he knew that there was no such thing as demon-possession?

(3.) This theory when applied in detail presents our Saviour in a light entirely inconsistent with his character as a divine teacher. It represents him not only as speaking of diseases as possession by demons, but as personifying diseases, and actually addressing them as demons, holding formal conversation with them asking them questions, and receiving answers from them, and permitting them to enter into the swine, etc. Force is added to this objection by the fact that this

* Luke. x. 17-18.

theory obliges us to regard our Saviour as voluntarily introducing this subject when not suggested by his disciples, as in the instance when he speaks of an evil spirit as going out of a man, and wandering in dry places, etc.*   On the supposition that demon-possession was only a Jewish superstition how can we regard our Saviour as voluntarily adopting a course which could only tend to mislead his disciples and confirm them in gross misapprehension, when he might so easily have corrected this mistake, as he did so many others, by simply saying that these were not cases of possession but only of disease.

(4.) This theory represents our Saviour as making use of an unfounded superstition to substantiate his claim of divine authority.   When he sent forth his disciples to preach "The kingdom of Heaven is at hand," the power to cast out demons was given them as a divine attestation to his mission. †   That which the disciples and those to whom they were sent regarded as one of the principal reasons for accepting their testimony, was the fact that "even the demons were subject unto them through Christ's name," which according to this theory was not a fact but a delusion.‡

We regard the above reasons as quite sufficient to warrant us in discarding the theory in

* Matt. xii. 43.   Luke xi, 24.

† Matt. x, 1.   ‡ See note on page 262.

question as in the highest degree unreasonable and untenable.

Third. There is another view held by prominent teachers in the Christian church who, while they insist on the reality of demon-posesssions in Apostolic times, and the possibility or even probability of them now, teach that we have little practical interest in the matter at present, as divine knowledge or inspiration is necessary to determine what are real cases of demon-possession, and what are not.

This view is inconsistent with the facts stated in the Scripture. Nearly every case which the Bible presents to us, is brought to our Saviour as a case of "possession," the fact of its being such having been decided not by our Saviour or his disciples, but by the people. We read of no instance of our Saviour's informing the people that they were mistaken in their diagnosis of the case; no intimation that they were incompetent to decide upon these cases; or that there was any serious difficulty in so doing. There may have been many cases in Judea in which the symptoms were not sufficiently marked to indicate their character unmistakably, but those brought to Christ seem to have been clearly developed and pronounced.

Fourth. Another theory is thus presented in the "Encyclopedia Britannica."* "Some theologi-

* Ninth edition, article "Demonology."

ans, while in deference to advanced medical knowledge they abandon the primitive theory of demons causing such diseases in our times, place themselves in an embarrassing position by maintaining, on the supposed sanction of Scripture, that the symptoms were really caused by demoniacal possessions in the first century. A full statement of the arguments on both sides of this once important controversy will be found in earlier editions of the Encyclopedia Britannica, but for our times it seems too like a discussion whether the earth was really flat in the ages when it was believed to be so, but became round since astronomers provided for a different explanation of the same phenomena. It is more profitable to notice how gradual the change of opinion has been from the doctrine of demon-possession to the scientific theory of disease, and how largely the older view still survives in the world."

This theory is without foundation. The theologians represented as occupying the "embarrassing position" have been brought into it, not by the teachings of Scripture, nor by established conclusions of science, but by giving too ready credence to the unverified hypothesis that so-called "possessions" are only certain forms of physical disease. It is not improbable that the Encyclopedia Britannica may find itself obliged again to revise its utterance, in accordance with more recent and reliable scientific knowledge.

Fifth. There is another theory of interpretation still more specious, and probably more generally accepted than the previous ones; viz; that the records of the evangelists are colored and distorted so as not to present facts as they actually occurred; that our Saviour, simply cured diseases, never himself speaking of them as "possessions," or regarding them as such, but his disciples wrote the narratives of these events in a form in accordance with their own and the prevailing popular beliefs. This theory is thus presented in "Chambers' Encyclopedia of Religious Knowledge" in the article on Demons. "When the contemporaries of Christ beheld the miraculous effects of his power on the bodies and spirits of the so-called demoniacs, it was natural that they should speak of it in language intelligible to their age and in harmony with its general notions.". . . . "Under the conditions of the popular belief it is difficult to see that there was any other course open to the evangelical historians, even if they did not share the common belief of their countrymen, than to adopt the current representation."

The same theory is thus presented by Dr. A. D. White, formerly of Cornell University. In speaking of the prevalence of the false idea of diabolic agency in mental diseases, he says: "In the New Testament the various accounts of the casting out of devils, through which is refracted the beautiful and simple story of that power by which Jesus of Nazareth soothed perturbed minds by his presence, or quelled outbursts of madness by his word, give abundant examples of this."*

This theory will be at once rejected by those who hold even the lowest views of the inspiration and authenticity of the Scriptures. Dr. White, while seemingly disposed to save the reputation of Jesus by sacrificing that of the evangelists, still represents our Saviour as selecting and using as the transmitters of his teachings and the founders of his church, men incapable of writing an authentic account of the simplest facts, who have given to the world, instead of an actual history of their Master's life, a "refracted" perversion of it. Aside, however, from any special considerations of Scripture authority, the fallacy of this theory may be shown by the following considerations.

(1.) It proceeds on the assumption that the Jews regarded mental diseases as possession by demons, which assumption has been shown to be gratuitous and inconsistent with facts.

(2.) This theory is utterly inconsistent with the minute and circumstantial details of the Gospel narratives. If our Saviour only "soothed perturbed minds by his presence, or quelled outbursts of madness by his word" how could the disciples without an overwhelming sense of false-

* On Demoniacal Possessions and Insanity. Pop. Sci. Mo. Feb. 1889.

ness and dishonesty, give details of imaginary conversations with demons, recording the very words used by both parties, and also controversies with the Jews growing out of these cases of casting out demons, and further, the Jews' recognition of the fact of casting out demons, their manner of accounting for it, and our Saviour's reply.* Have any other professed writers of history in any age ever been accused of such wanton substitution of fiction for fact?

(3.) This theory is utterly inconsistent with the minute and verbal correspondences of the Gospel narratives. If the authors of the Gospels recorded facts as they saw them, and words which they heard, the correspondence is natural. If each man gave an account of the events "refracted" by his individual preconceptions and fancies this minute and verbal correspondence is inexplicable.

(4.) If Christ never spoke of demon-possessions, but only of disease, how could such a marked departure from what this theory supposes to have been the current belief of that age have failed to be noticed by his disciples, and to lead to questions on their part, and special teachings on the part of our Lord?

(5.) Supposing this theory to be true, how are we to account for the fact that such misrepresentation of the records and perversion of truth

---

* Matt. xii. 22-29, Mark iii. 22. Luke xi. 15.

met with no challenge or rebuke from any of the contemporary eye-witnesss of the events, either Christians or Jews?

(6.) The accounts given of this same class of phenomena by writers of different nationalities and ages, and notably the accounts given from China in this treatise, show an undesigned and complete correspondence even in details, thus proving that the records of the evangelists, present facts as they actually occurred. If we are correct in this conclusion, then not the evangelists but Dr. White and others who hold with him, have given a view of events in our Saviour's life not as they actually occurred, but as they are refracted by their own prejudices. The fact that a theory so gratuitous, and so beset with difficulties and inconsistencies, can find its way into a scientific magazine, and meet with some degree of acceptance, furnishes the clearest evidence that in the interpretation of psychological phenomena, the present age, no less than those which preceded it, is dominated by its own prevailing ideas and prejudices.

We believe then that the language of the Bible with reference to demon-possession is to be interpreted in its ordinary literal sense; that it represents actual occurrences; that there were unseen spirits in Judea; that they sought opportunities to possess themselves of the bodies of men; that they did so, and while in possession of those bodies, gave evidence of that possession which was palpable and unmistakable. They conversed through the organs of speech of the persons possessed, and gave evidence of personality, of desires, and fears; and acknowledged God's authority over them. Our Saviour cast them out by his word, and gave the same authority to his disciples, though it does not clearly appear in the Scriptures how long that power was to continue.

In a word we believe that our Saviour said just what he meant; and that he was perfectly acquainted with this whole subject in all its facts and bearings.

It thus appears that the hypothesis of demon-possession may claim a divine sanction, as well as the common consent of all nations and ages. The question of such events being repeated in the world's history is simply a matter of evidence. Let us determine then by comparison how far the manifestations or symptoms of demon-possession as they appeared in the previous chapters of this treatise, correspond with those presented to us in the New Testament.

(1.) In China persons afflicted are of both sexes, and of all ages. The same is true of the cases presented in Scripture.

(2.) A marked characteristic of the cases which have been met with in China is that the attacks are occasional, and commence with some physical disturbance or bodily convulsion. This corresponds with the cases given in Scripture: "Lo a spirit taketh him and he suddenly crieth out; and it teareth him that he foameth again, and bruising him hardly departeth from him." Luke ix. 39. Compare Mark ix. 18 and Luke viii. 29.

(3.) In many of the cases which have come before us the demon declares that he will never cease to torment his victim unless he submits to his will. The subject bemoans his deplorable and hopeless condition; and sympathizing friends intercede for him. Frequently the victim pines away and dies. The correspondence of these characteristics to the cases given in Scripture is too obvious and striking to require pointing out.

(4.) We have had presented in some of the cases before us instances in which the subject has received bodily injuries or scars as if from an unseen hand. So we read of the cases in Scripture, that they were thrown down, torn and bruised, and that one cut himself with stones.

(5.) Some cases before us are easily cast out, and others with great difficulty. The Scripture narrative presents the same difference.

(6.) We see a correspondence also in the individual peculiarities of the spirits, more or less wicked, more or less violent, and more or less daring, the cases bearing a general resemblance, while each one has its own special peculiarities.

(7.) Another point of resemblance in some of

the persons possessed is the shameless tearing off of clothes, and an utter disregard of propriety and decency in language and behavior.

(8.) Nothing has excited more surprise in connection with these manifestations in China, than the fact that the subjects of these manifestations have in some cases evinced a knowledge of God, and especially of our Saviour; and acknowledged our Saviour's authority and power. The correspondence of this fact with the statements of Scripture is apparent.

(9.) We notice in cases of possession in China and in those given in Scripture, in some instances, a kind of double consciousness, or actions and impulses directly opposite and contrary. The woman in Fuchow, whose case is given in Chapter vii, though under the influence of a demon whose instinct it was to shun the presence of Christ, was moved by an opposite influence to leave her home and come to Fuchow to seek help from Jesus. So the demoniac who dwelt among the tombs "When he saw Jesus afar off, he ran, and worshiped him", although the spirit still manifested a feeling of antagonism and dread, saying: "What have I to do with thee, Jesus, thou Son of the Most High God? I adjure Thee by God that Thou torment me not." (Mark v. 6, 7. Compare Matt. viii, 28-29; Luke viii. 27-28.)

(10.) We have had cases before us in which

17 *Demon*

the same human body was possessed by several demons, three, six and more. So in Scripture we have cases of possession by seven demons and by a legion. (Lk. viii, 2. Mrk. v, 9.)

(11.) One of the most common characteristics of the cases met with in China is the instinct or longing of the spirit for a body to possess, and their possessing the bodies of inferior animals as well as men. So in Scripture we have spirits represented as wandering about to seek rest in bodies, and asking permission to enter into swine. (Matt. xii, 43; viii, 31).

(12.) In the cases before us, as well as those given in Scripture, we have the spirit cast out seeking to return again. (Matt. xii, 44.)

(13.) We have exact correspondence also in the assertion of a new personality, and the instinctive recognition of this new personality by all present, long conversations being carried on with this new personality, precisely as between two human beings, the possessed subject being in most cases entirely ignored. In this distinguishing feature of possession the correspondence between cases of demon-possession generally and those found in Scripture is very striking.

(14.) We have another correspondence in the fact that in attempts to cast out demons in the name of Christ there has been no failure.

(15.) Demons are cast out by others than Christians and by different methods, so in the

Scriptures. Witness the existence of exorcists in Judea, and our Saviour's words, "by whom do your sons cast them out?"(Matt. xii. 27. Lk. xi. 19.)

(16.) We have cases of casting out demons by those who have afterwards been guilty of gross immorality, and have been cast out of the church. So our Saviour declares "many shall say unto me in that day, have we not cast out demons in thy name," etc., to whom He will declare "I never knew you." (Matt vii. 22, 23.)

(17.) There is a correspondence in the effects produced by casting out demons in the name of Christ. When the gospel was first preached in Judea, and now when it is first preached in heathen lands the effect produced by casting out demons has been to arrest public attention, and give evidence readily appreciated and understood by the masses, of the presence and power of Christ, thus convincing men of the divine origin and truth of Christianity, and preparing the way for its acceptance.

(18.) In the case related by Mr. Innocent in Chapter vi, we have specific testimony given to the character of the missionary, similar to that given by the damsel in Philippi to the character of the Apostle Paul and his associates in the words: "These men are the servants of the most high God which show unto us the way of salvation." (Acts, xvi. 17.)

(19.) The cases in China and in the Scriptures

are recognizable by the people who speak of them as if there could be no reasonable doubt concerning them.

(20.) There is an exact correspondence in the representations given of the condition of these spirits as free, and for the present, roaming about at will, though still under limitations and control, such as are by these spirits clearly understood and fully acknowledged.

(21.) The evil spirits spoken of in Scripture are represented as belonging to the kingdom of Satan, and in direct and acknowledged opposition to the kingdom of our Lord. In China, as a rule, the cases which we have been considering are directly or indirectly connected with heathen temples and idolatrous worship. The Chinese attribute these cases to unclean and malicious spirits, who are the enemies of men, and are constantly seeking to injure them.

(22.) In case D in the Appendix we hear of a female slave possessed by a spirit, who was highly prized and used by her master as a means of gain. Compare the case given in the 16th chapter of Acts.

(23.) The testimony upon which the cases of demon-possession and demon-expulsion in the New Testament rest is of virtually the same character as that upon which the authentication of the cases presented from China rests; viz., the testimony of intelligent, unbiased, common people who were eye-witnesses of the events. The assumption so often heard now-a-days, that no testimony should be received in such investigations but that of so-called "experts" finds no sanction in the Scriptures. In investigations of this kind, *who* are the "experts?"

(24.) In reviewing the cases of "demon-possession" in China, we find that they are very rare in large cities, and that they occur principally in rural and mountainous regions. The same is true of the cases recorded in the Scriptures. We read of none occurring in Jerusalem. One occurred in Capernaum, in the very beginning of our Saviour's ministry: Mark i: 21-28; Luke iv: 31-37. The others were met with in Galilee, Gadara, the region of Tyre and Sidon, and that of Caesarea Philippi.

As the result of the comparison which has been made we see that the correspondence between the cases met with in China and those recorded in Scripture is complete and circumstantial, covering almost every point presented in the Scripture narrative. The frequent assertions, made in extracts which we have taken from a variety of authors, that the possession phenomena of Judea found in the Bible are identical with those of other lands seems justified, and we may inquire in the language of Bishop Cardwell of India, "If the cases now-a-days differ from those of the Hebrews in the time of Christ, will any one point out the exact bound and limit of the difference?"

Now as we have the highest authority for referring the phenomena presented in the scriptures to the agency of evil spirits, the conclusion that the same phenomena met with in China and other lands is referable to the same cause is irresistible.

It was my hope when I began to investigate the subject of so-called "demon-possession" that the Scriptures and modern science would furnish the means of showing to the Chinese, that these phenomena need not be referred to demons. The result has been quite the contrary.

"In discussing James IV : 7, 'Resist the devil,' etc., Dr. Plummer declares that James, quite as much as Peter, Paul, or John, speaks of the chief power of evil as a person. The passage, he holds, is not intelligible on any other interpretation. James 'was probably well aware of the teaching of Jesus Christ.'

'If the belief in a personal power of evil is a superstition, Jesus Christ had ample opportunities of correcting it; and He not only steadfastly abstained from doing so, but in very marked ways, both by His acts and by His teaching, He did a great deal to encourage and inculcate the belief.'"
—(From *The Old and New Test. Student*, Sept. 1891, page 182.)

"The emphasis which Jesus Christ lays on diabolic agency is so great that, if it is not a reality, he must be regarded either as seriously misled about realities which concern the spiritual life, or else as seriously misleading others. And in neither case could he be even the perfect Prophet?"
—Charles Gore, Canon of Westminster, author of *Lux Mundi*, in *Thoughts on Religion*, by George John Romanes, p. 192. (Chicago, Open Court Pub. Co , 1895.)

(See pages 191, 251.)

The papers by Dr. A. D. White referred to on these pages have now been embodied in his *History of the Warfare of Science with Theology in Christendom.* 2 vols., 8vo., D. Appleton & Co., N. Y., 1896.

CHAPTER XV.

TEACHINGS OF SCRIPTURE CONTINUED.

The authorized English version of the New Testament is less clear in its presentation of the subject of demon-possession than is the original Greek, in consequence of its translating *diabolos* and *daimonion* and *daimon* by the one word "devil." In the revised version the first of these words is translated "devil," and the other two "demon," the important distinction of the original being thus preserved.* The word *diabolos* (devil) meaning "slanderer" or "false accuser" is in the New Testament only used in the singular, and appears more than thirty times as a descriptive title of Satan. In its adjective form it is used three times to represent men as accusers or slanderers.† The words *daimonion* and *daimon* are used very frequently in the New Testament, both in the singular and plural, but never interchangeably with *diabolos*, and always in a sense different from that of *diabolos*. Whenever the words *daimonion* or *daimon* occur the margin of the newly revised version gives *demon* as their

* So in margin. † 1 Tim. iii; 11. 2 Tim. iii; 3. Tit. ii; 3.

proper translation or equivalent. Its synonym is "evil" or "unclean spirit." There is then in the Scripture only one devil, but the number of demons is indefinitely large. We are never told of a person's being possessed by the devil; but all the cases of possession are possessions by demons. It may be well to add here that the expression "possessed by a demon" so frequently used in our English translation of the New Testament, is the rendering of a single word in the Greek, which might be translated "demonized." In Acts xvi: 16, the expression in our authorized version, "a certain damsel possessed with a spirit of divination," would be literally translated "a certain damsel having a spirit of Python" or a "Pythian spirit."

The Scriptures are not more explicit in making a clear distinction between the devil and demons, than in teaching us the relation which subsists between the devil and demons. The Jews accuse our Lord of casting out demons by the power and authority of Beelzebub, the prince of the demons. * Our Saviour replied, "Every kingdom divided against itself is brought to desolation; and every city or house divided against itself shall not stand; and if Satan cast out Satan he is divided against himself; how shall then his kingdom stand, etc." Here Beelzebub and Satan are used as exchangeable terms, and the statement

* Matt. xii, 22–30; Mark iii, 22–27; Luke xi. 14–23,

of the Jews that Beelzebub or Satan is the prince of the demons is accepted by our Saviour as true. We are confirmed in this conclusion by other teachings of our Saviour. We are told that "the seventy returned again with joy, saying, "Lord, even the demons are subject to us through Thy name." And He said unto them, "I beheld Satan as lightning fall from Heaven. Behold I give you power to tread on serpents and scorpions, and on all the power of the enemy; and nothing shall by any means hurt you. Notwithstanding, in this rejoice not, that the spirits are subject unto you; but rather rejoice because your names are written in heaven."(*)

The Apostle Peter also referring to the infliction of sufferings by demons, says of our Lord, that he "went about doing good and healing all that were oppressed of the devil."† What is done by demons, is here as elsewhere in Scripture ascribed to the devil as their leader or head. Owing probably, to the frequent use of "devil" for "demon" in the authorized version of the New Testament, we often find in Christian teachings, oral and printed, that many things are attributed to the devil which should be attributed to demons. We are thus led, by conceiving of Satan as in so many places, and doing so many things at the same time, almost to consider him omnipotent. This shows the importance of adhering

* Luke x; 17-20.
† Acts x; 38.

to Scripture usage in keeping up the distinction between these two words. In matters of gravest importance Satan probably appeared himself personally, as the acting agent. This is notably the case in the temptation of our Saviour.

The intimate connection between Satan and demons invests the subject which we have been considering with a new importance. These demons are the "power of darkness" with which we have to contend. They are enemies, the more dangerous because working in the dark, unperceived and unsuspected; not few in number untrained and inexperienced, but a martialed host of veterans, composed of the "prince of this world" as its head, and the "principalities and powers," and "rulers of the darkness of this world," with legions of Satan's angels or messengers who are his willing subjects.*

The popular conception of the devil, in whatever way it may have been derived, is quite different from that which a careful and unbiased reading of the Scriptures will give us. He is to most persons who really believe in his existence, a being ghostly, hideous, and repulsive, of whom we have the vaguest and most shadowy conceptions.

In the Bible though he is represented as the embodiment of all wickedness and malignity, he is still never spoken of lightly. Our Saviour refers to him as the "Prince of this World"; †

* Lu. xxii, 53. Col. i, 13. Eph. vi, 12.　† John xii, 31; xiv, 30; xvi, 11;

as the "strong man armed;" * and when Satan asserts the authority to give to our Lord "all the kingdoms of the world" † that authority is not denied. When the seventy were sent forth to preach the gospel Satan and his agents with whom they had to contend are spoken of as "all the power of the enemy." ‡ He is represented as the "great dragon." § "Michael, the arch-angel, when contending with the devil" "durst not bring against him a railing judgment." ‖

The Book of Job gives us some conception, though the subject is full of mystery, of the character of Satan, and the relations which he as the "god of this world" is permitted to sustain to this world and its inhabitants. His distinguishing characteristics, as there presented are freedom, self assertion, consciousness of power, unbelief, undisguised opposition to God, taking pleasure in accusing God's people and inflicting injury on them. He is represented as coming audaciously, with "the sons of God," "to present himself before the Lord." ¶ His presence excites no surprise. He is received and addressed by God in a manner not unlike that which characterizes God's intercourse with men. His character and purposes as the avowed enemy

* Luke xi, 21
† Matt. iv, 8. 9.
‡ Luke x, 19.
§ Rev. xii, 9.
‖ Jude 9.
¶ Job, chap's i, ii,

of man are assumed to be well understood; and the right, or at least the privilege of accusing, tempting, and subjugating man, if he can do so, is implied. From the narrative as given in Job we may draw the following conclusions:

1. Satan has a kind of recognized, legal standing ground in this world, and (under limitations) liberty, authority, and influence.

2. It is his purpose to tempt and gain control over men, and to do this he is ever seeking opportunities.

3. He cannot carry out his purposes except by God's permission.

4. This permission is sometimes obtained.

These disclosures with reference to Satan in the Book of Job, are in perfect agreement with the teachings of the New Testament. Of this fact our Lord's temptation in the wilderness furnishes a striking illustration. Led by the Spirit, our Saviour, though possessed of divine dignity and power, in this as well as in other instances in his earthly life, voluntarily submits to the temptation of Satan as divinely permitted.

The temptation of Peter presents the same characteristics. We read in the revised version (which is in accord with the original Greek) "Simon, Simon, behold Satan asked to have you," (or, "obtained you by asking")"that he might sift you as wheat." *

* Luke xxii. 31. Compare Longfellow's poem, "The Sifting of Peter,"

The Scripture accounts of Paul's "thorn in the flesh," "the messenger of Satan," * and the "delivering unto Satan for the destruction of the flesh," † present the same features. It is a fact full of significance and hope, that in every one of the cases given above, Satan was foiled, and his temptations overruled for good.

Access of demons to the divine presence, and their connection with the divine councils by way of permission, is further illustrated in the fall of Ahab. ‡

The question naturally arises, who were, or who are these demons? Whence do they come? The Greeks used this word "demon" to designate the disembodied spirits of deceased men.§ It would appear that the same idea of spirits which "demonize" men has been held by all nations since the time of the Greeks, including the Chinese of the present day. The inquiry in what sense do the Scriptures use the word demon is pertinent and important. To this question the Scriptures do not give a specific answer. The opinion which is probably most generally adopted is that they were originally one with the holy angels, but that they have fallen from their

* 2 Cor. xii, 7,

† 1 Cor. v. 5.

‡ 1 Kings xxii, 18–22.

§ Primarily, of men who had lived in the Golden Age before the expulsion of Saturn. See Hesiod, "Works and Days," 109–126. Also ''Earth's Earliest Ages,'' by G. H. Pember. M. A., F. H. Revell Co. N. Y. pp. 70–73, and whole chapter. (Bohn Library Translation of Hesiod.)

original state by sinning against God. *

An ingenious hypothesis of Rev. James Gall, author of a work entitled: "Primeval Man Unveiled," † is worthy of notice in this connection. He believes that Satan and the demons who are his subjects, are the disembodied spirits of a pre-Adamic race, who once lived on this earth, whose human remains may yet be found, if they have not already been found in its strata. This race sinned, and fell from its original state as ours has since done. In consequence of sin, they suffered physical death. These are the "angels which kept not their first estate, but left their own habitation" (i. e. their bodies) ‡ and are "reserved in everlasting chains under darkness unto the judgment of the great day." Satan is the acknowledged head of these spirits, and probably by right of primogeniture. He was naturally envious of the race which succeeded him, and

---

* Greek writers speak of the worship of gods and demons as synonymous or interchangeable. Favonius, a philosopher of Adrian's time who at different periods of his life resided in Rome and Greece and the Lesser Asia, describes the religion of these nations indifferently as "the fear of gods and demons." Zenophon intending to commend the piety of Ageselaus king of Sparta says "he was ever a worshiper of demons."

Festus pronounces the accusations of the Jews against Paul to be (Acts xxv, 19,) "A question of their own demon worship," (*deisidaimonias.*) Paul calls the Athenians (Acts xvii, 23,) remarkable for their worship of demons, (*os deisidaimonesterous,*)

Augustine gives the Platonic conception of demons in Civ. Dei. lib. viii, Chap. XVI as follows; "In kind they are animal, in disposition passionate, in mind rational, in body carnal, in duration eternal, having the first three in common with us; the fourth peculiar to themselves, and the fifth common to them with the gods." This was probably the popular creed of the times. Imperial Bible Dictionary.

Article on Demons by Rev. James Henderson D, D. Glasgow.

† Primeval Man Unveiled: Or The Anthropology of the Bible." 2d edition. 1880. London, Hamilton, Adams & Co.

‡ Compare 2 Cor. v, 2. the only other place in which this word is used in the New Testament. In the revised version the Greek word used in the original is translated "habitation" as in Jude 6, 2 Peter, ii; 4.)

plotted and compassed its fall. After Adam's fall and loss of the proprietorship and control of the world, Satan reasserted his claim to it by right of precedence. He still contests the claim; the final issue of the contest being suspended on the success or failure of the redemption and restoration of men. In the meantime these disembodied spirits of a former human race, being accustomed to the occupation and use of human bodies constructed in all respects like our own, seek for ends of their own to possess themselves of them.

The question naturally arises here, is it possible for the spirits of deceased men, either good or bad, to hold communication with living men, and if so, are there actual cases of such communication? We know that angels may convey information to men by means of dreams and in other ways. We may also infer from the manner in which our Saviour in the parable of the rich man and Lazarus* treats the suggestion that Lazarus should be sent to warn the rich man's brothers, that such communication is not in the nature of things impossible. In the case of Samuel's appearance to Saul† it would seem that we have the evidence that spirits of the dead either by their inherent faculties or powers, or by special divine permission and arrangement, may as-

---

* Luke xvi; 19–31.

† 1 Sam. xxviii.

sume human bodies and hold conversation with men just as angels do. It seems also to be a natural inference from the injunction, "prove the spirits whether they are of God,"* that communications may be expected from the unseen world from spirits both good and bad. We not infrequently hear in the recital of personal experiences, and, in biographies and other books, instances of supposed communication with the spirit world. The Society for Psychical Research has collected many cases of this kind which seem to be authenticated. The present tendency is to account for them by thought transference or telepathy. A few occasional instances of supposed impression from the spirit world when the minds of those thus affected are roused to an abnormal state of excitement by fear and expectation, would not be remarkable. The frequency of these cases, however, renders them worthy of careful collection and examination. It is probable that these events are kept from publicity in most cases from fear on the part of those cognizant of them of being regarded as superstitious. The viewing of certain phenomena with a kind of ghostly dread and apprehension, which deters us from examining whether they represent important facts or only delusive appearances, is of the very essence of superstition. Dr. Horace Bushnell, in speaking of occurrences popularly

* 1 Jno. iv; 1.

called "supernatural" says: "What is wanted, therefore, on this subject, in order to any sufficient impression, is a full consecutive inventory of the supernatural events or phenomena of the world. There is reason to suspect that many would in that case be greatly surprised by the commonness of the instances." *

It does not admit of a reasonable doubt that in the cases of "possession" presented in the Scriptures and in the records of heathen nations, the motive which characterizes and dominates these cases is not a desire to instruct and benefit man, but the very opposite. Whether there is such a thing as "possession" from good motives and intentions is a question on which I have no sufficient ground for forming an opinion. I have met with one case which may seem to be of this character, which has not been given before in this book because it is exceptional, and insufficient of itself to warrant any reliable conclusion. It may be given here, however, as an intimation of the possibility of other similar and perhaps more pronounced and fully attested cases, which have not, so far as my information goes, been found in China.†

In one of our stations in Western Enchiu, in the village of Chwang-teo, we have two Christians, father and son of the family Sung. The inhabitants of this village are exceptionally rude

* See his "Nature and the Supernatural."   † Lu. xvi, 27.

18 *Demon*

and lawless.　These two Christians have suffered much opposition and persecution, not only from their neighbors, but especially from the female members of their own family, the elder Mrs. Sung, and her three daughters-in-law.　The opposition of these women was for several years bitter and persistent.　On one of my visits some years since I learned that the elder Mrs. Sung had recently died, and was surprised to find that the three daughters-in-law, and another son were studying Christian books and applying for baptism.　The reasons given for this remarkable change were the following: I was told by the two Christians, both of whom are very trust-worthy men, that some time after Mrs. Sung's death, one of the daughters-in-law passed into an unconscious state, manifesting symptoms very similar to those which characterize cases of "possession."　In one of these abnormal states, a voice spoke through her, purporting to be that of the deceased Mrs. Sung, declaring that she had gone to the land of spirits, that she was refused entrance to the abode of the blest, but had seen it from a distance.　She was asked if she saw there certain persons who had recently died in the village.　She replied with reference to each person specified, no.　When asked whom she saw there whom she knew, she replied that she saw a great multitude, but only recognized one individual, naming a woman who had recently died in a village some miles distant, who had for some years been a professing Christian. She informed them that her simple object in coming to them was to tell them that Christianity is true, and to urge them all to study Christian books, give themselves to Christ, and enter the Christian church. I was told that after this one communication the daughter-in-law regained her normal consciousness and had not been similarly affected since. The new interest in Christianity continued for some months, but proved to be only superficial and temporary. I visited the village, Oct., 1887. The two believers who were baptized about ten years previous are still living, and are respected by their neighbors as consistent Christians, but no others had up to that time been baptized in the village. The women in the family had ceased the violence of their opposition, and evince occasional impulses towards entering the Christian church, but their feelings and efforts are not sufficiently strong to effect their separation from idolatry, and the reformation of their lives.

To the question what is the motive which influences demons to seek to possess themselves of the bodies of men, the Scriptures furnish us with a ready answer. The Bible clearly teaches us that in all Satan's dealings with our race his object is to deceive and ruin us by drawing our minds away from God, and inducing us to break

God's laws and bring upon ourselves his displeasure. These objects are secured by demon-possession. Superhuman effects are produced, which to the ignorant and uninstructed seem divine. Divine worship and implicit obedience are demanded, and enforced by the infliction of physical distress, and by false promises and fearful threats. In this way idolatrous rites and superstitions, interwoven with social and political customs and institutions, have usurped the place in almost every nation in history of the pure worship of God. As regards the demons themselves it appears that they have additional personal reasons. The possession of human bodies seems to afford them a much desired place of rest and physical gratification. Our Saviour speaks of evil spirits walking through dry places and seeking rest, and especially desirous of finding rest in the bodies of their familiar or accustomed victims.* When deprived of a place of rest in the bodies of human beings, they are represented as seeking it in the bodies of inferior animals. †

The question is often asked, and very naturally, if demon-possession is possible and also actual in the world's history, why does it exist in the past rather than the present; in remote and inaccessible places, rather than in our immediate

* Matt. XII., 43-45.
† Matt. VIII.. 31.

presence; among ignorant and savage rather than civilized races? The usual answer to this question is that at the time of the introduction of Christianity God permitted demons to possess the bodies of men in order by the casting them out in the name of Christ, to display more conspicuously the power of Christ and the divine origin of Christianity. That the casting out of demons was among the most prominent and convincing of the evidences of the divine origin of Christianity in early times, the Scriptures leave no room for doubt. I believe, however, that the reason for the fact that cases of possession are less frequent now than formerly, and still less frequent in Christian countries, is to be found in Satan himself. He uses methods best suited to his ends. A form of possession adapted to advance his ends in heathen lands, may only be suited to subvert them in Christian lands; and this is a reason quite sufficient for its being discountenanced and suppressed. Satan acts under cover of darkness, concealing his purpose, his nature, and his presence. The Bible teaches that demon-possession is of Satan. So, for Satan to practice demon-possession in Christian lands (at least in its old forms with which the world is familiar) would be to reveal himself in his true character, and thus excite suspicion and opposition. Besides, the dispossession of demons in places where Christianity is introduced, would be injurious to Satan's influence. Furthermore demons had an intuitive apprehension that they could not hold their victims in the presence of Christ, and cried out, "What have we to do with thee?" "Art thou come hither to torment us before the time?"* In China the uniform testimony of the supposed demon is, "I cannot live where Christ is. I must go." There is something in the very atmosphere of Christianity which is repellent to them. Thus the best answer to this question comes from the demons themselves. As a matter of fact, cases of this kind disappear almost at once whenever Christianity is introduced, or continue in a modified and less pronounced form. They probably now exist and always have existed in all heathen nations, but, appear to our view, with comparatively few exceptions, only at the epoch when the advancing tide of aggressive Christianity comes into contact and collision with the storm-tossed sea of heathenism.

It may be objected that according to our above hypothesis the permission by Satan of any cases of possession in Christian lands, or in lands where Christianity is being introduced, is inconsistent with the doctrine of the wisdom of Satan and his control over his subordinate spirits. This objection is conclusive only on the suppositions that Satan has a complete knowledge of all that

Matt. VIII., 29.

is going on in the world, and that all demons are perfectly subject to his authority and control, neither of which suppositions is probable. Want of vigilance on the part of superiors, and personal ambition and gratification in subordinates may operate in Satan's administration to obstruct and delay changes, as well as in the affairs of men.

It may be objected, if association with Christians is repellent to demons, why are they constantly represented in the Scriptures as following and tempting Christians? We answer, possessing and tempting men are widely different. One implies a relation intimate, the other more remote; one internal, the other external; one may be regarded as unauthorized and illicit; the other as permitted. A screened position of nearness to an antagonist is eagerly sought for, while an exposed one is carefully avoided. Under our present circumstances Satan makes his attacks under subterfuges and disguises. The victim of his wiles proudly imagines that the artful sophistries by which he evades truth, stifles conscience, and justifies himself in his opposition to God, are the product of his own superior wisdom and insight. He regards the idea of the existence of such a being as Satan as a weak superstition, and the suggestion that he may be unconsciously acting under his influence and control with contemptuous incredulity.

It may be asked: Why is not our Saviour as willing to protect and rescue men from the more covert and insidious attacks of demons, as from their efforts to possess men's bodies? We can only say that the Scriptures clearly teach us that God permits the former but not the latter. The latter is an outrage against nature. It is robbing man of his very personality. It seems to some persons inconsistent with the character of God that evil spirits should be allowed to roam over the earth at will to seek the injury and distruction of his children. It is an obvious fact, however, that many evils are permitted in the present order of things which, no less than demons, destroy both the happiness and the lives of men. Pestilence and famine sweep away the earth's inhabitants by thousands and millions. These evils can, however, be mitigated or avoided by man's using the means which God has put at his disposal for his own protection. In the case of danger from demons the ability which God has given to man to protect himself is still more complete. They are allowed to tempt and injure man, but only under limitations and restraints, and if they are resisted in the name of Christ they will "flee from us."*

It may seem at first sight that the surprise and astonishment attributed to the Jews, on seeing our Saviour cast out demons, is inconsistent

* See Jas. iv, 7.

with their familiarity with the practice of exorcism, and with the words of our Saviour Himself; "By whom then do your children cast them out."* If we examine carefully the gospel narrative, the explanation of this seeming inconsistency will, I think, become apparent. We read in Mark's gospel: "And they were all amazed insomuch that they questioned among themselves, saying: What thing is this? What new doctrine is this? for with authority commandeth he even the unclean spirits, and they do obey him. And immediately his fame spread abroad throughout all the region round about Galilee." † Similar language is found recorded in other gospels. ‡ We read also in Matthew. "The multitudes marvelled. saying, It was never so seen in Israel." § There can be little doubt that the wonder of the people was excited not so much by the *fact* as the *manner* of our Saviour's casting out demons. It was "by authority," by "a word," or in the language of our Saviour himself, " with the finger of God,"‖ "by the Spirit of God."¶ What amazed the Jews was the contrast between the dread and apprehension with which their exorcists addressed demons, together with their frequent failures, and the calm dignity and authority with which our

* Matt. xii, 22-29.
† Mark i. 27, 28.
‡ Luke iv, 36, 37.
§ Matt. ix, 33.
‖ Luke xi, 20.
¶ Matt. xii, 28.

Saviour always addressed them, an authority which was in every case at once acknowledged and obeyed.

It is very noticeable that the multitudes or common people, and not the learned or educated classes, were specially moved and influenced by our Saviour's method of casting out demons. It is so at the present time. The higher evidences of our Saviour's divine mission have their weight with cultured minds capable of understanding and appreciating them. The poor and illiterate who are incapable of deep research, or close logical process of thought, find in these cases of casting out spirits an evidence of our Saviour's sympathy and divinity, palpable, and suited to their wants and capacities.* When the apostles were commissioned to go forth and evangelize the nations, among the "signs" promised to "follow them that believe," "in my name shall they cast out demons" stands first in the enumeration.† But when John the Baptist is pointed to our Saviour's wonderful works to confirm his faith in him as the promised Messiah, the casting out of demons is not mentioned.‡

Since the casting out of demons seems provi-

---

* Chinese Christians in different parts of the Chinese Empire have not only had their faith confirmed by the casting out of demons, but by numerous instances which they will adduce of the sick being restored to health in answer to prayer, and also remarkable deliverances and dreams and visions. These cases might be collected in great numbers by any one on the ground who has the leisure and the disposition to do so.

† Mark xvi., 17.

‡ Matt. xi., 3-6. Luke vii., 19-23.

dentially used as furnishing so striking an evidence of our Lord's mission as the Son of God and the Saviour of the world, why when the demons were cast out, and openly testified that Christ was the "Son of God," "The Holy one of God," * did our Saviour rebuke them, saying: "Hold thy peace," and on another occasion "straitly charge them that they should not make Him known?" † This command of our Saviour not to make him known is almost identical with that made to the twelve about two years afterwards; the reason is probably the same in both cases. It was the special function of the apostles to witness to the world that Jesus was the Christ, the Son of God, and this they did after our Saviour's resurrection repeatedly and persistently, in the face of persecution and death. Before our Lord's resurrection, the time for this public testimony had not come. A certain reserve was necessary. Our Saviour's earthly ministry was characterized by a nice balancing between revealing and concealing. He must reveal himself with sufficient clearness to furnish a ground for the faith of his followers, but not so clearly as to overawe his enemies, and prevent the crowning act of his mission on earth, his suffering on the cross. It was by this nice discrimination between revealing too little and

* Mark i, 24, 25.

† Mark iii, 12.

too much, this holding precisely to the middle course without diverging to the one side or the other that he was "straitened" until his baptism of blood should be accomplished.* It is remarkable that this testimony of the demons was given near the beginning of our Lord's ministry, showing that they knew his character at that time better even than the twelve who were daily instructed by him. It is possible that this testimony to our Saviour may have been purposely designed by Satan to interfere with Christ's plan, and defeat the great object He had in view. In this matter, however, as in all others, the demons were under divine control. The suppression of this testimony for the time being, and its being recorded in the Gospels afterward were no doubt alike for our good and the good of the church universal.

The Mosaic law denounced death against witches or wizards. This was evidently not because the wizard's art was a mere pretense or imposture, but because it was a natural and voluntary intercourse with evil spirits. The language of Scripture is too plain on this point to be misunderstood. "A man also or woman that hath a familiar spirit, or that is a wizard, shall surely be put to death; they shall stone them with stones; their blood shall be upon them." †

* Luke xii., 50.
† Lev. xx. 27.

"There shall not be found among you an en-chanter, or a witch, or a charmer, or a consulter with familiar spirits, or a wizard, or a necro-mancer."* The demoniac is an object of com-pasion as one overpowered and enslaved, the 'wizard' is a willing slave of demons, and, among the Jews, consciously engaged in the service of those who were the opposers and enemies of God.†

The facts which have come to our notice in connection with spirit-manifestations in China may perhaps assist us in understanding the dif-ferent phases of spirit-manifestations recorded in Scripture, as they are related to each other in a course of progressive development.

Four Stages of Obsession and Possession.

First, we have the initial stage of demon in-fluence which may be called that of obsession. It is the stage of the first approach, and the intro-ductory or tentative efforts of the demon. In this stage cases are often unpronounced in their character, leaving it difficult to determine whether they are to be classed with demon-possession, idiocy, lunacy, or epilepsy. In many cases of de-mon possession this stage is wanting, the second stage described below being the first.

Second. The stage marked by a struggle for possession, in which the unwilling subject resists and sometimes successfully, but generally pines

* Deut. xviii, 10–11.   † See p. 428.

away until he yields an involuntary subjection to the demon's will. This may be called the transition stage or the crisis. It is comparatively of short duration.

Third. This stage may be designated, with regard to the subject, as that of subjection and subserviency, and with regard to the demon, as that of training and development. The condition of the subject is most of the time healthy and normal. He is peaceful and quiet except in the paroxysm, which occurs in passing from the normal to the abnormal state. This stage may continue for years.

Fourth. In this stage the demonized subject has developed capabilities for use, and is willing to be used. He is the trained, accustomed, voluntary slave of the demon. He is called in China *Tu Shien*, "spirit in a body," or *Wu-po* "woman sorcerer;" in the language of the Old Testament, (according to the particular line of his development and use) a witch, or a "soothsayer", or a "necromancer;" in modern English phrase a "developed medium."

The above are only general distinctions, which must be understood as allowing marked variations in individual cases, and in the periods of time between them. In each stage also individual cases may never pass from that stage to the succeeding one.

It is important to understand the Scriptural

distinctions between forms of demon influence. These may be presented as follows:

Four Forms of Demon Action Upon Men Which Are Noted in Scripture.

First. Temptation in the form of spiritual suggestion. This mysterious influence from an unseen world, to which believers and unbelievers are constantly exposed, is referred to very frequently in the Bible, especially in the New Testament.

Second. Absolute demon control, the result of voluntarily and habitually yielding to temptation. Men work "all uncleanness with greediness;"* and give themselves up to the control of Satan with reckless abandonment. In the history of Judas this form or degree of demon influence is in the Scriptures clearly distinguished from the former one. In the second verse of the 13th chapter of John we are told that the devil had already "put it into the heart" of Judas to betray Jesus. In the 27th verse of the same chapter we read "Then entered Satan into him." In the present day we often meet with men, desperately wicked, almost Satanic, but they are not possessed. Though fearfully under the influence of Satan, they are perfectly free, follow the direction of their own wills, and retain their own personality.

Third. Bodily inflictions in the form of dis-

* Eph. iv., 19.

eases.   May not Job's afflictions, the woman
who had a "spirit of infirmity,"* and was bound
by Satan fourteen years," and Paul's "thorn in
the flesh, the messenger of Satan"† be regarded
as illustrations of demon influences of this kind?
Cases of idiocy, lunacy, and epilepsy as they
are witnessed now-a-days are sometimes strongly
suggestive of demon influence.   It is probably
impossible to determine whether any of these
cases are or are not referable to demon influence.
Supposing such a thing, however, it would still
be a case of physical disease and quite distinct
from one of "demon-possession."

Fourth. Demon-possession, one chief characteristic of which is a new personality.   To persons of this class alone is the term "possession"
properly applied.

We have yet to consider what is probably the
most important passage of Scripture relating to
this subject.   I refer to the last petition in the
Lord's Prayer. ‡   The rendering of the Revised
Version "deliver us from the evil one" gives us,
I believe, the true meaning.   In fact, a careful
study of this passage in the Greek, and of other
passages in which the same word occurs, seems

* Luke xiii., 16.

† II Cor. xii., 7.

‡ Matt. vi., 13. Luke xi., 4. With this may be named the nearly identical petition of John xvii. 15, the only one strictly common to both
prayers.

to necessitate the new rendering as the only legitimate one. *

If the conclusion above expressed is correct we see what our Saviour's view is of our position and danger; what our views and feelings should be as a prerequisite to the intelligent and sincere use of these words "Deliver us from the evil one" as the divinely appointed expression of our emotions and desires.

It is objected that to believe in these alleged cases of casting out demons is to lower and degrade the miracles of our Saviour by representing weak converts just emerging from heathenism as performing miracles, similar to his. But our Saviour declared that, after his ascension, his disciples should do greater things than he did. † What they should do, however, would be done by them only mediately as agents, but actually and properly by Christ. ‡ Our Saviour often honors humble Christians if they only have a strong and simple faith in him. § It is not for us to say when Christ shall work wonders, or through whom.

As to the character of these events they are wonderful as giving evidence of the presence of unseen opposing powers, and the sovereignity of our Lord; but they are far less wonderful than

* For an able defence of this new rendering, see the elaborate and exhaustive treatment of this subject in "The Person and Kingdom of Satan" by Rev. Edw. H. Jewett, S.T.D. Whittaker, New York 1889.

† Jno. xiv, 12.

‡ Gal. iii., 5. Alford: "He then that supplieth unto you the Spirit and worketh mighty works in you."

§ Matt. xvii 19.

19 Demon

the fact of the every-day miracle of the quickening of dead souls by the life of Christ through the agency of the Holy Spirit. What renders those cases of demon-expulsion wonderful to us is the fact that in them spiritual being and spiritual events come, in a sense, within the range of our observation, and become to some extent tangible and palpable. But why after all has it in this age of the church come to be regarded as a marvel that Christians should be able to cast out demons? We believe that Christ is present with his people, and that his Spirit dwells in them. Is it strange then that demons, recognizing Christ's presence with his people should instinctively escape from a Christian atmosphere? Need we be surprised that in the early church the presence of one Christian was sometimes, we are told, sufficient to drive demons at once from the bodies they had possessed?

In a review of this book, in its first edition, printed in the *Mid-Continent*, St. Louis, March 27, 1895, Rev. Jas. H. Brooks, D. D., writes as follows: "The word *demon*, in its substantive and verbal forms, occurs seventy-eight times in the New Testament, although in our Authorized Version it is usually translated *devil*. It is foolish to regard what is said of demons as due to the lack of medical science, and to the ignorance of the times, for they are particularly distinguished from epilepsy, lunacy, and all ordinary forms of disease and suffering. It is worse than foolish, it is irreverent. Our Lord Jesus Christ distinctly calls them demons, spoke to them as demons, cast them out as demons; and the man is treading upon perilous ground who calls in question his wisdom and veracity, or denies the strict truthfulness of the inspired narratives. No intelligent person who believes the Bible, can refuse to accept its testimony, that Demon-possession was an awful reality in the days of our Lord and his apostles; and if then, why not now?

"It has been so ever since Satan tempted and ruined our first parents in Eden. The Jews offered sacrifices unto devils in Egypt, Lev. xvii. 7; Deut. xxxii. 17, and again and again were they warned against demons, familiar spirits, witches and wizards, as controlled by the god of this world. If this is not literally true, Exodus, Leviticus, Deuteronomy, 1 Samuel, 2 Kings, 1 Chronicles, 2 Chronicles, Isaiah, Micah, Nahum, must all be set aside as incredible. The profound impression, therefore, that prevails universally in China, India and Africa of Demon-possession is a well founded conviction. The same devil-power is often exerted in more favored lands."

CHAPTER XVI.

HISTORICAL SKETCH OF DEMONISM.

Alleged communications with the unseen world have characterized the religious beliefs and practices of all nations from the earliest times.*

Something may be learned relative to the demonism of ancient Egypt from the Old Testament. We have three references to the magicians of Egypt performing wonders similar to those wrought by Moses.† It is to be noticed that we have here a record, not of the beliefs or superstitions, either of Jews or Egyptians, but of visible facts, inseparably linked with one of the most important events in Jewish history. Such statements as these cannot be ignored or discredited by those who receive the Bible as the word of God.

The book of Daniel gives evidence of the existence, and official recognition in the Babylonian court, of "Magicians," "Astrologers," and "Sorcerers," whose special province it was to disclose

---

* For a clear and comprehensive presentation of the historical developments of these beliefs, see article on "Witchcraft" in *The Century* January 1892. by the Rev. J, M. Buckley D.D. This has since been republished in a volume, entitled: "Faith Healing, Christian Science and Kindred Phenomena," By Dr. J. M. Buckley. N. Y. The Century Co, 1892.

† Ex. vii, 12, 22, viii: 7,18.19.
See Robinson's *Pharaohs of the Bondage and Exodus;* 153-169, also Appendix ii, 8, of this volume.

the secrets of the future and of the invisible world. *

The early books of the Old Testament make frequent reference to persons who had "familiar spirits." Christian writers who reject the doctrine of demon-possession are led to put strained interpretations on these passages. It is said that although death is denounced against persons who have "familiar spirits" yet we are not to infer from these denunciations the reality of "familiar spirits," † but only the existence of a class who *professed* to have "familiar spirits." It is also said that the misconception expressed in this language is to be referred to the prophets who were limited in knowledge, and were influenced by the beliefs and superstitions of their age. Direct statements of Scripture utterly preclude such an interpretation. In a repetition or republication of sundry laws given to Moses, this law respecting "witches" is directly referred to Jehovah as its author, by the familiar formula "And the Lord spake unto Moses saying."

Furthermore the passages themselves will show to what authority they are referable. "Regard not those that have familiar spirits, neither seek after wizards to be defiled by them; I am the Lord your God!"‡ Again, "The soul that turneth after such as have familiar spirits and after wizards,

* Daniel ii, 2.

† See Dr. Buckley on Witchcraft. Also G. H. Pember on page 428.

‡ Lev. xix: 31.

to go a whoring after them I will even set my face against that soul, and will cut him off from among his people."* That God and not Moses is represented as the author of this law is unquestionable. That these repeated denunciations against those who have familiar spirits should refer only to the mere pretence of being "witches," without any intimation in Scripture of any such pretense, is inconceivable. As the words of the New Testament are inconsistent with the supposition of its being impossible to determine the reality of pronounced cases of so-called demon-possession, † so it is implied in the teachings of the Old Testament that there was no difficulty in determining who were and who were not "witches."

The case of the damsel in Philippi who had (as it is in the Greek) a spirit of Python or a Pythian spirit, ‡ gives us further insight into the spiritism of the ancient Greeks. The reference is to the famous oracle at Delphi. Aside from any preconceived hypothesis respecting spirits, and in accordance with the general teachings of the Scripture it is obviously implied in this passage that, First, this damsel was possessed by a spirit; Second, that this spirit was akin to that which possessed the prophetess of the Pythian oracle; and Third, that the utterances of this damsel,

* Lev. xx :6.

† See page 249 of this book.

‡ See Revised Version Acts xvi: 16.

like those of the Pythian oracle, proceeded from the possessing spirit. This passage of Scripture is important as connecting and identifying the demonology of the New Testament with that of the Greeks.

The Apostle Paul also teaches us that the connection of demons with the worship of idols is a reality. In speaking of idolatry he says "the things which the Gentiles sacrifice they sacrifice to demons and not to God."* In the previous verse he repeats the assertion so often made in Scripture, that an idol in itself is nothing. He teaches us that the gods worshiped under different names are imaginary, and non-existent; but that, behind and in connection with these gods, there are demons who make use of idolatry to draw men away from God; and it is to these that the heathen are unconsciously rendering obedience and service.

The fathers of the early church also uniformly taught the reality of demon agency in connection with idolatry and pagan oracles.

Cyprian, says "These spirits lurk under the statues and consecrated images; they inspire the breasts of their prophets with their afflatus; animate the fibers of the entrails; direct the flight of birds; rule the lots; give efficacy to oracles; are always mixing up falsehood with truth; for they both deceive and are deceived." "Nor have

* I Cor. x. 20. Also, Ps. cvi, 28, 34-38. Lev. xvii, 7. De. xxxii, 17.

they any other desire than to call men away from God, and to turn them from the understanding of the true religion to superstition with respect to themselves."* Clement of Alexandria says: "It is evident, since they are demoniac spirits that they know some things more quickly and more perfectly than men, for they are not retarded in learning by the heaviness of a body." "But this is to be observed, that what they know they do not employ for the salvation of souls, but for the deception of them; that they may indoctrinate them in the worship of false religion. But God, that the error of so great deception might not be concealed, and that He himself might not seem to be a cause of error in permitting them so great license to deceive men by divinations and cures and dreams, has of His mercy furnished them with a remedy, and has made the distinction of falsehood and truth patent to those who desire to know. This therefore is that distinction; what is spoken by the true God, whether by prophets or by diverse visions is always true; but what is foretold by demons is not always true." "There may occasionally be a slight mixture of truth to give, as it were, seasoning to the falsehood."

"Augustine remarks," says Rollin, "that God, to punish the blindness of the Pagans sometimes

---

* Cyprian on The Vanity of Idols.

permitted the demons to give answers according to the truth." *

We are not to suppose that the cultivated Greeks and Romans were led to consult the oracles without any evidence of superhuman knowledge connected with them. On the contrary, these oracles were sometimes subjected to severe tests. Croesus, King of Lydia, before consulting the oracle at Delphi, sent messengers to inquire at a specified day and hour what the king of Lydia was doing. At that time the king proceeded to boil in a brazen cauldron, with a brazen lid, the flesh of a lamb with the flesh of a tortoise. It is said that the oracle, at the time the king was thus engaged, minutely described this event to his messengers.

"The Emperor Trajan made a like demand of the oracle of Heliopolis by sending a sealed letter to which he required an answer. The oracle replied by sending to the emperor a bit of blank paper nicely folded and sealed. Trajan was amazed to find the answer in perfect harmony with the letter sent, which contained nothing but a blank paper."

The ancients claimed that the spirits which aided them were the spirits of their demi-gods, heroes and departed friends.

Pliny mentions conversations with disem-

* See Spiritualism Unveiled, by Lieut. Gen. Sir. Robert Phayre, K. C. B.

bodied spirits and inferior deities. It is not improbable that the Sibylline oracles were nothing more than productions of writing mediums.

It is an interesting question whether the origin of Mahometanism should not be referred to the agency of evil spirits. Its character as a principal foe to Christianity and modern civilization makes such a supposition a plausible one. Mahomet's history is marked by two stages, clearly distinguishable; the former characterized by wonderful earnestness as a seeker after truth, and the latter as swayed by evil influences, the whole tenor of his character being thus changed. Dean Stanley says of him: "It is now known that at least for a large part of his life he was a sincere reformer and enthusiast." . . . . "The story of his epileptic fits, a few years ago much discredited, seems now to be incontrovertibly reestablished, and we have a firmer ground than before for believing that a decided change came over the simplicity of his character after the establishment of his kingdom in Medina."*

Fisher in his "Outlines of Universal History" presents these two stages in Mahomet's life, and the transition between them as follows:† "He retired for meditation and prayer to the lonely and desolate Mount Hira. A vivid sense of the being of one Almighty God and of his responsibility to God entered his soul. A tendency to hysteria,

* History of the Eastern Church. p. p. 360, 361. † Fisher, p. 224.

in the east a disease of men as well as women, and to epilepsy, helps to account for extraordinary states of body and mind of which he was the subject. At first he ascribed these strange ecstacies or hallucinations to evil spirits, especially on the occasion when an angel directed him to begin the work of prophesying. But he was persuaded by Kadija (his wife) that their source was from above. He became convinced that he was a prophet, inspired with a holy truth, and charged with a sacred commission." It was certainly a strange form of "epilepsy," which instead of impairing the mental powers and capabilities of its subject, increased and intensified them. (See footnote on page 313.)

Without doubt the beliefs of the nations of antiquity; the teachings of the Old and New Testaments; and the teachings of the Fathers of the early church, are all in accord as to the existence and agency in this world of superhuman intelligences. Such a concurrence of testimony is certainly of great weight. Before setting it aside, or discrediting it, we may well pause to inquire whether the assumption that we are wiser than all the ages, is justified by our actual and verified discoveries.

We come now to consider the more recent phases of belief in spirits which have continued until the present time. After the introduction of Christianity in the Roman empire the responses of the oracles ceased, and spirit manifestations assumed new forms, until about the time of the Reformation a belief in the actual prevalence of witchcraft seemed to take possession of the different nationalities of Europe, and their colonies in America. The trials and executions of persons charged with "witchcraft" form one of the darkest and most mysterious chapters in modern history.

In studying this subject a definite and discriminating use of terms is a matter of the greatest importance. For want of thus discriminating there is perhaps no field of inquiry into which so much confusion has been introduced.

"Magic, ascribed by the Greeks to the hereditary caste of priests in Persia, still stands in the East for an incongruous collection of superstitious beliefs and rites, having nothing in common except the claim of abnormal origin and effects. Astrology, divination, demonology, soothsaying, sorcery, witchcraft, necromancy, enchantment, and many other systems are sometimes included in magic, but" (and this is the point to which the attention of the reader is especially called) "each term is also employed separately to stand for the whole mass of confused beliefs which, outside of the sphere of recognized religion, attempt to surpass the limitations of nature. For this reason the title of a work on this subject seldom indicates its scope." *

* Rev. J. M. Buckley, D. D., "Faith Healing," &c., pp. 197-9.

It is evident that most of the terms in this quotation are associated with debasing forms of superstition, and demonology is often indiscriminately classed with mere superstitions, and regarded as equally baseless and unreal. Whoever avows his belief in demon-possession is likely to be regarded as giving the same credence to the mixed pretensions of spiritualism and witchcraft. Most of the above designations are so loosely employed that it may be hard to make distinctions between them both clear and just. Fortunately the two terms in which we are specially interested, demon-possession and witchcraft, are specific and self-defining. The meaning of the former has been sufficiently indicated in previous chapters.

A "witch" is defined in the Capital Code of Connecticut A.D. 1642, as one who "hath or consorteth with a familiar spirit." This is in accordance with the teachings of the Old Testament. We may then regard a "witch," and "a person who has a familiar spirit" as synonomous. Witchcraft is now thought to embody three distinct ideas: first, that it is a witch's craft; second, that its intent is to injure the person who is the object of it; and third, that the agent through whom this injury is to be effected is the "familiar spirit," in union and compact with the witch. This is the generally accepted and quite intelligible meaning of "witchcraft." Dr. Buckley in the article above referred to says: "Witchcraft has been restricted by usage and civil and ecclesiastical law till it signifies a voluntary compact between the devil, the party of the first part, and a human being, male or female, wizard or witch, the party of the second part,—that he, the devil, will perform whatever the person may request." Dr. Buckley further says: "The sixth chapter of Lord Coke's Third Institute concisely defines a witch in these words: 'A witch is a person which hath conference with the devil; to consult with him to do some act.'" The trials for witchcraft during the seventeenth century all implied, or were based upon the above theory; they presented specific charges against alleged "witches" for effecting certain injuries or torments through the agency of evil spirits. Now, if we assume this to be the only legitimate use of the word "witchcraft," we may inquire what evidence the world presents, or has ever presented, of the existence of witchcraft as a real thing.

Some writers on the customs and experiences of the American Indians, and the tribes of Africa, and the South Sea islands, imply the existence of such witchcraft in those places; and occurrences described seem to give no little countenance to this belief. It is desirable that persons residing in those countries should make a searching inquiry as to whether the alleged practice be real or only apparent, and what its special features are. Without expressing any opinion on this subject with regard to places and races of which we have imperfect information, and confining our inquiries within limits in which we have reliable material on which to base our judgment, we may at least make some progress in answering this question.

There is no evidence of the existence of witchcraft in this conception of it either in the Old Testament or the New. There are numerous references to witches in the Old Testament, and four to witchcraft.* Witches were the instruments through which demons acted. The presence of demons was invoked by them, at the instance of those who applied to them, in order to obtain information or advice; but the idea of these mediums inflicting injuries on men by the aid of demons is foreign to the Bible. The word witchcraft occurs once in the authorized version of the New Testament, in Gal. v: 20, but our translators used it in a vague sense as a translation of the Greek *pharmakeia*, which word means "sorcery by the use of drugs." The Revised Version gives in the place of "witchcraft," "sorcery."

Witchcraft in this sense does not appear in those cases of "possession" found in China, India, Japan and other nations which have been presented in previous chapters of this treatise. I would not venture to assert that there is no

* 2 Chro. xxxiii, 6; 2 Ki. ix, 22; Mi. v. 12; Na. iii, 4.

such thing in China, for I have heard rumors of something like it. I only say that no evidence of it has appeared in communications received in the course of my inquiries respecting demon-possesion.

In speaking of witchcraft we can hardly avoid reference to that deplorable episode in our American history, the Salem Witchcraft trials. Case after case was formally tried, and one after another of the accused, after what was regarded as full and conclusive evidence, was condemned to suffer the penalty of death. The judges of the court seem to have had a profound sense of the solemnity of the occasion, and of personal responsibility, and a sincere desire to do right.

In the trial of one such case, Judge Hale "prayed the God of heaven to direct their hearts in the weighty thing they had in hand; for, to Condemn the Innocent, and let the Guilty go free, were both an Abomination to the Lord"* The decisions of the court were sustained by the general sentiment of the people. And still it is now universally acknowledged that every one of the condemned persons was innocent, and in all these cases it is generally doubted if there were any such thing as witchcraft.

How it was possible for the intelligent and cultured people of New England to be thus de-

---

* See Cotton Mather: "The Wonders of the Invisible World." p. 119.

luded, is a question which has puzzled thinking men from that time to this.

There is no difference of opinion as to the fact that the accused were convicted principally on the testimony of a class of persons generally called the "afflicted" or the "bewitched." Cotton Mather says in his account of one of the trials, (and the statement is applicable to them all;) "To fix the Witchcraft on the Prisoner at the Bar, the first thing used, was the Testimony of the Bewitched."*

Its general character may be succinctly stated as follows: First, The bewitched would in the presence of the accused, or when brought into court to bear testimony, be thrown into "fits" and a state of insensibility. This was regarded as an evidence that the accused had mysterious superhuman power over them. These "tortures" are constantly referred to in the course of the trials. We are told for instance, in one case, that "It cost the Court a wonderful deal of Trouble, to hear the Testimonies of the Sufferers; for when they were going to give in their Depositions, they would for a long time be taken with Fits, that made them incapable of saying anything."†

Second, When in these "fits" or "tortures" the "afflicted" ones would accuse by name those whom they declared to be the cause of their sufferings.

* Ibid p. 130. While a variety of other testimony was used by way of corroboration, this testimony is everywhere the most prominent.

† Ibid, p, 122.

This kind of evidence was very common in the trials and had great weight with the juries and judges.

Third, Further evidence of the guilt of the accused was found in the fact that they had, as it appeared, an influence over the "bewitched" when they were in a state of unconsciousness, which influence no one else possessed. For instance it is said of one case: "It was also found that the Sufferers were not able to bear her Look, as likewise, that in their greatest Swoons, they distinguished her Touch from other Peoples, being thereby raised out of them."*

Fourth. Still further evidence was found against the accused in the fact that the "bewitched" were restored to their normal condition when the accused were convicted. Numerous cases of this kind are given in evidence.

That the decision of these cases turned on the testimony of the "bewitched" while in these abnormal conditions is further evidenced by Sir Matthew Hale's charge in the trial of Rose Cullender and Amy Duny. "The Judge told the Jury, they were to inquire now, first whether these Children were bewitched; and secondly, whether the Prisoners at the Bar were guilty of it."†

Proceeding on the concluson that the principal

* Ibid. p. 149.
† The Wonders of the Invisible World. p. 119.

20 Demon

ground of the conviction of those accused of witchcraft was the evidence furnished by the "bewitched," what opinion are we to adopt with reference to the character of these witnesses, and of their depositions? Some have attempted to show that their testimony is to be attributed wholly to fraud, and have regarded the "afflicted" as adroit actors and deceivers. Perhaps much that appeared in these trials is referable to deception; but to endeavor thus to explain all the phenomena presented is to attribute a degree of ignorance and obtuseness to the intelligent men of that age which is inconceivable. It is to suppose that a few ignorant children were able for months together to deceive the wisest heads of New England; and that in that age intellectual ability was at its maximum in childhood, and diminished with increasing age.

Most writers have acknowledged something in the "bewitched," not to be accounted for on ordinary principles, which they have attributed to *hallucination, nervous disease, hysteria and hypnosis.* Any attempt, however, to explain in detail the acknowledged phenomena by any of the above hypotheses, will show how unsatisfactory they are, and how inadequate to cover the whole ground.

The author of the last and one of the ablest works on "Salem Witchcraft" gives the following estimate of his own theory, and of those previously propounded, for explaining these events. "I only desire to suggest what may have been; something which offers, perhaps, a rational explanation of the beginning of this horrid nightmare. Certainly such a course is as plausible, as reasonable, and has as much basis of fact as any of the theories heretofore advanced. We know nothing about these things as matter of knowledge; all is conjecture."*

There is another theory for explaining the phenomena of the so-called "Salem Witchcraft" which deserves more attention from writers on this subject than it has hitherto received. It is the theory which was held by some of the accused. Not a few of them when under trial evinced a consistency, truthfulness, and conscientiousness worthy of Christian martyrs, preferring to die rather than falsify themselves. They seem to have been the only ones who in that time of excitement manifested mental poise, cool judgment, and composure. These they maintained even in the turmoil of the court, and on the scaffold. When asked in court how the tortures and abnormal conditions of the "afflicted" were to be accounted for, if they were not "bewitched," their answer in several instances was that they were *caused by the devil*; and I am strongly inclined to agree with them. What reason is there to prevent us from supposing that the "afflicted"

* Witchcraft in Salem Village. By W. S. Nevins. p. 52.

were controlled by demons directly and immediately without the intervention of a human
instrument, the so-called "witch"?

This hypothesis furnishes a consistent and adequate explanation of all the facts without discrediting honest testimony, or requiring any
stretching or straining it to cover the ground.

It is recommended by the fact that many of
the pathological and psychological symptoms
of the "afflicted" correspond to well known symptoms of demon-possession. On this hypothesis,
the actions and words of the "afflicted" are seen
to be natural and consistent. When in their
tortures, they uttered fiendish accusations against
the innocent, they were but the mouth-pieces of
demons. We are no longer required to puzzle
ourselves to account for inexperienced and uneducated girls succeeding, by such strange and un-
precedented methods, in turning the heads of
juries, judges and the populace; but these results
are referred to an agency both competent and
morally suited to the work. The fact of these
girls declaring, when in their normal condition
that they had no ill-will towards the accused,
and did not know what they had said when accusing them, as well as the remorseful confessions
of some of them years afterwards, entirely har-
monizes with this theory.

This hypothesis also goes far to explain the acts
and vindicate the character of the judges and

jurors. They proceeded on the conviction that the "fits" of the "afflicted" were abnormal—that they could not be accounted for on natural principles, and were to be attributed to evil spirits. If the theory now proposed is the true one, they were not deluded on this point, but simply made the mistake of regarding the innocent accused, instead of the "afflicted," as the instrument of evil spirits; being misled by the view of witchcraft so common in that age, and by the law which they themselves were administering.

When we consider this hypothesis as it is related to Satan, and his character, and designs, everything is natural and consistent. All his attributes as a deceiver, a liar, a murderer, and a false accuser, re-appear conspicuously in this one transaction. The Christian world was amazed and paralyzed while Satan the active agent, concealed behind the mask of "witchcraft," though recognized, was totally misplaced.

It is the habit of writers now-a-days, shunning any intimation of Satanic agency, to speak of this calamity as a "moral cyclone," "a wholesale delusion," "a neighborhood insanity," all produced by that vague impersonal intangible something called "witchcraft," which attacks individuals and communities like the plague, and from which there is no sure means of escape.

So the term witchcraft, which seems to have been so largely misconceived, and often so

grievously misapplied, though an integral part
of the English language from Anglo Saxon times,
is one about which men write essays and books
as the Chinese do about the dragon and phœnix.
Even where the devil's agency has been plainly
seen and acknowledged, men have been totally
deceived as to the real direction and character of
his operation, and have thus become his ready
prey.

Were it not well to substitute "devil-craft" for
"witchcraft;" to believe in the Bible doctrine of
Satan as an actual and personal enemy? Had
the courts in Salem proceeded on the Scriptural
presumption that the testimony of those under
the control of evil spirits would, in the nature of
the case, be false, such a thing as the Salem
tragedy would never have been known.

It is possible that the definition is at fault
which conveys the popular conception of a witch
and witchcraft. If we should broaden the definition, and say that a witch is a person in collusion, either voluntary or enforced, with a demon;
and witchcraft is whatever act or art such a
person may practice in the proper character of
a witch—then real witchcraft would seem not to
be wanting. In this case we need not assume
that the witch has necessarily made a deliberate,
formal and voluntary compact with the devil;
nor yet that the witch, in her own person, freely
designs to inflict an injury upon others. But

we can identify the witch and her arts as one in kind with the ancient Delphic priestess and the modern medium, with their arts, and as subject to some form of demon-possession. Perhaps to the same family belong the founders of some false religions, the medicine men of the American aborigines, the fetish priests of Africa, the magicians of Ancient Egypt, and of modern India. But on this hypothesis, there were no witches in Salem, but rather demoniacs, and these must be identified with the "afflicted," not the accused.

I am well aware that the views here presented, of the continued presence and agency of Satan in individual and public affairs, will be scornfully rejected by many persons of education and culture. These views, however, have the sanction of many names which command universal respect.

From one of these, Frederick Denison Maurice, I beg to introduce the following quotations. In speaking of the belief in the influence of evil spirits over bodies and souls of men, he says: "This belief we may often have been inclined to look upon as the most degrading and despicable of all, from which a sounder knowledge of physics, and of the freaks and capacities of the human imagination has delivered us. Are we sure that the deliverance has been effected? Are we sure that the fears of an invisible world, of a world not to come, but about us, are extinct? . . . Are we sure that all our discoveries, or supposed discoveries respecting the spiritual world within us, may not be appealed to in confirmation of a new demoniac system? Are we sure that the very enlightenment, which says that it has ascertained Christian stories to be legends, will not be enlisted on the same side, because if we only believe *these* facts, it will be so easy to show how *those* falsities may have originated?

"Oh! let us give over our miserable notion that poor men only want teaching about things on the surface, or will ever be satisfied with such teaching. They are groping about the roots of things, whether we know it or not. You must meet them in their underground search, and show them the way into daylight, if you want true and brave citizens, not a community of dupes and quacks. You may talk against deviltry as you like; you will not get rid of it unless you can tell human beings whence comes that sense of a tyranny over their own very selves, which they express in a thousand forms of speech, which excites them to the greatest, often the most profitless, indignation against the arrangements of this world, which tempts them to people it, and heaven also, with objects of terror and despair.

"There is no disguising it, the assertion stands broad and patent in the four gospels, construed according to any ordinary rules of language:— the acknowledgment of an evil spirit is characteristic of Christianity."*

* Theological Essays pp. 32-34.

Another and more recent form of spiritism will be considered in the next chapter.

The highest authority in English upon the life of Mahomet is Sir William Muir, LL. D. See his "*Life of Mahomet from original Sources, New Ed. [Abridged from the first Ed., in four vols.] With an index, London. Smith, Elder & Co.,* 1878" The entire third chapter of this work, pp. 38–59 on "The Belief of Mahomet in His Own Inspiration," may be read in this connection with great interest.

In a review of the present work, in its first edition, printed in *The Nation*, N. Y., Aug. 22, 1895, the writer speaks as follows:

"The phenomenon which announces itself as demon-possession has never ceased since men were men, and is probably as frequent at the present day in New York and Boston as it ever has been at any time and place in history. It follows at all times the local and temporal fashions and traditions, and from causes which, once more, would form a highly interesting problem to unravel, it has with us assumed a benign and optimistic, instead of a diabolical and hurtful form, constituting what is familiarly known to-day as *Mediumship*. It differs from all the classic types of insanity. * * * Of its causes, apart from suggestion and imitation, absolutely nothing definite is known, the psychical researchers being the only persons who at present seem to believe that it offers a serious problem for investigation. The Charcot school has assimilated it to *hysteria major*, with which it unquestionably has generic affinities, but just why its specific peculiarities are what they are, this school leaves unexplained. The name hysteria, it must be remembered, is not an explanation of anything, but merely the title of a new set of problems."

CHAPTER XVII.

SPIRITUALISM.

The number of "Spiritualists" in the world has been reckoned at 20,000,000. This is probably an overestimate. Making all allowance for exaggeration the number is very large, and, until recently at least, has been rapidly increasing. As early as 1875 spiritualists had forty periodicals advocating their peculiar views. Besides these they have their book literature, their lecture halls, and their popular conventions.

Spiritualism—or more properly spiritism—is avowedly based on communications with disembodied spirits. As one of the great intellectual forces entering into modern thought and civilization it challenges our serious consideration. In the present chapter it is not proposed to enter upon an elaborate examination of it; such an undertaking being foreign to the object and scope of this work.

We assume that the phenomena which spiritualism presents have a large substratum of truth. This conclusion is adopted because the Scriptures imply that physical phenomena resulting from the

314

agency of spirits are in accordance with natural laws, and may be expected as ordinary events of experience; because large numbers of educated men have been influenced by the evidence which it presents to acknowledge the reality of certain of its phenomena, and to add their names to the increasing numbers of its adherents; and also because experts and specialists in Germany, France, England and the United States, have carefully examined its alleged facts, and declared to the world that they have found phenomena which could not be explained by any known physical laws.

The above assumption is not invalidated by the not infrequent discovery of fraud among the adherents of spiritualism. A score of impostures will not overthrow the evidence of one fact. Though it may be admitted that the existence of numerous impostures tends to produce a presumption that all is imposture, it is equally true on the other hand, that on the supposition of the phenomena of spiritualism being real, imposture is to be expected. This is true to a greater or less degree of almost every known science. For instance, how much fraud, imposture and failure to effect promised results are found in the history of medical practice. Spiritualism is not the only system in which untrained and incompetent persons, bring reproach upon themselves and those of whom they are the self-appointed representatives.   Even persons who have facts to present, often add to these facts and phenomena meretricious accessories, in order to increase their attractions and make them more startling to the public eye.   We must remember that the deceit of the fictitious accessories may be detected , and the author of them unmasked, while the actual facts remain unaffected.

The British "Society for Psychical Research," and the more recently organized "American Psychical Society," have, by their investigations elicited many facts that illustrate this discussion. But the facts which they gather from the credible testimony of others who have witnessed them in their ordinary surroundings, are, in general, much more striking than those which the investigating committees witness in the course of their own experiments.

In 1887 there was published in Philadelphia, by J. B. Lippincott Co., "A Preliminary Report of the Commission Appointed by the University of Pennsylvania to Investigate Modern Spiritualism, in Accordance with the Request of the Late Henry Seybert."   The well-chosen members of this commission took much time and care to arrive at satisfactory evidence and explanation of spiritualistic phenomena.   But it is hardly to be wondered at that their efforts did not result in any very decided conclusions.   On the supposition that spiritualism is only a system of delusion and deception, no results were to be expected. On the supposition that spiritualistic phenomena, when genuine, are produced by demons, it is hardly reasonable to suppose that these demons would voluntarily, gratuitously and without restraint, submit themselves to an examination which might only serve to disclose their actual character, instead of confirming false pretensions, or might thwart the very object of their manifestations.

Any experiment to be successful must conform to all the conditions of the case. An experiment with spirits can never be like one made in chemistry or physics. A spirit is an intelligent and moral being who may be supposed to have some choice as to where and how to exhibit its presence and power. A spirit must be sensitive to the moral conditions and atmosphere that surround it, and must be governed by moral affinities and antipathies. Things that a spirit will do in one company it cannot or will not do in another. If spirits have anything to do with these phenomena they have some purpose in what they do, and are seeking to accomplish some end. They will naturally do most where the conditions are most favorable to this end.

We may suppose some medium, or witch, or pythian oracle to be powerfully possessed by a familiar spirit, and both the spirit and its subject eager to exhibit that power in pursuit of its usual aims. Yet in the presence of persons in whom there may be recognized a sufficiently pronounced moral antagonism, the medium or spirit may be utterly helpless, or so guarded that nothing is done. If evil spirits are the agents in question, then obviously they would show forth their true character principally in those communities or companies most congenial to them, and most thoroughly under their sway, and they would suit their wonders to their hopes of securing the confidence and subserviency of their witnesses. But if mankind is so beset by evil spirits we may herein gratefully recognize our source of safety, being sure that those have least to fear who are most indwelt and possessed by the Holy Spirit of Christ and of God. And just as an evil spirit will come to those who seek it, so the Holy Spirit is sensitive and responsive to our faith.

"Ye are of God, little children, and have overcome them; because greater is he that is in you, than he that is in the world."*

"You may then," to use the words of Dr. Austin Phelps,† "take the crude mass of the phenomena alleged, and set aside a certain proportion, large or small, as you please, to the account of the rascality which the system somehow attracts to itself as a ship's bottom does barnacles. Strike off another portion, as probably due to the honest

* 1 John iv. 4.
† Spiritualism pp. 24.25.

exaggeration of credulous or prejudiced observers. Cancel another section, as explicable by electric laws, or by principles of the animal economy, and especially by laws of disease well known to science. Ignore, if you must, everything else which is purely physical, as likely to be one day explained by physical laws yet to be discovered. Eliminate something more for the incertitude of psychological research, when pressed beyond the facts of the general consciousness. After all these deductions spiritualism is apparently right in claiming that a residuum of fact remains, which goes straight to the point of proving the presence and activity of *extra human intelligence*. For one, I must concede that, at least, as a plausible hypothesis."*

The above admission will no doubt be regarded by many as a dangerous concession to spiritualists. We, however, concede nothing which is peculiar to spiritualism, but only the existence of certain phenomena with which the world has been familiar in all ages, and to which multitudes at the present day are eye-witnesses in all lands. The effect of denying the existence of these phenomena is to lose influence over those who witness them; to confirm the assertion of spiritualists that we are only blind guides, and to leave those who are

---

* In the work entitled "Ten Years With Spiritual Mediums" to which reference has been made in Chapter xii, while the author rejects and combats the assumption of the agency of spirits in producing the phenomena of spiritualism, he still does not question the *reality* of the phenomena.

honestly seeking an explanation oɪ facts of consciousness to the instruction and guidance of spiritualists. Dr. Phelps well remarks "that no very *attenuated* hypothesis of any kind, in explanation of the phenomena in question, can meet the case as it presents itself to the popular mind. Shadowy conjectures on the subject will seem so glaringly inadequate, that they will only shift the charge of creduality to ourselves."

Proceeding on the assumption that communications are received from spirits, the question remains, from *what kind* of spirits do they come? Are they good spirits, or are they bad spirits? Do they tell us truth or falsehood? Is it their object to benefit or to injure us?

It would be difficult to find any discussion of this subject more candid, or more thorough, than the nine lectures delivered by Joseph Cook in Boston in 1880.*

In these Mr. Cook remarks† that "Two points are in debate concerning spiritualism—the reality of communications between spirits and men, and the trustworthiness of these communications as a source of religious knowledge." * * * "The great error oɪ our time in dealing with spiritualism is that we do not sufficiently emphasize the fact that the question between the biblical view

* Full reports of these are to be found in *The Independent*, N. Y. 1880, Jan. 29 to March 25. A few supplementary lectures based on later material, would if prepared make the whole series well worth republication.

† See *Independent*, March 4. 1880.

and the spiritualistic view of the world is not as to the reality of communications of spirits with men, but as to their trustworthiness?"

This issue can be determined only as moral tests are used as well as those which are physical, and rational.

In comparing the phenomena of spiritualism, alleged or actual, with those of demon-possession as presented in previous chapters, we are struck with the remarkable correspondence between them. Some obvious points of resemblance may be given in general as follows:

1st. The use of a medium for the purpose of holding communication with spirits.

2d. Necromancy, or professed communications with the dead by the intervention of a medium.

3rd. The invoking or summoning of spirits by means of hymns or prayers.

4th. Receiving communications from spirits by writing, through methods more or less direct and immediate.

5th. Gradual "development" or training by which the medium or subject, and the spirits, are brought *en rapport*, so that the medium becomes ready and responsive in performing his new functions.

6th. Obtaining prescriptions and healing diseases by spirits, though the intervention of a medium.

7th. Carrying on communications with spirits through a medium by the use of spoken language, or by raps, or other arrangements and devices.

8th. The mysterious appearance and disappearance of lambent lights and flames.

9th. Levitation, suspension in the air, and transference from one place to another of crockery, household utensils, and other objects, including also men, either in a conscious or unconscious state.

10th. Haunted houses, mysterious opening and shutting of doors, and other similar phenomena.

11th. The moving of furniture and other objects without physical contact.

12th. Rappings, clattering of dishes, and unusual noises and disturbances, without any physical cause which can be found.

13th. Impressions by unseen hands, sometimes gentle, and sometimes violent, producing physical pain and injuries.

14th. The nervous and muscular symptoms peculiar to the demoniac, and often to the medium during possession, or its initial stage.

The above points cover the general phenomena connected with what is called "spiritualism," and show that it is in accordance with the demonism of China, and other countries, and of the Bible. We have seen that the Scriptures categorically and authoritatively attribute such manifestations to demons, the agents of the devil.

It is a striking fact that the Chinese uniformly attribute these phenomena to evil spirits whom they fear and hate. To be possessed by an evil spirit they consider a misfortune and a disgrace. Mediums, those who invoke and hold intercourse with spirits, are, from a supposed necessity, often consulted, but are never regarded with respect or affection. The general name given to all forms of spirit manifestations is "sie", a term which combines the ideas *corrupt, injurious, demoralizing, debasing.*

Spiritualists will no doubt insist that the assertion that the phenomena in question are the work of evil spirits, and none others, is both gratuitous and malicious. Is not "mediumship", however, in the very nature of the case evil? I believe it to be but another name for demon-possession. What are the moral accompaniments and sequences of mediumistic practices? Who does not know them? What is their moral tone? What is their final tendency? What type of character most widely prevails among confirmed and persistent spiritualists? How do they stand related to the New Testament Christ?

The Bible teaches us that to have intercourse with a "familiar spirit" is a voluntary act of disloyalty to, and rebellion against God. It is forsaking God, and holding intercourse with, and becoming the agent of his avowed enemy, the devil.

There were instructions given in the New
Testament, specific, simple and infallible for determining the character of spirits holding communications with men.   There was a command,
"Believe not every spirit, but try the spirits
whether they are of God; because many false
prophets are gone out into the world."*   And a
test was given "Every spirit that confesseth not
that Jesus Christ is come in the flesh is not of
God." †   But in applying this Scripture test to
spiritism in the present age we meet at once with
difficulties.   First, because some spiritualists
may not deny the fact of our Saviour's having
come in the flesh; and secondly, from the want
of such an authorized presentation of the tenets
of spiritualism as will be accepted by its adherents. Spiritualists have never, so far as we are
aware, published an authoritative statement of
their beliefs.   Their representative literature,
however, furnishes evidences of its tendency and
temper which are unmistakable.   From a mass
of this kind of material a few specimens only can
be given here.

In a long article in a spiritualist "Weekly Journal "there appeared the following under the title
"The Genuine Teachings of Jesus, The Synopti-
cal Gospels and John, Jesus and the Talmud," etc.

"It is to Paul, not to Jesus, we owe the abro-

---

* I John, iv, 1.
† I John. iv. 3.

gation of the law; it was to Paul's influence that the writer of Hebrews opposed sacrificing bulls and goats. Jesus had nothing to do with it."

. . . "Jesus had defects and imperfections like all other men.". . . . "It is an absurd idea that Jesus was a perfect man, or any more Divine than any other man. He was a simple Jewish enthusiast and religious reformer, foolishly supposing himself the Messiah, thereby coming to an untimely death."*

A letter to the editor of the same Journal presents the claims of spiritualism as a new and better religion than Christianity in these words: "How can professed spiritualists scout the idea that spiritualism is a religion? Has not spiritualism done a thousand fold more for us than theology or 'Christ and him crucified,' in opening the portals, and giving us real glimpses of the life to be, giving us line upon line of philosophy of existence in both spheres?"

The following extracts are from a somewhat elaborate work on "Moral Philosophy" highly recommended by spiritualists. Speaking of Christian obedience the writer says: "To believe the Bible and obey the Christian church is the obedience intended. We unqualifiedly say that a man owes no such obedience, and has no such duties." . . . "The slow relinquishment of the personality of God has left this doc-

---

* Religio-Philosphical Journal January 14, 1880.

trine in a most precarious state, and with its fall Christianity ceases to exist."*

The following gives the author's estimate of Christ's work of atonement. "Slaughtered oxen, hecatombs of human victims, or ten thousand bleeding Christs will not atone for the least transgression of the laws of our being." . . . . "The true redemption is not through the blood of Christna of India, a pilgrimage to the shrine of Mohammed, or the efficacy of Christ's blood, but by compliance with the laws of the physical and spiritual worlds." . . . . . "Terrible is the significance, and humiliating to the student of history are the words, 'peace with God,' 'lost from God,' 'reconciled unto God,' 'atonement,' 'salvation through the blood of the lamb,' 'regeneration,' an endless vocabulary which is fossilized ignorance, credulity, folly, selfishness, fear and rascality." Quotations of this kind might be multiplied indefinitely.

There is little room for doubt that spiritualism antagonizes all the distinctive doctrines of Christianity, especially the doctrine that "Jesus Christ has come in the flesh," though it adapts itself to the moral and religious state for the time being of those whom it would influence, and many would not be entrapped in its snare if at times, it had not, at least, an outward veneering of Christianity. This however is for the timid novitiate not

* Ethics of Spiritualism—A System of Moral Philosophy, etc,. p. 99.
Ibid., pages 101-102.

for the advanced spiritualist. Dr. T. L. Nichols, a distinguished spiritualist, says: "Spiritualism meets, neutralizes, and destroys Christianity. A spiritualist is no longer a Christian in any popular sense of the term. Advanced spirits do not teach the atonement of Christ; nothing of the kind."*

It is an important fact that spiritualists do themselves acknowledge that the world is full of lying spirits, that they themselves are constantly deceived by them; and the difficulty of determining whether they are or are not being deceived, troubles them not a little. A spiritualist writing on "Test Conditions" says:

"This is a topic on which a great deal has been said, and is still being said, within the ranks of the spiritualists. Those outside know nothing of 'test conditions' beyond their own crude ideas of the manner in which spirits should manifest, if there be any spirits, which they doubt or deny. A 'test condition' with them is that which brings the phenomena of spiritualism within the category of physical miracles. Many so-called spiritualists are on the same plane."

* * * * * * *

"With the believing spiritualist it is different. He is supposed to have passed beyond the mere test plane. He is thoroughly and *finally* con-

* Monthly Magazine of Social Science and Progressive Literature.

vinced that there are spirits, and that they do communicate and manifest. Then what are physical "test conditions" to him? He wants *truth*. He knows that deceiving spirits exist by millions, that some spiritual tramp may come and personate his father, for example, and, hence, he wants a *spiritual* condition that will prevent this.

"Locking or tying up the medium will not accomplish this, for material bonds are nothing to spirit power. The lying, deceptive spirit in the medium, if it exist, must be exorcised. Who wants to spend his time and money for such Dead Sea fruits as catering to the sports or tricks of low, deceptive spirits? Here is a medium, for example, that is discovered in a palpable fraud, the toggery found upon her being publicly exhibited; and yet spiritualists sustain her, because she is really a medium; and it is, they say, the spirits that perpetrate the fraud, while the poor medium is innocent. Her mediumship hallows all she does, whether good or bad. Let me ask, is fraud any less a fraud because it is perpetrated by a spirit?

"If Spiritualism is to be a cloak and an excuse for crime, away with it; and if mediums are to be sustained in lying, cheating and swindling, let it all perish. This constant cry of 'Sustain the mediums, right or wrong', because they are mediums, charging all their offences—their low disgusting trickery—on the spirits, is a delusion and a snare, and will, if it is continued, sink our great cause so low that the sun of truth and righteousness will never be able to shine upon it?"*

Another writer says: "For seven years I held daily intercourse with what purported to be my mother's spirit. I am now firmly persuaded that it was nothing but an evil spirit, an infernal demon who, in that guise gained my soul's confidence, and led me to the very brink of ruin."†

The law of moral affinities precludes the idea that these rapping, roistering table-tipping, lying spirits invoked by modern spiritualists are in any sense good spirits. Good spirits would instinctively shrink from such companionship and methods. The good "demon" of Socrates is an appellation made use of by writers who succeeded Socrates, and was not used by Socrates himself. He spoke of this mysterious guiding influence as the inward "voice." It seems to have been conscience, or the voice of God, which was to him so distinct and authoritative that he was almost disposed to attribute to it personality. Dean Stanley speaks of the extraordinary disclosures which Socrates has himself left of that "*divine sign*" which by later writers was called his demon, his invoking genius, but which he himself called by the simpler name of his prophetic or supernatural "voice."‡

* Spritualism Unveiled by Miles Grant p. 35.
† Religio-Philosophical Journal Dec. 24. 1887.
‡ History of the Jewish Church. vol. iii. p. 224.

The connection in which Marcus Aurelius uses the word *demon* shows clearly that it is only a personification of conscience.

We have endeavored to present the real tenets of spiritualism by extracts which are typical and representative. For a fuller and more minute presentation of its doctrines the reader is referred to its own publications, a careful perusal of which will leave no room to doubt that spiritualism, off its guard, denies the existence of a personal God, utterly rejects the Bible as a Divine revelation, and especially denies the Divinity of Jesus Christ, and His work of atonement.

As to the adaptiveness of spiritualism to its ends, let me quote again from Dr. Phelps—"Senseless as it seems to sedate and Christian logic, it is very crafty as a compound of temptations. Look at the ingredients. What are they? Here are some truths for the honest ones, converse with the dear departed for the bereaved, gushing messages for the affectionate, marvels for the curious, revelations for the credulous, gossip for the idle, mummery for the frivolous, swelling words for the mystical, a loosening of marriage-ties for the impure, and an anti-Christian supernaturalism for minds famished by life-long skepticism. Surely, so far as it goes, it is a cunningly-laid snare. Very foolish it may be to be caught in it, yet it is a subtle thing in the hands of the fowler. Considering the material he has to deal with, is it not worthy of the great hierarch of evil?"

It has been reserved for inhabitants of cultivated and nominally Christian nations of the 19th century to court that intercourse with spirits from which many of the more intelligent heathen shrink with aversion. They present the spectacle of thousands and millions of men and women, many of whom have been reared in Christian homes, and are possessed through heredity, education, and national and social ties, with all the advantages of Christian culture, who have adopted a religion ignoring a personal God, who have "changed the truth of God into a lie, and worshiped and served the creature more than the Creator."* Avoiding communion with the infinite, everpresent Spirit of Holiness, and in flagrant disobedience to His will, they deliberately throw themselves open to the access and incursion of miserable, wandering, finite spirits, that work in darkness, abound in deeds that are either paltry or vicious beyond expression, and who, even when they seem to confer a benefit, show by results that they do it that evil may come. This is a religion which, notwithstanding its vaunted intercourse with the spirit-world for many years, has added nothing to our knowledge of truth or virtue, or to our motives to a better and higher life.

* Rom. 1; 25.

I cannot think that I fail in the duty of Christian charity in affirming my belief as I have already done, that the phenomena of spiritualism are plainly referable to *demons*; in the main identical with phenomena which have been referred to demons by the common consent of all nations, and are declared to be such by the authoritative teachings of Scripture.

To briefly sum up all: It would seem that every age and country present phenomena which exhibit, in some variety of form, the reality of demon intercourse with men, and of demon-possession.

The demoniac is an involuntary victim of possession. The willing subject becomes a medium. This general term includes others more specific, and is often but the modern name for witch and sorcerer.

History is full of facts which illustrate the demonology of the Bible, and seem to find in that neglected doctrine their only sufficient explanation.

CHAPTER XVIII.*

THE FACTS AND LITERATURE OF THE OCCULT.

The facts that make the foundation for the discussion conducted in the present volume have not been drawn from literature, but from life. A considerable body of carefully sifted and well authenticated facts are offered to be accounted for, which yet are but specimens of a much larger collection made. They are gathered from the author's personal observation and the agreeing testimony of many trustworthy and living witnesses, having no collusion with each other.

Such facts, however unfamiliar to many readers, are not confined to any distant antiquity, but are still occurring. They are not the half seen, half remembered, and many times exaggerated phenomena out of which myths of were-wolves and changelings are evolved. They are everyday facts which can be examined at first hand in many places, and substantiated at every point by any person who will take the pains.

Nor are these facts of an isolated kind. For nothing is more obvious than that they belong to an enormous class, with important subdivi-

* In regard to this chapter, prepared by the Editor of this volume, see Note of Explanation, pp. 6-7.

sions, and that they exhibit an unfailing vitality,
a persistence of recurrence, and a relation to
human welfare which gives them a commanding
claim to be understood. The designation of their
class in most instances involves some theory of
their origin, and varies with different persons.
They are said to belong to the order of the
supernatural. They are called preternatural,
supernormal, superhuman, supersensuous, miraculous and occult. One describes them in terms
of medical science. Another regards them as
myths, and no testimony will convince him that
such facts have ever existed as this volume and
many other books report.

But the same thing called by one name will
often get a hearing which, called by another, is
ignored.

The term most used is supernatural, and no
other is more loosely used and misunderstood.
What it may mean depends upon each man's
conception of nature. To one man nature only
includes the range of his own experience, still
further limited by the defects in his analysis of
that experience. What is beyond that is beyond
nature. To another it is all of the visible or
sensible world. But, in its fullest sense, nature
is all that is *natus*, born, produced or made.
It is the entire finite universe, in distinction from
the infinite Creator.

The distinction, it is right to say, is not that

between the seen and the unseen, nor that between matter and spirit; but that between the contingent and the absolute, the finite and the infinite. Paul's splendid climax in the eighth chapter of Romans may be said to express the sum, and contain an inventory, of nature. It is as if he had said: Though all nature were against me, it could not separate me from God. Death, life, angels, principalities, powers, things present or future, far or near, or whatsoever created thing, must all and equally fail to accomplish that.

All is nature that is not God. Nature is the synonym for the divine creation.

Strictly speaking, there is only one supernatural being, and whatever is done as the immediate act of God is supernatural. The commonest function of nature directly maintained by his operation is, in the best sense, supernatural quite as much as original creation, or any unusual effect which he may produce, and which is called a miracle. But the immediate act of a finite will, intelligence or power may properly be regarded as a natural act, and any effect proceeding from it as a natural effect.

There are doubtless many planes of natural being and action little known to men. And each must have its special laws, yet all may interact, and stand related to each other in some comprehensive plan. The phenomena under review are those which have all the outward seeming of proceeding from the interaction with the familiar human plane of another natural plane of intelligent being less well known. This is an inference that they inevitably suggest even to the most incredulous.

They do not appear as effects of divine action. The cause at work is not the first cause, nor the familiar human cause, or at least not that alone; but an intermediate cause that operates in much obscurity, yet betrays the marks of intelligence and a certain variable quality of moral character.

Perhaps no better designation for this class of facts can be had than the word occult. This convenient term commits no person to an explanation, and may be used in common by the advocates of every view. It merely implies that the phenomena in question are shrouded in mystery, and neither suggests an explanation, nor denies that one can be made.

Occult phenomena may counterfeit the supernatural while yet they are not such; nor are they to be thought anomalous. The laws of their manifestation, as is true of many other things, may be, in part, peculiar to themselves, and still may have their proper place in the general order of nature. Every kind in nature has laws after its kind. Great prejudice has been needlessly aroused against testimony affirming the occult by the assumption that such phenomena not only exist and are supernatural but are also outside the pale of law; as though the laws of the universe were not sufficiently comprehensive to include all beings and all events that have a place within it.

The modern conception of all-pervading law may yet become recognized as being no less Biblical than scientific, while those things in the Bible which, on a hasty reading, seem most anomalous, with deeper study show the very bloom of law, in which the moral and physical are perfectly blended and equally expressed. The miracles which later theologians have viewed as infractions of law, are never so considered by the Bible writers who record them. As early as the fifth century Augustine could say that a miracle was not opposed to nature, but only to so much of nature as is known. *"Portentum ergo fit non contra naturam, sed contra quam est nota natura."* (*De Civitate Dei, xxi. 8.*)

His memorable words should never be forgotten. They are suited still to answer all who fain would stand upon the quicksands that were chosen by David Hume.

Even to this knowing age known nature is almost an inconsiderable section of the whole. Although experience is a test of truth, no man's experience measures all the truth, nor would the collective experience of the race, could it be expressed, exhaust the facts with which we have to deal, nor can the lack of experience prove a negative.

Theologians have done hurt to their own cause by conceiving of the miraculous in a way not required by the Bible, and making a needless occasion of unbelief; also by confounding the terms *miraculous* and *supernatural.* Divine action is not always miraculous, nor are miracles always divine, but all divine action is supernatural, and all miracles are exceptional to common experience.

The Bible shows but one thing that is opposed to law, that abuse of free agency called sin. Sin is the only thing called in the Bible an anomaly. (1 John iii. 4.) But even sin has a law of its own (Rom. vii. 21-23), and this strange antinomy of divine providence is made to subserve a higher harmony of law than without it had been possible.

Between the occult and the supernatural the Bible exhibits not only an obvious difference, but often a moral antagonism. This is made impressively clear to the mind when the occult wonders related in this and other volumes, and in the Bible itself, are compared with its accounts of divine creation, miracle, inspiration, guidance, protection and provision. Every day instances and modern illustrations of divine action in human life may be profitably compared and contrasted with the occult, and are credibly reported in a multitude of books, of which three good specimens are these by *Horace L. Hastings:*

Tales of Trust; Embracing Authentic Accounts of Providential Guidance, Assistance and Deliverance.

Ebenezers; or Records of Prevailing Prayer.

The Guiding Hand; or Providential Guidance, Illustrated by Authentic Instances.

All published at 47 Cornhill, Boston, Mass.

There is reason to suppose that occult phenomena of some sort, occurring at some time, have given rise to many myths and many superstitions. But although the genuine phenomena have often suffered every exaggeration and spurious imitation, they are too numerous and well attested to be ignored. Unauthenticated instances pervade national and local traditions, and are abundantly scattered among different authors. Once they were accepted with undiscriminating credulity; now with an equally reckless scepticism they are denied.

Such is the temper of the present time that few persons who meet with these facts only in the course of reading ever give them a fair examination. After they have produced a passing wonder the facts go unexplained, or are hastily judged in accordance with some predilection, or dismissed with total disbelief. Many a student will do justice to any other subject sooner than to this. Many, again, of those who encounter it by some practical experience of their own go from one to an opposite extreme, and suddenly abandon all former views in favor of some newly learned hypothesis that at the moment seems most plausible.

But the incredibility of these events is much diminished when they are found to belong, in all senses of the word, to a *prodigious* class, of which countless cases have been as thoroughly proved as anything can be proved by human witness. Moreover, our general belief, resting on well assured evidence elsewhere gathered, may, without detriment to induction or conclusion, concede a corroborative value to many a story that lacks explicit proof.

But these facts are so wrought into the inmost fiber of history that no incredulous criticism can ever do them quite away. Their influence has so deeply penetrated the religion, mythology, poetry, art and customs of every race that even a sceptical science, which picks and chooses the objects of its interest and ignores the rest, is already beginning to feel it, and must be brought to close terms with it soon.

The facts are many and indisputable which make it look as if mankind were beset by a race of invisible intelligences, occupying a different but proximate plane of existence, having power to act directly upon the minds and bodies of men, and to produce various prodigies, even making themselves audible, and sometimes visible, and sensible to touch, and also the objects of worship.

These intelligences often claim to be, and seem like, the spirits of dead human beings. Like actors, they often appear to personate characters which incidentally they show are not their own. They often confess themselves to be lost souls, or even demons. They often act like demons while claiming to be gods demanding worship, and the nature of their claims and manifestations would seem to be largely determined by the company they are in, and the character and convictions of those persons whom they seek to approach or use.

Whether there be such a race of spirits, who they are, and what forms they can assume, is simply a matter of evidence. No man knows the whole of nature well enough to say that in the nature of things it can not be. And yet this unwarranted and jejune assumption is the only ground for absolute scepticism in this matter. No persons are so forward to employ it as some scientific scholars who make most of the importance of induction; for even careful scholars have been known to jump at a conclusion in the interest of some prepossession, and to reject good testimony which was hostile to their chosen views.

It does not appear to be any lack of good tes-

timony that makes men doubtful of spirit agency
in some cases of occult phenomena. It seems
rather to be ignorance of that testimony, or the
collision of that testimony with some prejudice.

The first question in the discussion is, What,
precisely stated, are the phenomena? The next,
What is their cause? and have spirits anything
to do with them? Hardly can the most incredulous person become familiar with the phenomena
and fail to have a spirit agency strongly suggested
to his mind. Then for those who accept the
spirit theory it remains to determine who the
spirits are.

Whether in the course of their ministry (Heb.
i. 13, 14)good angels ever manifest themselves,
or "the spirits of just men" (Heb. xii. 23);
whether the demons or "unclean spirits,"so often
named in the New Testament, are to be identified with the original Satanic race, or with lost
souls of men, as Josephus and other Jewish, and
some early Christian writers held; whether such
lost souls continue in the region of this planet
(and why should they not?); whether these spirits
are wholly without form or body because without
flesh and bones (Luke xxiv. 37-39); all these
and similar questions which follow the acceptance of the spirit theory are matters of experimental evidence, and cannot be determined *à
priori.*

Many who at first have utterly refused to be-

lieve in spirit agency have changed their minds,
and among them a number conspicuous for
their scientific training and achievements. Many
who have ceased to ridicule the spirit hypothesis
continue to pour their contempt upon the doctrine of demon agency which is found in the
Bible, endorsed by Christ, and illustrated in the
preceding chapters of this book. But in one
case, as in the other, the only criterion as to the
actual facts is that of experience. One's own
experience, so far as it may go, and the trustworthy testimony of others whose experience
causes them to know whereof they speak, must
be gathered and examined with the utmost candor and care. Those who accept as valid the
testimony of the Bible do so on the ground that
its writers were trustworthy men, who knew
much of what they reported by their own experience, and all of it by the instruction of one
who did know all.

But a vast amount of evidence is already in,
collected in former ages and our own. It is no
new theme of interest to mankind, but as old as
the history of the race; although new interest in
the old theme has in recent years been shown in
western lands, because the phenomena seem to
have multiplied. They have always elicited the
profound attention of many, whether in fear or
hope or wonder, especially of those whose contact with them has been of an experimental kind.

Inevitably all men come to the study of the subject with certain prepossessions, and are naturally inclined to make little of the testimony that does not agree with these pre-existing views. Happy is the man who can recognize his own prepossessions, and hold them completely in control; who can consent to learn from an enemy, and will do justice to evidence that is opposed to his cherished convictions. Only one who loves the truth indeed better than his own opinions is fit to find or handle evidence in a matter that appeals to prejudice. A certain moral factor, in the pursuit of truth, takes precedence of all intellectual qualities and attainments, howsoever invaluable these may be.

For a brief summary up to date of results in psychical research perhaps nothing better has been made than a paper sent to the Psychical Congress of Chicago, in 1893, by the distinguished naturalist, *Dr. Alfred Russell Wallace.* It may all be found in *Borderland* for October of that year, and is entitled:

Notes on the Growth of Opinion as to Obscure Psychical Phenomena during the last Fifty Years.

In that paper, among other memorable remarks is this:

"The whole history of science shows that whenever the educated and scientific men of the age have denied the facts of other investigators on *à priori* grounds of absurdity or impossibility, the deniers have always been wrong."

This statement is illustrated in a brilliant paper on "The Dogmatism of Science" by *Dr. R. Heber Newton* in the *Arena* for May, 1890. Dr. Wallace also remarks as follows:

"For myself, I have never been able to see why any one hypothesis should be any less scientific than another, except so far as one explains the whole of the facts and the other explains only a part of them.

"That theory is most scientific which best explains the whole series of phenomena; and I therefore claim that the spirit hypothesis is the most scientific, since even those who object to it most strenuously often admit that it does explain all the facts, which can not be said of any other hypothesis.

"The antagonism which it excites seems to be mainly due to the fact that it is, and has long been, in some form or other, the belief of the religious world, and of the ignorant and superstitious of all ages, while a total disbelief in spiritual existence has been the distinctive badge of modern scientific scepticism. But we find that the belief of the uneducated and unscientific multitude rested on a broad basis of facts which the scientific world scouted and scoffed at as absurd and impossible." The man who says these things himself belongs by common consent to the first rank of living naturalists.

THE LITERATURE.

And now, to further facilitate the efforts of such readers as may wish to examine this subject more thoroughly for themselves, something more will be said regarding the literature in which it can be studied to advantage.

The literature of the subject, like the phenomena which it describes, reaches through all periods of recorded history, is of immense extent, and may be found under many heads. No man could ever master all of it. No country ever had a literature of which a large part has not been devoted to the concrete representation, or the analysis of these very facts.

In the preceding pages of this volume about an hundred different writers are cited, most of whom were directly consulted in its preparation, and some large quotations from them are made. But no exhaustive comparison of the literature of the subject has been attempted. The Bibliographical Index which follows names all of the writers referred to. It also gives a more particular account of those whose testimony is regarded as important, but insufficiently known, and insufficiently described elsewhere in this volume.

In addition to these, some others will be presented in the present chapter that are significant for the data which they yield, quite irrespective of their various theories. While making no pretension to completeness, the list will serve to show the range and ramifications of this subject, and the various quarters in which information must be sought. But although it is practicable to distinguish the several departments of study in which the occult is treated, it is not possible to strictly classify all books; for these continually overlap one another's special province.

Many useful books have been written upon this theme that are not strong enough to stand alone. Many reviewers pass their hasty judgment upon some single or occasional work as though it bore an isolated testimony not worthy to be seriously weighed. But if any student be determined to search this matter to the end, to secure evidence from every side, and to deal with it at any cost to his own pleasure, he will find an astonishing mass of consenting testimony to the reality of the facts, their powerful influence upon the fortunes and character of men, and the inadequacy of those explanations that are most congenial to the modern mind.

If in the preceding chapters, and other similar accounts, the facts to be explained be correctly reported, then, whatever theory may be formed, it is obvious that they have important bearings upon several distinct regions of investigation. Pathology, psychology, mythology, folklore, witchcraft, magic, demonology and theology, each includes an extensive literature that discusses these occult phenomena from different points of view. Even medical jurisprudence may be supposed to have a concern in them. They are described in modern works of fiction, travel, biography, and history at large. Books written in the interest of modern and western spiritism are multiplying with great rapidity, and probably in many a city would rival the number and assortment of those which the Ephesians who "used curious arts brought together, and burned before all men," and "counted the price of them, and found it fifty thousand pieces of silver." (Acts xix. 19.)

It was stated in the periodical called *Light*, for June 19, 1886, that during the previous forty years two thousand volumes upon mediumistic wonders had been published, exclusive of tracts and pamphlets.

Probably no fuller Bibliography exists in this general domain than the following:

Graesses Bibliographie der wichtigsten in das Gebiet des Zauber, Geister und sonstigen Aberglaubens einschlagenden Werke. Leipzig, 1843.

But this does not include works issued since its own publication.

THE BIBLE.

The testimony of the Bible alone, even at its lowest estimate, is of high value. What the Bible has to say of sorcery, necromancy, divination and possession is never said as if these things were at all peculiar to the age or countries of which they are told. The Bible describes these experiences as if they were common to humanity, and always would be until the final overthrow of evil, and Satan's end. The Bible is a record of facts as well as of doctrines in this matter, and as such quite as worthy of regard as the latest report of hypnotic experiments, or the psychical researches of modern savants. There are good reasons for believing that all history is full of strictly parallel instances which confirm and vindicate its witness.

DEMONOLOGY.

Ralph Waldo Emerson, in his essay under this caption, as good as any penned from the rationalistic side, calls demonology the shadow of theology. And certainly no Christian theology can be formed which does not involve, in deep but inseparable contrast with its elements of glory, the factors of this somber theme.

The connection of demonology with the occult, however disallowed in our age, has been so intricate in the past that a student must read it perforce to get at a large part of his facts. Baxter, Glanvil and DeFoe are no less useful than they ever were in furnishing these facts from the experimental side, while others, like Charlotte Elizabeth, have incidentally treated them in connection with the Biblical doctrine.

A useful catalogue, prepared by *Henry Kernot*, was published by Scribner, Welford and Armstrong in 1874, and exhibited in chronological order a collection of books made by this firm at that time.

It is a pamphlet of 40 pages, 10¼x6¾ inches, entitled as follows: Bibliotheca Diabolica: Being a choice selection of the most valuable books relating to the Devil - - - comprising the most important works on the Devil, Demons, Hell, Hell Torments, Magic, Witchcraft, Sorcery, Divination, Superstition, Angels, Ghosts," etc., etc.

This includes many once famous and now almost forgotten books, which will bear to be read again in view of the more accessible facts of our own day.*

On modern cases of possession by evil spirits probably no treatise hitherto published takes precedence of the one by *Justinus Kerner, M. D.*, named in the Index, and quoted by Griesinger.†

Issued in Karlsruhe in 1834, and now largely lost sight of, it is a book of the utmost importance to those who want well accredited and well delineated facts from a medical psychologist of high rank, and some unusual opportunities in practice and observation. Whatever errors of judgment it may contain, it is an honest book of facts which cannot be easily explained away,

---

* Copies of this pamphlet may perhaps still be had through A. S. Clark, 174 Fulton St., N. Y.

† See page 125.

and such as corroborate in many particulars those exhibited in the present volume.

In close relation with this book and the one by Kerner, much better known, and called *The Seeress of Prevorst*, stands a book by his collaborator, possibly not translated.

Adam Karl August Eschenmayer, 1768-1852. M. D. of Tübingen. Prof. of Philos. & Med. at Tübingen. Conflict Zwischen Himmel und Hölle an dem Dämon eines Besessenen Mädchens beobachtet - - - Nebst einem Wort an Dr. [David Friedrich] Strauss. Tüb & Leipzig, 1837. Pp. 215. 7¾ x 5. (The Conflict between Heaven and Hell observed in the Demon of a Possessed Girl, etc.)

With these two writers may also most properly be named the once well-known Jung Stilling, whose Autobiography, first introduced to the world by Goethe, attained a wide celebrity on both sides of the Atlantic. It was published in New York by Harper Bros., in 1848.

Johann Heinrich Jung, 1740-1817. M. D. of Strassburg. His *Theorie der Geister-Kunde* was translated by Saml. J. Jackson (who also rendered the Autobiography), and issued under the title: Theory of Pneumatology. In Reply to the Question, What ought to be Believed or Disbelieved concerning Presentiments, Visions and Apparitions, According to Nature, Reason and Scripture? Translated from the German by S. J. Jackson, London, Longmans, 1834. Sm. 8vo. Pp. xxii., 460.

The first and best American edition was published by J. S. Redfield, N. Y., 1851. 12mo. Pp. xxiv., 286. Edited by Rev. George Bush, a well known Hebraist and Swedenborgian.

Modern demonology is discussed in this book only as a part of its whole theme. But this author Jung, with Kerner, Eschenmayer, Enne-

moser and Blumhardt, form a group of South
Germans who should be named together.   Four
of them were distinguished physicians, three of
them graduates from the then most sceptical
university in Europe.   All of them are among
the best qualified witnesses and historians of
occult phenomena, and the mental and pathological conditions which go with them.

Those who antagonize the spirit theory are apt
to object to all lay witnesses that they are not
scientific experts.   Then when highly trained
physicians testify favorably to the same view, it
is objected that they are visionary.   If the witnesses go further, and infer that some of the
spirits so engaged are demons, then, however
well informed, and inured to exact thought the
witnesses may be, it is objected that they judge
only in the interest of their theology.   Thus no
witness can be found on one side of this question
who is acceptable to its opponents, who prefer to
decide the whole controversy upon antecedent
grounds.

In the light of the facts exhibited in the present volume the writings of these men, which,
although once subject to much obloquy, were
also widely read, will repay a fresh perusal.

Besides them may be named the following:

Collin de Plancy, Dictionnaire Infernal, ou Bibliotheque
Universelle sur les Etres, les Personnages, les Livres, les
Faits, et les choses qui tiennent aux Diables, aux Apparitions,

a là magie, à l'Enfer, etc., etc., 4 vols. 8vo. Paris, 1818. Seconde edition entièrement refondue, 1825. Of this work Henry Kernot says an English translation exists which has not been published.

Abbé Lecanu: Histoire de Satan, sa Chute, son Culte, etc. 8vo. Paris, 1852.

Gustav Roskoff: Geschichte des Teufels. 2 vols. 8vo. Leipzig, 1869.

Among the more useful recent books assuming the Biblical ground are the following:

Wm. A. Matson, D. D. The Adversary, His Person, Power and Purpose. A Study in Satanology. Pp. 238. W. B. Ketchum. N. Y., 1891.

This book is not confined to doctrine, but with much ability illustrates the Scripture doctrine by many impressive incidents which confirm the conclusions of the present volume.

Jas. K. Ormiston, K. C. L. Vicar of Old Hill, Staffordshire. The Satan of Scripture. 2d ed. revised. Pp. 194. 7¾x5. John F. Shaw & Co., London, 1871.

Mrs. George C. Needham: Angels and Demons. Pp. 92. 7¾x4¾. Fleming H. Revell Co. Chicago 1891.

If it be said of the old books that they are full of absurdities, the same may be said of the new, even of those written by highly scientific men. Each reader must sift for himself as best he can both old and new, remembering that many things once thought absurd are so no longer, and much now looked upon as science will some day seem absurd.

ANGELOLOGY.

Incidentally the subject of angelology is involved in this connection, whether or not it may be rightly classed with the occult. The Bible exhibits the agency among men of good angels, as well as of evil spirits; and describes it as constant and perpetual. It describes the visible apparition and intercourse of angels, with no word to show that these might not always continue. Occasional instances of such appearances, especially to dying persons, or in the way of protection, are related in many books. A notable case is given by Krummacher, the illustrious court preacher to the king of Prussia, in connection with the earlier history of that country. The claims of some spiritists make it important that both in and out of the Bible this subject should be included in any comprehensive study of these matters. Even a secular daily journal like the *New York Herald* prints a long editorial on "The Ministry of Angels," in which it is assumed that the fact of this ministry, and human need of it, largely form the motive and justification for the doings of spiritists. (*Herald*, June 3, 1894.) The Bible, which teaches this ministry, does not teach that men should seek the approach of angels, but does warn them against the approach of bad spirits that come in a guise of the good. Two meager but useful books are these:

Rev. Chas. Bell: Angelic Beings, Their Nature and Ministry. Religious Tract Soc'y. London, 1875.

E. A. Stockman, Editor of *The World's Crisis:* Footprints of Angels in Fields of Revelation. Advent Christian, Pub. Soc'y. Boston, 1890.

A book of great originality and beauty is the following, which has to do with the Old Testament appearances of the Angel Jehovah.

Rev. Wm. M. Baker, D. D. The Ten Theophanies; or the Appearances of our Lord to Men before his Birth in Bethlehem. Pp. 247. 7¾x5¾. A. D. F. Randolph & Co., N. Y. 1883.

WITCHCRAFT.

The witchcraft excitement produced for two hundred years books affirming and denying that abound in data. Indeed, from the *Malleus Maleficarum* or *Witch Hammer* of 1489 down to *Sir Walter Scott's Letters on Demonology and Witchcraft* (Black, Edinburgh, 1831), and *Sir David Brewster's Natural Magic*, or the latest novel or medical treatise having occult phenomena for its theme, an endless succession of books deal with it. Several important works describe the criminal trials connected with witchcraft, and an extended history of these trials is *W. G. Soldau's Geschichte der Hexen processe, 1843*.

The New England witchcraft was a small affair compared with that of Europe at the time, and its literature is correspondingly limited. The most important works regarding it are still those written by *the Mathers*, father and son. Modern works repeat the original narratives, with the addition of blind efforts to explain them.

The principal book produced in England to oppose the then prevailing view of the subject was

Reginald Scott's Discoverie of Witchcraft, 1584, of which a new issue was made in 1886, edited by Dr. E. B. Nicholson, with Introduction, Notes and Glossary. 4to. E. Stock, London.

This was a notable book, and had an important influence in staying the persecution of suspected witches, and diminishing the fanatical excitement through which many innocent persons suffered.

The author did not deny that there might be genuine witches and apparitions, but in a very modern spirit he aimed to show how little witchcraft there was in much that was so called, how grossly blundering and cruelly false were many accusations.

He was answered by the King of England, *James I.*, who published a *Demonologie* in 1597. The view that there has always existed a genuine witchcraft continued to be ably maintained. In 1666 appeared the first edition of

Joseph Glanvil's Sadducismus Triumphatus, or a Full and Plain Defence concerning Witches and Apparitions. This contains some important data, best shown in the third edition, 1689, as does also

Richard Baxter's Certainty of the World of Spirits; 1691.

Glanvil was chaplain to Charles II., and one of the founders of the Royal Society. He has been rightly described, even in the *Popular Science Monthly* (August, 1892) as "a man of acute and original intellect." Many of his narratives are not duly authenticated, but his *Drummer of Tedworth* obeys the law of evidence quite as well as if its writer were a member of that same society to-day. His testimony has of course been ridiculed by those to whom his facts are an offense. But now, two hundred years after, men of science having the best repute and most modern training bear witness to entirely similar facts met with in their own observation.

Horsts Zauberbibliothek, 6 vols. Mainz, 1820-26, is called a perfect cyclopædia of the doctrine and methods of magic. In 1851 the new spiritism brought out from one of its adherents,

J. C. Colquohoun, a History of Magic, Witchcraft and Animal Magnetism. 2 vols. sm. 8vo; and about the same time, Victor Rydberg's Magic of the Middle Ages: Translated from the Swedish by A. H. Edgren. 12mo. N. York.

ANCIENT SPIRITISM.

The testimony of the ancient Greek and Roman authors to the existence and character of similar phenomena in their day, so ably summarized by Dr. Leonard Marsh (See p. 133, and Index) is also to be found recapitulated in Ennemoser and Pember, as mentioned elsewhere. With them the following may be named:

William Howitt: History of the Supernatural in all Ages and Nations, in all Churches, Christian and Pagan, Demonstrating a Universal Faith. 2 vols. London, Longman & Co. Am. ed. J. B. Lippincott, Phila., 1863.

L. F. A. Maury: La Magie et l'Astrologie dans l'Antiquité et au Moyen Age. Paris, 1864.

Bouché Leclercq: Histoire de la Divination dans l'Antiquité. 4 vols., 8vo. Paris, 1879.

J. A. Hild: Etude sur les Demons - - - des **Grecs.** 8vo. Paris, 1881.

MODERN SPIRITISM.

Under the one head *Spiritism* the catalogue of the Boston Public Library enumerates more than 250 titles, a far from complete collection. But Spiritism may be found discussed incidentally in many other books of the same library.

Probably the foremost places among recent writers, who themselves adhere to this doctrine and cult, belong to the two Frenchmen known by their pseudonyms as *Eliphaz Levi* and *Allan Kardec.*

Levi has an English exponent in **Arthur Edward Waite**, who has written

The Mysteries of Magic, A digest of the writings of Eliphaz Levi, with Biographical and Critical Essay. Dem. 8vo. Pp. XLIII., 349.

Waite has also written or edited the following works:

The Occult Sciences. A Compendium of Transcendental Doctrine and Experiment, Embracing an Account of Magical Practices; of Secret Sciences in connection with Magical Arts; and of Modern Spiritualism, Mesmerism and Theosophy. Pp. 292. Kegan Paul, Trench, Trübner & Co., London, 1891. The Real History of the Rosicrucians.

The Magical Writings of **Thomas Vaughn.** A Reprint, etc. Lives of Alchemistical Philosophers.

The principal work of *Allan Kardec* is, more than any other book, the Bible of European

Spiritists. It was done into English by Anna Blackwell from the 120,000 French issue, and an American edition was published in 1875, entitled thus:

Spirit Philosophy. The Spirits' Book; Containing the Principles of Spiritual Doctrine according to the teachings of Spirits of High Degree, Transmitted through various Mediums. Pp. 24, 234, 16mo, with Portrait (of Kardec). Colby & Rich, Boston.

(French title) Philosophie Spiritualiste. Le Livre des Esprits, contenant les principes de la doctrine spirite - - - selon l'enseignment donné par les esprits supérieurs à l'aide de divers mediums. Recueillés et mis en ordre par Allan Kardec. Diedier, Paris. (The English edition was published by Trübner & Co.)

Kardec was a man of fine education, and a proficient educator. Without being himself a medium, he collected from different mediums a large body of statements, given in trance, or by automatic writing, in response to his carefully prepared questions covering the principal problems of philosophy and religion. These questions and answers, thoroughly classified and edited, make up the Spirits' Book, which certainly exhibits a far greater coherence and solidity of matter, and skill of presentation, than most writings emanating from a similar source. His other books are these:

Livre des Mediums.
Instruction Pratique, etc.
La Spiritisme à sa plus simple Expression.
Qu'est-ce que le Spiritisme?
Caractère de la Revelation Spirite, etc.
All to be had from the Bibliotèque des Sciences Psychologiques, 5 Rue Petits Champs, Paris.

Kardec is well enough informed to rightly distinguish between the terms *Spiritualism* and *Spiritism.*   He regards the former as having its established use in philosophy as opposed to materialism, and designates his doctrine of spirits by the latter.   It would save much confusion of speech were this distinction generally heeded. Beyond its use in philosophy the word *spiritual,* in all Christian literature, has a religious use, describing what pertains to, depends on, or proceeds from the Divine Spirit; and this modern application of its related term, apart from philosophy, is, to an evangelical Christian, a species of sacrilege.

Strictly mediumistic writers are numerous. Among the best known are, *Judge John W. Edmonds, Andrew Jackson Davis,* and an English clergyman, an M. A., of Oxford, the *Rev. Wm. Stainton Moses. W. T. Stead,* the well-known editor, now claims to write as a medium, and under a "control" at will.

No one can compare the experience of these men with that of Mahomet, or even Swedenborg, and not recognize an extraordinary likeness, if not identity, in the sources and methods of their inspiration.

A practical study of mediums has been written by *Rev. Minot J. Savage,* called

Psychics: Facts and Theories. Arena Pub. Co. Boston, 1893.

Among American advocates of spiritism probably no writers have been more fair and highly accomplished than *Epes Sargent*, and *Robert Dale Owen*. The books of the former are named in the Index following. Of the latter are these:

Footfalls on the Boundary of Another World, with Narrative Illustrations. Pp. 528, 7½x5. J. B. Lippincott & Co., Phila., 1860.

The Debatable Land, with Illustrative Narrations. Pp. 542. G. W. Carleton & Co., N. Y., 1871.

A valuable study of spiritism, worth translating, was printed in Geneva in 1888, as the graduating thesis of a candidate in theology, named *Eugène Lenoir*.

The matter is handled under the three main heads of Historical, Contemporary and Experimental Spiritism. The writer views first the spiritism of India, Persia, Assyria, Chaldea, of the Hebrew Bible and Kabbala, of Greece and Rome, and of the time of Christ. Then the modern doctrines most widely diffused and the modern phenomena, with the experiments and researches of scientific men; and finally the author's conclusions, in nine admirably stated theses, make up the book, which is thus entitled:

Etude sur le Spiritisme. Thèse Présentée a la Faculté de Theologie Protestante de Montauban, pour obtenir le grade de Bachelier en Theologie, et sutenue publiquement, par Eugène Lenoir. Genève. Imprimerie Maurice Richter, 10 Rue des Voirons, 1888

The well known books on this subject by *Alfred Russell Wallace* and *Prof. Wm. Crookes*,

eminent zoologist and chemist, are among the
most important; also the

Report on Spiritualism of the Committee of the London
Dialectical Society; Together with the Evidence, oral and
written, and a selection from the Correspondence. Published
by the Committee without the authorization of the Society. Pp.
XI., 412, 8vo. Longman, Green, Reader and Dyer; London,
1871.

The identity in kind of occult phenomena in
Europe and India is obvious from many things.
An Englishman, *J. B. Brown*, writes upon

The Dervishes, or Oriental Spiritualism. 16mo. London, 1868.

A Frenchman, Paul Gibier, calls spiritism an
occidental fakirism in an important book containing ten pages of bibliography.

Dr. Paul Gibier, Ancien interne des Hôpitaux de Paris:
Aide naturaliste au muséum d'histoire naturelle. Le Spiritisme
(fakirisme occidentale) Etude historique, critique et experi-
mentale - - - avec figures dans le texte. Pps. 398. 12mo.
Octave Doin, Paris, 1887.

Also see

Spiritism. By Edelweiss. Pp. 366. 16vo. John W. Lovell.
N. Y., 1892.

Lionel A. Weatherby, M. D. The Supernatural? With a
Chapter on Oriental Magic and Theosophy, by **J. N. Maskelyne.** Bristol, Arrowsmith; London, Marshall, Kent & Co.,
1891.

Among books aiming to assume the Biblical
ground in dealing with these matters perhaps
none is better worth reading than the one by
Robert Brown described in the Index. But others
in the same line useful are these:

Wm. R. Gordon, D. D. A threefold Test of Modern Spiritualism. Chas. Scribner. N. Y., 1856. Pp. 408, 7⅝x5.

Rev. M. W. McDonald: Spiritualism, Identical with Ancient Sorcery, New Testament Demonology and Modern Witchcraft; with the Testimony of God and Man Against It. Carleton and Porter. N. Y., 1866.

Rev. A. B. Morrison, of the So. Illinois Conference: Spiritualism and Necromancy. Pp. 203, 12mo. Cincinnati, Hitchcock & Waldron; N. Y., Nelson & Phillips, 1873.

John H. Dadmun, Minister of the Gospel: Spiritualism Examined and Refuted; It being found Contrary to Scripture, Known Facts and Common Sense. Its phenomena accounted for, while all its claims for disembodied spirits are disproved. Pub'd by the author. P. O. Box 1241, Philadelphia, Pa., 1893. $1.50. per Copy, Postpaid. Pp. 468, 8¼x6.

This author has had much personal contact with spiritism, and has been an industrious collector of current information about it. The book embodies considerable material and keen observation. It is better worth reading than might be supposed from a hasty view of its obvious defects.

APPARITIONS.

Intimately connected with the subjects thus far named, and having a place in many of the books already described, is that of ghosts, phantoms or apparitions. The following books treat of it more at large. Although it may be easy and proper to dismiss the ordinary ghost story with a laugh, yet if it is to be known whether phantoms ever have an objective reality it becomes necessary to examine a good deal of testimony, and there is no lack of testimony for this purpose,

Even the rationalizing Kant said that "he did not feel himself authorized to reject all ghost stories; for however improbable one taken alone might appear, the mass of them taken together command some credence." The following books contain a mass of them.

Magica de Spectris et Apparitionibus Spiritum. Leyden, 1656.

Daniel Defoe, under the name of Andrew Moreton, Esq., wrote:

The Secrets of the Invisible World Disclosed; or the Universal History of Apparitions, etc. A third edition was published in 1738.

Augustine Calmet: The Phantom World; or the Philosophy of Spirits, Apparitions, etc., edited with an Introduction and notes by Rev. Henry Christmas, M. A., F. R. S., F. S. A., Librarian and Secretary of Sion College. 2 vols. Pp. 378, 362. Richard Bentley. London, 1850.

Calmet, abbot of Sénones, the learned, eminent and admirable Roman Catholic commentator on the Bible, lived from 1672 to 1757. This was his most popular work, and went through many editions. The translation follows that of 1751, which contained the author's latest corrections and additions. The translator calls it "a vast repertory of legends, more or less probable." By no means were all of these believed by the author himself, and some carry their own evidence of imposture. Yet many are of a kind for which there exists a large degree of corroboration in other and better attested narratives.

D'Ameno Sinistrari (L. M.) De la Démonialité et des An-
imaux Incubes et Succubes, où l'on prouve qu'il existe sur terre
des créatures raisonables autres que l'homme, ayant comme
lui un corps et une ame, naisant et mourant comme lui, et
capable de salut ou de damnation. Ouvrage inédit publié d'-
apres le manuscrit original, et traduit du Latin par Isidore
Liseux. Sm. 4to. Paris, 1875. Only 598 copies printed.

Of this book *Henry S. Olcott* says in *Posthumous Humanity*, Pp. 233, "Father Sinistrari's *De Daemonialitate et Incubis et Succubis*
learnedly and exhaustively deals with the whole
question," (and) "among others the Chevalier
G. des Mousseaux, a great modern Catholic
writer upon magic, . . . has entered at
great length into the discussion. In his *Les
Hauts Phénomènes de la Magie* he devotes an
hundred pages to it."

Adolphe D'Assier, member of the Bordeaux Academy of
Sciences: Posthumous Humanity. A Study of Phantoms.
Translated and Annotated by Henry S. Olcott, President of the
Theosophical Society. To which is added an Appendix show-
ing the Popular Beliefs current in India respecting the Post
Mortem Vicissitudes of the Human Entity. Pp. 360. Cr. 8vo.
Geo. Redway. London, 1887.

The French title of this book reads: "Essai sur l'Humanité
Posthume, et le Spiritisme, Par un Positiviste."

Regarding the spiritistic theory as a delusion,
this avowed positivist defends the objective reality of phantoms of the dead, offering an explanation of great ingenuity if not tenuity. His
book abounds in extraordinary illustrations and
facts acquired from first hand witnesses, and from
the most incontestable authorities. These he

undertakes to interpret, "to strip them of everything like the marvelous, so as to connect them, like all other natural phenomena, with the laws of time and space."

He is "forced to notice a mysterious agent revealing itself by manifestations of the most peculiar and varied nature. Averse from invoking a supernatural cause," he seeks some other, and discovers it in a magnetic fluid, a new application of the doctrine of odic force. Like all men who try to strip the universe of the marvelous, he totally fails to do it. The marvels left when his explanation is done are more incredible than those he attempts to explain, and which at the first aroused his own incredulous contempt.

But if these strange phenomena were never called supernatural, if it were freely granted that they are wholly within the range of nature, and of law, even should they be produced by intelligent beings occupying a plane of nature little known, one constant occasion of prejudice among scientific men would be removed. For nature surely is not the visible or familiar world alone.

The next work shows at their best so far the efforts of the British Society for Psychical Research. It is principally devoted to the two subjects, found to have a certain close relation with each other, of apparitions and telepathy. It is in two large volumes, crowded with illustrative data. These have been collected and authenticated with so great care that they would hardly be made more credible had every statement been sworn and witnessed before a notary. Some definite conclusions are reached, and others tentatively proposed, but all are offered with admirable modesty, soberness and caution, and good evidence of a desire for the truth alone.

Edmund Gurney, M. A., Fred'k. W. H. Myers, M. A., and Frank Podmore, M. A. Phantasms of the Living, 2 vols. Pp. 573, 733, demy 8vo (6x9). London. Rooms of the S. P. R., 14 Deans Yard, S. W.; and Trübner & Co., Ludgate Hill, E. C. 1886. Price one guinea. The first edition is now out of print.

Another more recent book written by a high authority in English folk-lore is the following:

Rev. T. F. Thistleton Dyer, M. A. The Ghost World. Pp. 447, 7½x5½x2. Ward and Downey, London; J. B. Lippincott Co., Phila. 1893. The subject is treated as folk-lore, and illustrated in its whole range.

Perhaps the most impressive and dreadful account of an apparition ever written, and claiming to be true in every particular, is to be found in *Blackwood's Magazine* for October 1888, entitled, "Aut Diabolus aut Nihil." The writer asserts that every statement may be proved by direct application to any of the persons concerned in his account, who were then all living. An apparition of Satan in his own proper person to a company of his avowed worshipers, is told in words that convey all the effect of having been inspired by an actual participation in this unique Parisian *séance*. The story may be fiction, but the impossibility of the occurrence can not be successfully maintained.

The fact that sects of acknowledged devil worshipers exist in India and other portions of the east has long been a matter of familiar history and observation. That such a sect exists at this day in France, deliberately offering formal worship to the Prince of Darkness in his recognized character, and including highly intelligent persons among its votaries, is a report which has attained some notoriety quite recently.

The practices connected with this worship, the persons engaged in it, and the causes which have led to it, have been made the basis of a work of fiction now (1894) in its 9th edition, and first published in 1891.

J. K Huysmans: Là Bas. Pp. 441. 7¼x4½. Tresse & Stock, Editeurs. Paris, 1891-4.

A further account of these Luciférians may be found in the Paris correspondence of the *Courrier des Etats Unis* for April 30, 1894 (N. Y.), and a condensed translation of the same letter in the *New York Sun* for May 3, 1894.

INCIDENT.

There are books valuable for their data that can not be strictly classed with any of the preceding nor of the following departments named, although trenching upon all of them. They are chiefly books of incident, furnishing more or less well accredited examples of the occult of every sort. It is true that in these books, as in all the literature of demonology and witchcraft, a good deal may be found that may fairly be called rubbish. It is true that certain stock stories continually reappear, being passed around from writer to writer. But amid the mass of unauthentic tales are many well attested, and no amount of lying or romancing invalidates good testimony in any single case where it is found.

Moreover frequent repetitions, under similar conditions, of the same kind of phenomena often make a degree of intrinsic probability in favor of the genuineness of reputed facts. A book of incident extremely popular at one time is this:

Mrs. Catherine Crowe. The Night Side of Nature; or Ghosts and Ghost-Seers. London, 1848. (Reached in England its 16th thousand in 1854.) Am. ed. Pp. 451. J. S. Redfield. N. Y. 1850.

Of this book the *Athenæum* said: "It shows that the whole doctrine of spirits is worthy of the most serious attention." The *Boston Post:* "It is not a catch-penny affair, but an intelligent inquiry into the asserted facts respecting ghosts and apparitions, and a psychological discussion upon the reasonableness of a belief in their existence." The *Boston Transcript:* "In this remarkable book Miss [Mrs.] Crowe, who writes with the vigor and grace of a woman of strong sense and high cultivation, collects the most remarkable and best authenticated accounts, traditional and recorded, of preternatural visitations and appearances."

The title of the book is worthy of attention, for it describes the phenomena recorded as being neither preternatural, supernatural nor unnatural, but as belonging simply to the more deeply hidden part of nature.

John Tregortha (possibly a pseudonym): News from the Invisible World, or Interesting Anecdotes of the Dead; In a number of Well Attested Facts, showing their Power and Influence on the Affairs of Mankind. With Several Extracts and Original Pieces from the Writings of the best Authors. The whole designed to Prevent Infidelity, Show the state of Separate Spirits, and Evince the Certainty of the World to Come. A new and Improved Edition. "There appeared Moses and Elias talking with him." Pp. 454. 9x5¾. Manchester, J. Gleave, 1835.

This book in its arrangement shows little literary skill, and the attestation of its stories is quite insufficiently shown. But the internal evidence of historical probability is in many of them not lacking, and in some of them such as can only be refused by assuming the natural impossibility of the events. This assumption, so legitimate in its place, is made to serve all kinds of sophistry in the interest of any reigning prejudice. Both morally and psychologically considered, these tales form a rare collection, and are profoundly suggestive of thought.

In 1852 Harper & Bros. (N. Y.) published the following:

Chas. Wyllys Elliott: Mysteries or Glimpses of the Supernatural. Containing Accounts of the Salem Witchcraft, the

Cock Lane Ghost, The Rochester Rappings; The Stratford Mysteries; Oracles, Astrology, Dreams, Demons, Ghosts, Spectres, etc. (The author writes only as a sceptic.)

In the next division belong works by *Andrew Lang*.

MYTHOLOGY AND FOLK-LORE.

The religious mythology of antiquity, and the folk-lore of existing races, contain important features, to whose meaning such phenomena as are reported in the present volume may furnish a true key. It is by no means a key to be hastily applied to all mythology, for this is made up of various factors and is a complicated thing. It may well be true of many myths that they originate in the effort of unscientific minds to explain the ordinary phenomena of nature; that they are what John Fiske calls "the earliest recorded utterances of men concerning the visible phenomena of the world into which they were born." *

There can be no doubt that the transformations of myths are largely due to the accidents and vicissitudes of language. But mythology is not made up of poetic elements alone. Myths and legends, which are different things, have become inextricably blended. The imaginative and traditional elements are combined, and there are many reasons for believing that the more important traditions have some historical ground. The events that seem to arise from an occult agency, whatever that may be, are quite

*See Myths and Mythmakers, Pp. 16, 21, 47.

sufficient to account for many legends and beliefs.

It is the strong and growing tendency of modern thought to regard all demonology as so much mythology. Many even of those Christian scholars, who still claim to accept the Biblical view of the world, shrink from committing themselves decidedly to Biblical demonology. To a great extent they practically ignore it, and often do not seem to know, in any thorough manner, what the Bible doctrine is.

On the other hand good reasons have been given, and not yet shown to be invalid, for regarding a great deal of mythology as only a perversion and expansion of the Biblical demonology. Not that it has been borrowed from the Bible, but from the same original fund of facts and teachings which the Bible writers used.

The Persian Ahriman, the stories of Titans, heroes and demigods, and the views of spirits and demons always maintained in pagan lands, all have a closer accord with the Biblical statements than is commonly recognized. Even missionaries who carry the Bible to the heathen sometimes fail to see how much it has in common with the heathen views.

In the *Missionary Herald* for Jan., 1894, p. 6, a missionary in China is quoted as saying: "During this month more money will be spent in propitiating spirits that have no existence than all the churches in the United States give in one year for foreign missions."

Christians often think of the devil and his emissaries as safely shut up in hell. Whether the Bible hell be an existing, or still future, condition or place, man's world is regarded as the present sphere of Satan's operation, and as swarming with man's invisible foes.

With this view the heathen everywhere readily agree. Of the truth of the statements made in Ephesians vi. 12, and supported by the entire Bible, the Chinese are vividly and over-whelmingly convinced, while the missionary sometimes is not.

Perhaps there is no more able nor interesting popular exposition of mythology in accordance with the principles of philology, and the defini-tion given by Mr. Fiske, than his own book, which since its first appearance has passed through some seventeen editions.

John Fiske: Myths and Myth Makers. Old Tales and Super-stitions Interpreted by Comparative Mythology. (Copyrighted first in 1872.) Pp. 251, 12mo.

Max Müller's interpretations of mythology, with some reservations and modifications, and supplemented by Tylor's view of animism, finds in Mr. Fiske at once an admirable expositor, disciple and critic. The theories elucidated in his book are unquestionably valid for much, but as surely not for all the matters to which they are applied.

Since the publication of this work, and of *Tylor's Primitive Culture*, so largely quoted in another part of the present volume, there has appeared *Herbert Spencer's Principles of Sociology*, of which the first volume more particularly deals with the same class of facts that is handled by Tylor. Mr. Spencer finds in spirit or ghost worship the beginning of all religion. To show that it may be the beginning of every polytheistic cult would be a much easier task.

Under the present heading only three other works will be named. They are each written by men of rare ability and scholarship, though with very different convictions. Yet incidentally the books supplement and confirm each other in a remarkable degree.

François Lenormant: The Beginnings of History. According to the Bible and the Traditions of Oriental People, from the Creation of Man to the Deluge. Translated from the French edition, with an Introduction by Francis Brown, Prof. in Union Theological Seminary. N. Y., Chas. Scribner's Sons, 1882.

The seventh chapter discusses the *crux interpretum* of the first part of Genesis, the passage regarding the sons of God and the daughters of men. On purely philological grounds Lenormant, who has no superior as a judge, concludes that, whatever the historical facts may have been, the text unquestionably asserts an intercourse of fallen angels with humanity, and the consequent production of a race of demigods corresponding with the traditions of the Greeks and other peoples.

He also claims in his favor "the great majority of modern exegetes, and specially of all those who evince the most profound philological knowledge of the Hebrew," (p. 318), together with the general agreement of the ancient rabbinical teachers, and of the Christian fathers for some centuries after Christ. He regards the story as a legend only, though as one divinely authorized to convey a moral lesson. For the common explanation of recent times he, and his many strong authorities, leave no exegetical standing room whatever, and hold it to be an accommodation to common prejudice. And so they leave no choice to those who stand by the historical validity of all the Bible narratives but to find a very different meaning in the passage from that conveyed by popular interpretations.

Once viewed in this light, the bearing of this text upon mythology, and also upon still existing possibilities of demon activity, becomes apparent. The same view, together with the historical character of the events, has been elaborately defended by various German writers, and also in an English work, whose combined merits of learning, logic, style and temper are far above commonplace. Its author is the

Rev. John Fleming, A. B., Incumbent of Ventry and Kildrum,

Diocese of Ardfert; Rural Dean; and Irish Society's Missionary. The book is called, The Fallen Angels, and the Heroes of Mythology, the same with "The Sons of God" and the "Mighty Men" of the sixth chapter of the First Book of Moses: - - - Hodges, Foster & Figgis, Dublin. 1879. Pp. 216, 8¾x5¾.

This bold and surprising argument is maintained with a degree of scholarship and cogency that few would anticipate finding. The books of Pember and Gall, named elsewhere, should be read with this, as being profoundly suggestive, even if somewhat fanciful in their conjectures.

Another author, of a different sort, and popularly known, is *Chas. Godfrey Leland*, an American, who is President of the British Gipsylore Society, and who in the subject of folk-lore is an authority unsurpassed. A new and elegantly illustrated work of unique research, by Mr. Leland, is called,

Etruscan Roman Remains in Popular Tradition. Pp. 385, 11x8. C. Scribner's Sons, N. Y. 1892.

This exhibits a form of spiritism or witchcraft, prevalent among the Italian peasantry, which the author identifies with the ancient paganism. The invocations, and other ceremonies and practices have an immemorial antiquity, and the spirits retain the names of the classical divinities. It is a religion of magic that survives and persists under the perpetual interdict of the Roman church, and its relation to modern spiritism on the one hand and pagan mythology on the other is singularly marked. It is so with the voodooism of semi-christianized negroes in America, and the obi practice of the blacks in Jamaica and Africa. They are all forms of spiritism, which in its last result becomes polytheism, accompanied with acknowledged demon-worship, idolatry, fetichism, and consecrated immorality.

How and why this comes to pass the first chapter of the Epistle to the Romans offers to explain.

Mr. Leland's book will serve as a connecting link between some others that, without it, would not seem to be nearly related. A reviewer in the New York Tribune, Jan. 16, 1893, says: "The Romagnan peasants use what they call *the old religion* for purposes of magic, and call those imaginary beings spirits whom their ancestors worshiped as gods."

But how far these beings are imaginary is the question. (See note on page 463.)

It is certain that the apostle Paul held a somewhat different view of them (1 Cor. x. 19, 20). It is certain that the entire Bible supports and inculcates the view that spirits other than men in the flesh have access to men, and power over them. It is certain that a deep conviction of this as truth pervades the entire pagan mind of every race, and has done so from the beginnings of history to this day. This conviction has also been shared by no small portion of those peoples among whom some form of Christianity has prevailed, nor was it ever lost until the sway began of the modern sensualistic philosophy of Europe. The conviction has ever been fostered and maintained by occurrences of the occult order, extraordinary prodigies, and facts of divination that seemed to have no other explanation.

Epes Sargent quotes it as a common saying of the ancient Romans that if divination is a fact there are gods—"Si divinatio est dii sunt." This conviction lies at the base of every polytheistic system, if indeed it be not the principal source of all such systems. The dreadful sense of dependence on the favor of these spirits resulting from this conviction makes spirit or ghost-worship the most universal and fundamental characteristic of pagan religions, and it may be the initial form under which they commonly exist. (See Appendix, page 438.)

The close affinity of western spiritism with oriental polytheism is strikingly illustrated in the recent theosophical movement associated with Madame Blavatsky, Col. Olcott and Mrs. Annie Besant. The latter, a cultivated English lady, while traveling in India, has not hesitated to tell the Hindus that Krishna is her god and Hinduism her religion, to go barefoot through their temples and do obeisance to their idols. (See letter from India in *The Congregationalist, Boston, April 19, 1894, Pp. 556.*)

BIOGRAPHY.

Many things may be found in biography. Occult incidents, and those closely like them, are scattered throughout its whole range. But especially to be read in this connection are the lives and legends of the famous sorcerers and magicians of all time.

Many a man reads one such book, and wonders and doubts, and then thinks no more about it. But let any reader follow up this line, and learn all he can of many such careers, and then form his conclusions.

Simon Magus, Apollonius of Tyana, Jamblichus, Merlin, Michael Scott, Cornelius Agrippa, Jerome Cardan, Nostradamus, Dr. Faustus, Dr. Dee, Cagliostro—however great charlatans these men may have been, however legendary the accounts of their lives, it must be borne in mind that little or nothing is told of them which cannot be paralleled and witnessed in our own day among Hindu fakirs and western mediums. The mediums Home and Eglington must be accounted for in the same way, or are quite as inexplicable as any magician of ancient or mediæval times. The lives of Mahomet and Swedenborg should be studied, and such books as the following:

Wm. Godwin: Lives of the Necromancers. 8vo. Chatto, London, 1876.

Arthur Edward Waite: Lives of the Alchemistical Philosophers. - - - To which is added a Bibliography. Pp. 315. demi 8vo. George Redway, London, 1888.

Geo. C. Bartlett: The Salem Seer, (or) Reminiscences of Charles H. Foster. Pp. 157. sm. 8vo. U. S. Book Pub. Co., (copyrighted) 1891.

In the case of this medium intelligent and correct responses in foreign languages of which he had no knowledge was one of the frequent features of his sittings.

D. D. Home: Incidents in my Life. Pp. 288, 7¾x5. Longman, Green, Longman, Roberts & Green, London, 1863.

In the case of Home levitation and sensible apparitions were often witnessed.

Arthur Lillie: Modern Mystics and Modern Magic. Containing a Full Biography of Rev. Wm. Stainton Moses, Together with sketches of Swedenborg, Boehme, Madame Guyon, the Illuminati, the Kabbalists, the Theosophists, the French Spiritists, the Society of Psychical Research, etc. Swan, Sonnenschein & Co., London; Chas. Scribner's Sons, N. Y. 1894.

TRAVEL.

After biography books of travel may be profitably searched for cognate data. *Lane's Modern Egyptians* and *Buyers' Northern India* are two of many containing such information. Many of these have been written by missionaries regarding the countries of their labor. Of such works Tylor, Spencer and Sir John Lubbock have made large use, more particularly in collecting the facts of savage life.

PATHOLOGY AND PSYCHOLOGY.

These are hard to separate in the prosecution

of this theme. Psycho-physics, medical psychology, mental pathology are names that show the blending of these departments in which are treated the phenomena of possession, trance, clairvoyance, hypnosis, animal magnetism, telepathy, illusion, hallucination, and the outward sounds and signs that accompany these.

It may be that with the exception of possession not one of these phenomena is necessarily to be ranked with the occult. They exhibit static and dynamic conditions and possibilities of the human being which are incidentally involved with occult phenomena, but may also be quite as independent of them as ordinary somnambulism, sleep and dreams. Yet there are dreams which do connect themselves with the occult, and all of these phenomena may also be incidentally involved in supernatural action, using the word in that sense in which in this chapter it has been defined.

Explanations physical, psychical and combined are broached by many physicians and psychologists, who do not long remain in agreement, but are frequently shifting their ground. The confusion of possession with epilepsy and insanity brings the literature of these subjects within this circle of research.

The materialistic trend of modern psychology is by no means shared by all the strongest thinkers in this field, though men like *Ribot* pay much more attention to these matters than writers of a purely spiritual school, and the metaphysicians. Among formal and extended treatises upon psychology perhaps no other gives so much space to them as that by *Dr. Wm. James*, which is largely quoted in this volume.

Books like *Sir Henry Holland's* and *Dr. Chas. Elam's Physician's Problems*, may already be considered a little old, although immensely interesting still. But most recent books are in a state of rapid change, and fast grow obsolete. Only three others will be mentioned.

Daniel Hack Tuke, M. D. Illustrations of the Influence of the Mind upon the Body in Health and Disease, Designed to Elucidate the Action of the Imagination. 2d. Am. from 2d. Eng. ed. Henry C. Lea. Philadelphia, 1884.

Franklin Johnson, D. D. The New Psychic Studies, in their Relation to Christian Thought. Funk & Wagnalls. N. Y., 1887.

Thomson Jay Hudson: The Law of Psychic Phenomena. A Working Hypothesis for the Systematic Study of Hypnotism, Spiritism, Mental Therapeutics. Pp. 409. A. C. McClurg & Co., Chicago, 1893.

This last is a disappointing book of large promise and small fulfillment. In the way of new facts it contributes almost nothing. In the way of explanation it is likely to seem most plausible to those who are least acquainted with the character and range of facts which have to be explained. It is likely to be highly commended by those reviewers who have only a confused notion of these facts, and are ready to grasp at any theory, especially if it relieves them from serious consideration of spirit agency in all portions of these phenomena. The merits and shortcomings of the book are sufficiently indicated by *W. T. Stead* in "Borderland," July, 1893, p. 78; and by *Dr. Richard Hodgson* in the Proceedings of the S. P. R., June, 1893, p. 230.

FICTION.

Many useful studies of the occult have appeared in works of fiction, and the number is constantly increasing. This is a straw on the tide. Both the supernatural and the occult are important features in the romances of Hawthorne and Scott.

The widely known story by *Robert Louis Stevenson* called "The Strange Case of Dr. Jekyll and Mr. Hyde" vividly illustrates some features of the subject of possession, and may be profitably compared with such facts as are shown in the present volume. Among other books the following may be mentioned as exhibiting various aspects of the occult.

W. D. Howells: "The Unknown Country."

David Christie Murray and *Henry Hermon:* "One Traveller Returns."

F. Marion Crawford: "The Witch of Prague;" "Khaled."

W. Meinhold: "The Amber Witch."

Mrs. Margaret B. Peeke: "Born of Flame."
Katherine P. Woods: "From Dusk to Dawn."
Franklyn W. Lee: "Two Men and a Girl."
Anna C. Reifsneider: "Ruby Gladstone, or A Return to Earth."

The Salem witchcraft has newly attracted attention owing to the two hundredth anniversary of its occurrence. Some years ago it was treated by *Longfellow* in his New England Tragedies. Recently it has been handled by *Miss Mary E. Wilkins* in dramatic form, in Giles Corey, Yeoman, A Play. Harper Bros., 1893. During 1893 at least three different novels were first published having this same theme.

John R. Music: The Witch of Salem, or Credulity Run Mad. Funk & Wagnalls, N. Y.

Constance Goddard DuBois: Martha Corey, A Tale of Salem Witchcraft. A. C. McClurg, Chicago.

Augusta Campbell Watson: Dorothy the Puritan. E. P. Dutton & Co., N. Y.

JOURNALISM.

Finally, the journalism devoted to the occult has in a short time grown to enormous proportions. The number of periodicals published in Europe and America as the organs of spiritism, theosophy and the many forms of magic would greatly surprise those readers who have not had their attention especially drawn to the matter, and this number keeps continually growing.

There are also the journals of societies organized for the scientific investigation of the occult,
and of the peculiar mental phenomena, which,
although associated with it, are by no means
to be inseparably identified with it.

The British Society for Psychical Research
issue their *Proceedings* several times a year,
and a monthly journal for private circulation
among its members. The American Psychical
Society began to publish its quarterly magazine
in 1892. And now the most conspicuous of living journalists, the editor of the Review of Reviews, Wm. T. Stead, has entered upon the
publication of a large popular magazine devoted
to all branches of this subject.

Borderland is at present issued quarterly.
It may attain to such a circulation as to require
a more frequent issue. It is crowded with matter that will cast a spell upon multitudes of
readers.

Every number has a long catalogue of the
current articles and books within the range of
its discussions, showing a most rapid and extraordinary growth of general interest in these
things. The variety of strange phenomena and
practices displayed in its pages would immeas-
urably astonish many intelligent people, who
yet are not prepared to learn that all the mysteries of pagan temples, Babylonian, Greek and
Roman, Chinese and Hindu, are now being

searched and practised on every hand in the cities of so-called Christian lands.

The editor proposes that in the interests of truth his readers shall everywhere form circles and *séances*, to make their knowledge as full and experimental as may be; while a correspond-ent offers property for the establishment of a college in which experts may be trained, like the neophytes in the colleges of priests connected with the temples of antiquity.

Already in circles of wealth and rank the oc-cult is followed as a fad, while the signs and advertisements of trance-mediums and fortune-tellers are so many in our modern streets and papers that Boston and Paris may yet outdo old Ephesus and Antioch and Rome in their cultivation of what was once known as Black Art.

It is certain that the interests of truth and morals call for a proper understanding of these phenomena and practices. A search-light should be thrown upon them of the highest power, that no more doubt may remain as to what they are in their real character and whence they emanate. On every side, and daily, old and young are be-ing swept off their feet by a mad curiosity to experience these wonders the reports of which are being so widely spread. The nations that for three hundred years have lived in the face of an open Bible have for the most part only known these things as sporadic, and infrequent and much circumscribed events. But in pagan Africa and Asia they are an every-day affair, frequent and frightful in proportion to the darkness and degradation of any people. Now in Europe and America may be beheld a rising flood of the same tide by which the orient has for ages been submerged.

Those who ignore it now cannot ignore it long. For good or evil it must be recognized and understood. But that which all history shows to be obviously fraught with danger to truth and morals needs not to be practised in order to be adequately known. It must be sufficiently observed to have its character defined and its danger advertised. But the tree of the knowledge of good and evil still bears fruit which allures full many to destruction.

CONCLUSION.

The one fact of demon possession so unmistakably exhibited in this volume as an experience of our own age, if this be granted, is a fact in the natural history of man which has far-reaching implications. It is one that concerns the welfare of us all. At once we see what power among men these hostile beings are able to exert, and what they may be likely in far more subtle and less obvious ways to do.

For it can not be supposed that they would

always betray or parade their inimical purpose by an overt act. They are much more likely to approach their victims in disguise, and for one person who is made aware of their presence and intentions countless others may be subject to their insidious influence and unobserved approach.

The further fact of telepathy, or the direct conveyance of thought from mind to mind without any operation of bodily sense, has been put beyond all question by the labors of the society for Psychical Research. Let him who laughs at this read Gurney's book (Phantasms of the Living), and he will laugh no more.

This also is a fact in natural history of manifold importance. In his first book and public manifesto issued in 1836, called *Nature*, Ralph Waldo Emerson well said that "the use of natural history is to give us aid in supernatural history." For the universe is a unit, and a marvelous and purposed correspondence runs through its successive planes of being, from the lowest to the highest. To the human mind, in the ascent of its activities, each lower plane becomes an object-lesson, and furnishes the symbols and the language by which to apprehend what lies beyond.

Possession and *telepathy*, these two acquired facts in the history of nature and man, have a value beyond estimate in the effort to account for some relations between man and God. All of the various functions sustained to the human spirit by the Spirit of God are described by the New Testament writers as the effect of an *inworking* or *energizing* act of God. By this one method of action God divides sever- ally, as he will, to men manifold gifts and graces. (I Cor. xii.) By this contact and en- ergy of the Holy Spirit in the spirit of man God communicates with man in all degrees; im- presses, influences, draws, guides, regenerates, or imparts of his own nature, sanctifies, or sep- arates man from sin, makes him sensible of the divine presence, love and will, attracts and con- trols his heart, empowers his will, reveals Christ, explicitly instructs, abundantly illuminates, or plenarily inspires, just as he sees fit. Much more is attributed in the Bible to this invisible action of "God, who worketh all things in all men," (I Cor. xii. 6) and who maintains the throbbing life of all nature by the ceaseless influx of his power. (Ps. civ. 30.) But all of these offices are sustained to man through an inworking of the Spirit, an act whose general name is energy, while the act by which man voluntarily conveys his thought to the mind of God is principally known as prayer. This is the telepathy be- tween man and God which makes all true re- ligion possible. (See page 437, Ap. II., 9.)

There is also a telepathy between man and

man, and it may be between man and other spirits, which would open up many possibilities. The very same term used to describe the operation of the Holy Spirit is applied by the New Testament to "the spirit that now worketh in the children of disobedience." (Eph. ii. 2.) The now burning question of divine inspiration, and the manner in which either divine grace, or temptations to sin, may be communicated to the mind of man, find in this subject of telepathy much illustration, and in Gurney's book a strong side light which makes it one of the most profitable that can be read.

Again, as the spirit of man may fall under the complete possession and control of an evil spirit, who enters in and dwells in man, using directly his organs as well as his mind, even so may a man come under the complete possession of the Spirit of God, who desires this control for man's own good, and jealously resents the intrusion of an alien. (Jas. iv. 4, 5. Alford's Version.) Yet in assuming it he does no violence to the human personality, but exalts it to the highest degree of freedom and strength.

This is the New Testament doctrine as to a man's becoming filled with the Holy Ghost, a condition which is held out as the duty and privilege of all believers, and to be attained by a free and entire submission to God's will, with believing prayer, and acceptance of his promises.

While there may be all degrees of this attainment, the apostle Paul prayed that the Ephesians "might be filled up unto all the fullness of God. . . . according to the power that worketh in us." (Eph. iii. 19, 20.) All men are invited to this intimate fellowship with their Maker, the Father of spirits (Heb. xii. 9), and all are exposed to the approach of wicked spirits, whose influence also is of all degrees. An adequate resistance to this approach is to be found in the Christian faith alone. Whoever is without this, or fails to vigilantly act upon it, becomes a ready prey. So in this faith is also found the only adequate means of linking the human spirit to the Divine, and of promoting and perfecting their communion.

This is the Bible view, which ancient and modern experience abundantly and equally confirms. But now as formerly "Sadducees say that there is no resurrection, neither angel nor spirit; but Pharisees confess both." (Acts xxiii. 8.) Of all books that report upon this boundary land of human life the Bible is most credible, if for no other than this reason, that it so perfectly preserves the moral proportions and relations of the facts which it describes.

The Bible describes many interviews of men with angels, and it nowhere indicates that such communications should permanently cease. But an angel who spoke with John called himself "a fellow servant . . . of those who keep the sayings of this book." (Rev. xxii. 8, 9.) The self styled angels who in our day appear to men, and seek to establish with them a *rapport*, are commonly such as set aside "the sayings of this book," or accommodate them to the predilections of human nature unrenewed.

The Bible permits men to address themselves to angels or spirits good or bad, who, unsought, have appeared to them and spoken; but it absolutely interdicts all efforts on the part of men to seek communication with the dead, and evidently requires that men who wish to approach the spirit-world shall address themselves to God only. Otherwise they cannot fail to invite the guile of lying spirits who would gladly divert the interest of men from its proper object to themselves. For if by any means such spirits could entice men from the worship and service of God, and from confidence in his well accredited word, we may suppose that they would wish to do it, and would show themselves proficient in the art.

The Bible requires that the messages of spirits shall be tried (1 John iv. 1-3), and evidently tried by "the sayings of this book," and the testimony of Jesus Christ.

In this nineteenth century and *fin du siècle* many consummations of history may be observed. If at this time some should depart from the

Christian faith by giving heed to seducing spirits, and teachings of demons, who with their cauterized consciences speak lies in hypocrisy within the hearing of men, it would be only what the Spirit of God long since expressly said should come to pass; while the servants of God were admonished to keep the brethren in remembrance of these things. (1 Tim. iv. 1, 2.)*

The man through whom this prediction was conveyed elsewhere wrote that "even Satan transformeth himself into an angel of light. It is no great thing, then, if his ministers also transform themselves as ministers of righteousness."(2 Cor. xi. 14, 15.) And again he wrote: "Though we, or an angel from heaven, preach any other gospel unto you than that which we have preached unto you, let him be accursed." (Gal. i, 8.)

The world makes light of the testimony of Christ and his apostles. But there are still those in it who, however doubtful of all others, believe there is one expert in these things who can be wholly trusted. All other testimony, and all other spirits, they will prove by their degree of conformity with his who is "the Faithful Witness, the First Begotten of the Dead, and the Ruler of the Kings of the earth." (Rev. i. 5.) His verdict and his views, so far as they can be known, are still, with many minds, **a**

* See note on page 415.

valid and supreme criterion by which to "prove all things, hold fast that which is good, (and) abstain from every form of evil." (I Thes. v. 21, 22.)*

. Far more than poet's fiction to these minds is that magnificent piece of English writing, Marlow's *Faustus*, almost three centuries old, and yet so pertinent to our own day. Its eloquent lesson they would lay to heart, fleeing from all unnecessary commerce with those

"Unlawful things,
Whose deepness doth entice such forward wits
To practice more than heavenly power permits."

---

* It will be observed that the texts quoted from the Bible in this chapter do not always follow the King James version, but also the Westminster, Dean Alford's, and other approved translations.

APPENDIX I.

MORE CHINESE INSTANCES.

(a)

EXPERIENCES OF CHINESE CHRISTIANS IN PINGTU AND CHU-MAO.

In the year 1874 we were not a little perplexed by occurrences in connection with the Christians in Ping-tu and Chu-Mao, in which a native preacher, Liching-pu, was the principal actor. Reports of these occurrences came to me from several independent and trustworthy eye witnesses; I have obtained from them separate accounts which are mutually confirmatory. The various witnesses will appear in the narrative. I have taken down the story chiefly from the lips of Lichung-pu, and it is as follows:

"In the spring of 1874 I went to a 'hwei'* east of Len-ko to preach. I saw there a company of twenty or thirty women who came to worship at the temple of Lai shan shing mu,† the most of whom I personally knew. While there a relative of mine pointed to a woman standing by, belonging to the Sie family, and said: 'That woman suffers fearfully from a demon which gives her no rest; and in obedience to whose command she has come here to worship.' The woman hearing the remark hung her head in shame. I addressed the group of

---

* A market, or large gathering of people for the purpose of trade and idolatrous worship. These large gatherings are held annually, or semi-annually, generally in connection with a temple, and continued for several days.

† "Holy Mother of the Great Mountain." The name of the goddess of the sacred mountain, Tai Shan, situated in the western part of the province of Shantung.

women, assuring them that they need not fear evil spirits, as such spirits can not harm any one who believes in God and Jesus Christ.

"On hearing this another woman, Mrs. Ku, from a place six *Li* * (two miles) distant addressed me as follows: 'Do you say that there is no reason for fearing spirits, I am a *hiang-to*† of twenty year's standing, and am in communication with three spirits. I have at home a beautiful picture of Kwan-yin (the goddess of mercy). If my spirits are afraid of you and your doctrines I will have nothing more to do with them, and will give my painting of Kwan-yin to you and become a Christian myself. If you like to come to my house we will see whether my spirits are afraid of you or not.' I could not decline this challenge, and an arrangement was made that I should visit her that same afternoon. I went accompanied by a Christian Liu Chung-ho‡ to the house of a relative of mine who lives in Mrs. Ku's village. In this family are two Christians, and there was also stopping there at the time a pupil from the girls' boarding school at Teng Chow-fu. After conversing with these persons for awhile Mrs. Ku entered. She said that of her three 'familiars,' she would summon the one which was the most powerful, and who manifested herself in the character of a girl named Tse-hwa. I then told the crowd that I had been challenged to meet this woman to see whether her spirits were afraid of the true God or not; that we would now pray to God; and if they did not wish to engage in this act of worship they might withdraw. Appar-

* A *Li* is a Chinese mile, which is about a third of an English mile.

† A medium. Literally a leader of incense burners.

‡ The same person refered to in a previous narrative. See p. 13.

antly from fear they all left. I read a chapter
of the Bible and prayed. Mrs. Ku then burned incense, and prayed to the demon Tse-hwa. In a few
moments Mrs. Ku sank down on her *kang**, her
frame rigid, her hands clenched and cold, and her
lips and face purple. A few moments later she sat
up again. Looking around her she saw her child
standing by, and without any provocation struck
her a severe blow. I said to the spirit, 'The religion of Jesus Christ which has now been brought to
this village is opposed to you and all your ways.
You are an enemy of the truth and a disturber of
man's peace, and as Christ's religion has come here
and must prevail you must leave.' The reply was
'I know that wherever the Christian religion is there
is no place left for me. I know too that this religion is good and true, and if my *hiang-to* wishes
to become a Christian I must leave her.' After a
considerable conversation all of this same tenor the
demon said, 'I will go.' Mrs. Ku then returned to
consciousness with the air of one disappointed and
frightened, and soon after took her leave saying,
'I must certainly suffer for this.'

"From this place I went to the village where Mrs.
Sie lives. Her husband received me very kindly, saying, however, that his wife during the intervals of
her attacks appeared as other people, and at this
time she was quite well. But it happened that a
few moments later a child came running in saying,
'Mrs. Sie has another seizure, and is under the influence of the demon.' I went immediately in to
the part of the dwelling where she was. When she
heard us coming she rolled herself up in a mat
on her *kang* where she kept up an incessant laugh-
ing and tittering. I said to her: 'What is your

* A bed made of earth and brick very common in North China.

name?' She replied: "I will not tell you. Tse-hwa gave you her name and you have sent her away. She has just been here to tell me of it. There are eight of us, and I am employed in finding a place for the rest.' After prayer a conversation followed similar to the one described in the visit to Mrs. Ku and with a like result. The woman on returning to consciousness rose from the *kang* and entertained her guests with much politeness. Pointing to a recess in the wall covered by a curtain, where was an image and an incense urn, she told us that the demon exacted worship of her three times a day before that shrine. I tore away the curtain, removed the articles used in worship, and exhorted Mrs. Sie never again to believe in or fear these beings, but to trust only in Christ. It being almost dark I left promising to come back the next day, and then returned to the village of Mrs. Ku the medium.

"The next morning Mrs. Ku came in with one cheek swollen and red. The 'familiar' Tse-hwa (so she said) had beaten her the previous evening and upbraided her as follows: 'Why do you requite me thus? After helping you these twenty years to make money and get a living, why do you call in these Christians who would drive me away?" while Mrs. Ku was thus speaking her appearance changed and she seemed to be under the influence of the demon again. I then addressed the demon as follows: 'After having promised yesterday that you would leave, why have you come back again?' The answer was 'I have something to say. If my *hiang-to* wishes to be a Christian I cannot prevent it, and in that case I will never visit her again. But I will tell you something about her. She is a bad woman; if she enters your religion you will have to look after her carefully. I advise you to have nothing to do with her.' Liching-pu continues 'Mrs. Ku after recovering consciousness asked what Tse-hwa had said. I informed her, and begged her to sever at once her connection with evil spirits, and be a disciple of Christ. I have since heard that after our interview the villagers, unwilling that the spirit Tse-hwa should leave them, because they were in the habit of consulting her through Mrs. Ku for healing their diseases, besought Mrs. Ku to pay homage to the demon and induce her to remain, which she did. I have met Mrs. Ku several times since, but she always hangs her head and turns away from me, and will not speak to me.

"Early the same forenoon agreeably to my promise I started out to visit Mrs. Sie again. When I had gone half way to the village I met an old woman who begged me to hurry on saying: 'The demon has taken possession of Mrs. Sie, and she is to-day very violent. She attacks everyone who comes near her, and none of the family or the villagers dare enter her room. She is breaking utensils, scattering about the grain, and threatens to kill anyone who dares come to call you.' I said, 'How then did you dare to come?' She replied: 'I am more than sixty years old, I care little for life, and I determined that I would come.' I found Mrs. Sie's husband outside of the house with the rest, none daring to go in where his wife was. She had bolted the door of her room, but when she heard me outside she unbolted it, and ran into another room, and rolled herself up in a mat as she had done the day before, saying: 'I am not afraid, I am not afraid.' After we had prayed the demon said: 'I will go as I promised yesterday, but I have first a few words to say,' Then addressing a certain member of the family it said: 'I must be revenged on you. You have brandished swords at me. and fired fire-crackers before me, thinking to frighten me and drive me away. If it were not for the restraint I am under I would tear you to pieces.' I commanded the demon to leave Mrs. Sie and never to return, and thereupon Mrs. Sie was restored to consciousness, and spoke to us in a most pathetic way of herself. At this time she was reduced to a mere skeleton, and was so weak that she could hardly speak, though when in her abnormal state she had almost superhuman strength. She told us that she had not eaten food for three days. I urged her to trust wholly in Christ, and told her that if she did so she need not fear for the future. As far as I have been able to learn she has not been troubled since, and is, as she was before she was possessed of the demon, a strong, well woman. She is not a professing Christian."

APPENDIX. I.
(b)
EXPERIENCE OF MRS. LIU.

Mrs. Liu, a widow about 65 years of age, lives in the market town, Shin tsai, about 230 miles west of Chefoo. She belongs to a respectable and what was formerly a "well-to-do" family. Twenty years ago her husband fell into the very common vice of gambling, and, to escape from his creditors went to Manchuria where he probably died, as he has not since been heard from. Mrs. Liu was left in reduced circumstances with a large family to support. When she became a Christian thirteen years ago she was entirely illiterate. She can now read the Bible and other Christian books with ease, and is a very apt and earnest teacher of others. Chiefly through her influence more than a score of her friends and neighbors, mostly women, have become Christians. The religious services of the little church in Shin tsai have been held in her house from the first. Indeed she was the founder and continues to be the chief support of this church. I have hardly known a woman in China who has more fully illustrated Christianity in her life, or one who has exerted greater influence for good. She has never been in the employ of the Mission, and her labors for Christ, which have been abundant, have also been spontaneous and gratuitous. Her meekness and firmness under trials and persecutions, and her many acts of kindness to others have, for several years past, disarmed prejudice and opposition, and gained for her a "good report of them which are without."

My attention was first called to the narrative which follows by persons living at some distance from Mrs. Liu's home. I afterwards gathered the particulars from her, and they are given below in her own words. The account is confirmed in every point by the sons of Mrs. Liu, who have frequently visited the Chang family referred to, and by Mrs. Fung, who occupies so prominent a place in the narrative as Mrs. Liu's companion, and by Mrs. Fung's husband, who generally accompanied the two women on their excursions.

"In the village of Chang-Chwang Tien-ts, lives a Mr. Chang, about fifty-seven years of age. who is a literary graduate of some wealth. His home is six miles from Shin-tsai. His family is related to ours by marriage, and I have been for years familiarly acquainted with the members of it,

"In 1883 this family was afflicted by a demon or demons. It appears (or they appeared) as possessing different women of the family, and occasionally two at the same time. It demanded that worship should be paid to it, that a special shrine should be erected to it in the house; and public services performed in the temple; and that its commands in general should be implicitly obeyed. The women at first complied, and spent a considerable amount of money in paying homage to it. When these proceedings came to the knowledge of Mr. Chang, the head of the family, he felt indignant, and determined to oppose the whole thing, ordering the women to disregard and defy the spirit. The spirit then took possession of one of the women and repeated its demands. Mr. Chang refused. The spirit threatened revenge and commenced executing it immediately by attempting to burn the house; by stealing and wasting the substance of the family, and by making trouble generally. Food, clothing, and valuables were stolen from the house in the most mysterious way, even when they were secured by lock and key; furniture .and dishes shook and rattled without any perceptible cause; and three women in the family were, at different times, possessed. Fires broke out without apparent cause, and, on one occasion, destroyed a number of buildings.

"In the summer of 1883 Mrs. Chang, having heard that the Christian religion gives to its adherents immunity from the inflictions of evil spirits, came to Shin tsai to see and consult with me. She related to me her trouble, and said that she had come to seek help, through me, from the God I worship. She arrived at my house physically weak and emaciated, reporting that the demon had not allowed her to eat anything for a long time;— that when her food was prepared and brought to her, before she could take it, she was seized with an irrepressible aversion to it and obliged to turn away from it: After staying a few days with me Mrs. Chang's health was restored. She requested me to go home with her, but as this was impracticable at the time, Mrs. Fung, (another Christian) went in my stead, and remained with the Chang family some days. She exhorted the women to worship the true God, and trust in Christ as their Saviour, and taught them also, elementary and easily understood truths of Christianity. In a short time comparative quiet was restored in the family, and Mrs. Fung returned home.

"Before many days had passed a messenger came to me from the Chang family, informing me that their troubles had increased, and begging me to come to their help. They told me that two women in the family had been possessed by demons for several days, and were still in a state of unconsciousness. Mrs. Fung and I returned with the messenger. Arriving about noon, we found all in great confusion. Buckets and jars of water were set in different places about the house to put out fire whenever it might appear on the thatched roof, and men were constantly on the watch, prepared with water and step-ladders for mounting the house if necessary. They informed us that fire frequently broke out where it was least expected. We were first shown to the room of Mrs. Chang's eldest daughter-in-law, a person of about forty years of age. She was under the influence of the demon and demanded wine, which she drank in large quantities, though ordinarily she would not touch it. Followed by some servants and attendants we entered the apartment where she was lying, and stood observing and talking about her for a time, she the meanwhile reclining on the bed, tossing her arms, and staring wildly and unnaturally. We then requested most of those present to withdraw, so as to leave the place as quiet as possible, that we might read the Scriptures and pray, The demon seemed aware of our purpose and turning to us said: 'You profess to be Christians do you? And you read the book from Heaven, and think you are going to Heaven yourselves; and you have come here from Shin tsai to cast me out; you need not flatter yourself with any such expectation. I have been here thirty years and I am not cast out so easily.' We replied: 'We have no strength to cast you out, but we have come to do it in the name and by the, power of Jesus.' The demon replied: 'I acknowledge the power of

Jesus but I am not afraid of you. You have not
faith enough to cast me out. You have not faith
as much as a mustard seed.' We replied: 'We came
trusting in Christ. and in his name we will cast
you out.' The possessed person replied by a contemptuous smile followed by a fit of weeping. We
then proceeded to hold a religious service. We first
sang the hymn 'The judgment day will surely come,'
and read the 10th chapter of Matthew. Then each
of us in succession prayed, after which we sang.
When we had finished the service the woman was
lying perfectly quiet, apparently unconscious or asleep.

"We then went to the apartment where the other
woman was lying. She is a widow, When under the
influence of the demon she was constantly watched
by her only daughter, as she had a fixed propen-
sity to commit suicide by jumping into a well
or pond, or by hanging herself. We held a similar
service with this woman, and left her in a state of
insensibility.

"As we were leaving the room of the second woman, the one first visited came to find us, greeted
us very cordially, and said she had just awakened
from a long sleep, and had heard from others of
our arrival, and all that had followed. Her manner was perfectly natural; she was her old self again.
She had no idea whatever of what happened during the abnormal state from which she had recovered.

"About this time, just before dark an extraordinary commotion occurred among the fowls, which
rushed and flew about in great consternation without any apparent cause, the family and servants
having difficulty in quieting them, and restraining
them from running away. After awhile they cow-
ered up in the corner of the yard in a state of

fright. The swine also belonging to the family, more than a dozen in number, occupying a large pen or walled inclosure near by, were put into a singular state of agitation rushing about the inclosure, running over each other and trying to scramble up the walls. The swine would not eat, and this state of disquiet continued until they were exhausted. These manifestations naturally excited a great deal of interest and remark, and were accounted for by the supposition that the demons had taken possession the fowls and swine.*

"The next morning the second woman also made her appearance. She seemed perfectly well and natural. We remained in the Chang family several days instructing the women in the truths of Christianity, I have visited them frequently since at their request. The women have made very encouraging progress in the knowledge of Christianity. Five in the family regard themselves as Christians, are continuing the study of the Scripture, and meet for a religious service on Sunday, even when we are not with them." So ends Mrs. Liu's narrative.

This state of things has continued for nearly six years. No foreigner has visited the place as yet, and it is not thought expedient to do so. Mr. Chang, the head of the family, gives his free consent to the women to study the Bible, worship the true God, and trust in Christ as their Savior, and reads Christian books himself. and expresses his belief that Christianity is true; but is not willing that the women in his family shall, at present, make a public profession of their faith. The manifestations which drove them to Christianity for relief have entirely disappeared.

* See Mark v, 12, 13.

APPENDIX I.
(c)
A CASE OF SUPPOSED POSSESSION IN SA-WO.

A case of supposed possession which occurred in Sa-wo in June 1882, was, for the time, the one sub-ject of interest and conversation in that neighbor-hood, and there is hardly a person in the village who is not familiar with all the details of it.. A Christian from Sa-wo , who was an eye-witness to many of‘ the incidents of the case, gave me a mi-nute account of it. During the year 1887 I had an opportunity of a long conversation with the Chris-tian, Chu wen yuen, who was the principal actor in the affair. The followiug account was obtained from him, and written out as given in his verbal narrative. It differs from others only in having more minuteness of detail. His narrative is as follows:

"In the village of Sa-wo, there is a woman of the family Chu, who has two sons Wen-heng, and Wen-fa. The mother obtained a wife for Wen-fa from the family Li, and while she was very young took her into their own family to bring her up. The girl was harshly treated by her future mother-in-law, and drowned herself. Some years after another daugh-ter-in-law was secured from a family named Yang, and it was agreed that she should remain in her own home until the time for her marriage. A few days before the marriage she was taken ill with what seemed to be possession by an evil spirit.

On the night of the wedding and after the wedding

ceremony, when most of the guests had left the house, the bridal pair were conducted to their apartments, and left to drink wine together, as is the custom with us in our neighborhood. At this time the bride, changing to an unnatural appearance, and with the voice and manner of the deceased daughter-in-law Li, and a strength almost superhuman flew upon the unfortunate bride-groom in a fury of passion, and seized him by the throat, exclaiming, 'You never treated me in this fashion; you never gave me wine to drink. My life in this family was a very wretched one.' Wen-fa cried out for help, aud other members af his family ran to his assistance, and with difficulty extricated him from the relentless grasp of the young woman who seemed transformed into a fiend.

"After this the wife of the elder brother Wen-heng was similarly affected. In the transition into this abnormal state she was at first rigid and insensible, and then she would regain consciousness and laugh, and cry, and talk, always assuming, like her sister-in-law, the voice and manner of the deceased sister-in-law Li, recounting the bitter trials which had driven her to commit suicide.

"Her husband Wen-heng, came to me, and begged me to go and cast out the demon in the name of Christ. I could not well refuse. My brothers, (I have five brothers, none of them Christians) remonstrated. They said: 'Why should you meddle with such matters and disgrace yourself and us? The whole thing is disreputable; besides you will certainly fail and make yourself ridiculous.' I said: 'l cannot fail for the promise of Christ is sure.' One of them replied: 'If you succeed in casting out this spirit we will all be Christians.

"I arrived at the house in company with several

other Christians, about the middle of the afternoon. A large crowd had collected to see the result of the matter, most of them entirely out of sympathy with us, and openly expressing their opinion that we should fail. I addressed the spirit in this language. 'You have no right to come here to trouble this family, and we have come to insist on your leaving.' The reply was: 'I will leave, I will leave,' but it did not leave. We then knelt down and invoked God's help, and when we arose from our knees both women seemed perfectly well and normal. The people generally were favorably impressed, others said that it was certainly a very happy coincidence, and still others that the women would probably have recovered just the same if we had not been called. Wen-fa said: 'This spirit-business is all a delusion, You women are a weak set specially given to this sort of thing. Let the spirits take possession of *me* and I will believe in them.' The crowd then dispersed. Wen-fa went to his own room, and the other Christians returned home. I stayed sometime to converse with those who had not dispersed. In a few minutes Wen-heng came running in to inform us that Wen-fa was really possessed of a demon, and had entirely lost consciousness. He urged me to go to him and cast the demon out. I declined on the ground that I was alone, the other Christians having gone to their homes, or their fields, and besides, Wen-fa was an unbeliever and opposer, and if we should succeed in casting out the demon it would probably return. After I went home Weng-heng came to me again urging me to go home with him, as he and the other members of the family believed in the power of Christ, and he had no resource but to come to me. I told him to return home and if Wen-fa should be very bad in the evening to come again, and I would try to gather a few Christians and go back with him.

"After dark, and just after several of us Christians had had prayers in the chapel, Wen-heng appeared, saying that his brother was very violent, and it required several men to hold him. We were told that a great crowd had gathered at the house, and that they had interrogated the demon, and had long conversations with it. Among others these questions and answers were reported, 'Who are you? 'I am a friend of Wen-fa and have come to see him.' Where do you come from?' 'My home is south-west of here,' 'It seems that you are a friend of Wen-fa, how do you like these Christians? Are they your friends, too?' 'No, they are far from being my friends,' 'We propose to send for them to drive you out.' 'I am not afraid of them.' Wen-fa's mother asked: 'Why do you not take possession of me instead of Wen-fa?' The reply was: 'Oh, every one has his affinities and preferences; we do as we please in this matter.'

"Arriving at the house we made our way through the crowd into the inner court with difficulty. To our distress we found the two women apparently again possessed and they and Wen-fa were all together in the same abnormal state. Wen-fa was more violently affected than the others and I directed my attention particularly to him. When I entered he seemed very restless and uneasy. He said to me: 'Why do you trouble yourself to come here to see me? I do not need your services.' I replied: 'Other friends have come, why should I not come also.' He said he wished to leave the house for awhile, and I requested those who were restraining him to release him, and he tried to run through the crowd. His brother followed him and with the help of several others brought him back. We then engaged in prayer, invoking the presence and power of Christ to cast out the evil spirit. During prayer he was rolling and tossing himself about on the *kang* (earth-bed), his mother removing everything from the *kang* for fear he would injure himself. When we rose from prayer all the persons affected seemed perfectly restored, and in their natural state. The villagers present asked Wen-fa a great many questions to satisfy themselves that he was quite himself again. It was evident to all that when he came under the influence of this spell he was not himself, and when restored he had no recollection of anything he had said or done. A large proportion of the villagers were now won to our side. There was still, however, a company of unbelievers and opposers, one of the most prominent of whom was the employer of Wen-fa, a man who kept a *tanfang*, an establishment for beating and cleaning cotton. The Chu family was delighted with having found a way in which they could rid themselves of their unseen and unwelcome visitors. They urged me to remain after the other villagers had returned. While they were preparing food, (as most of the family had hardly eaten anything for the last twenty-four hours), they asked me a great many questions about Christianity. They said they all wanted to learn, and requested me to come in any time I could and teach them. I remained there teaching them the Lord's prayer until a late hour. Wen-fa did not oppose his wife and the rest of the family in their wish to learn the new doctrine, but he evidently had no heart in the matter.

"The next day Wen-fa went to the *Tan-fang* to work, and there was naturally a great deal of conversation about what had happened the night before, most of the workmen having been at Wen-fa's house. They said: 'You stay here among us, no demons will dare to come here.' (It is believed that an influence emanates from the bodies of strong men in active exercise which resists and drives away evil spirits.) There

was one person present who was favorably disposed
to Christianity, who demurred to their speaking so
lightly of the subject, and being so self-confident. A
warm discussion arose in which Christianity was denounced. Before this controversy was closed Wen-fa
fell down in a fit. He was perfectly rigid and breath-
less, apparently dead. His companions at once ran
for guns and swords, especially an executioner's sword
which spirits are supposed to be particularly afraid
of, and shouted and brandished their weapons to intimidate the demon, but all without effect. Wen-fa
still remained ghastly and insensible. Fearing that
he would die on the premises the head of the establishment ordered his men to carry him out. About this
time his muscles relaxed and he became limp, though
still motionless and insensible. When they reached
the street a great crowd gathered, which was soon
joined by Wen-fa's mother. Some one raised the cry,
'take him to the chapel.' His mother and others cordially assented, and the men who carried him directed
their steps that way. As they turned from the main
road to enter the chapel Wen-fa commenced resisting,
and it required the men in charge to use their utmost
strength to prevent him from breaking away from
them. By dint of great effort they dragged him into
the chapel. Arriving there he fell down apparently
exhausted and insensible. He soon got up, however,
perfectly himself again, and asked, 'What are you all
here for? What are you about? What does this
mean?' He had no idea of what had happened.

"After this all |the villagers, including Wen-fa, ac-
knowledged the power of Christianity to cast out evil
spirits. They said if this had only happened once we
might have thought it a mere coincidence, but the connection of Christianity with these cures was too evident to be doubted. To this day all the villagers take

this view of the matter. Wen-heng, his mother, wife, and sister-in-law all commenced studying Christian books, and seemed very much interested, and made remarkable progress. The new year, however, came on in the course of a few weeks with its many idolatrous ceremonies and offerings. They agreed together to do away with the usual ceremonies, and pass the new year as Christians, but a wealthy and influential uncle opposed and over-ruled them. Having yielded to his commands to pass the new year in accordance with Chinese customs, they gradually gave up the study of Christianity, and have had but little intercourse with us since. They, however, seem very kindly disposed to us, and grateful for what we did for them. They have had no further trouble from evil spirits. Cases of this kind were very frequent in our village some years ago, but since the introduction of Christianity we hardly ever hear of them."

APPENDIX I.
(d)
CASE OF A SLAVE GIRL.

In the south-eastern part of the district of En-Chiu, in the village of Yang-kiatswen, lives a man of the family Niu, who had an experience supposed to be attributable to an evil spirit. The case is familiarly known and often referred to by the villagers in that neighborhood. Several Christians living from two to four miles distant from Yang-kiatswen, are well acquainted with the story which they related to me. It is as follows:

"Some years since Mr. Niu was very much troubled by spiritual manifestations in his family. Strange noises and rappings were frequently heard about the house. The buildings were also set on fire in different places in some mysterious way. Everything went wrong. These misfortunes were supposed to be caused by a demon, which at times took possession of a female slave in the family. Mr. Niu made every possible effort to get rid of the demon but without success.

"A Christian visited him about this time and urged him to become a Christian in order to be free from the inflictions of demons. He found him, however, very reticent and timid. He talked as if he thought some one was overhearing him, and ready to call him to account for what he said. A short time afterwards he was visited by another Christian whom he frankly told that he did not care to get rid of the demon, in fact that he had made peace with it by worshiping it,

414

and giving it a recognized place and authority in the family. It had taken permanent possession of the female slave. It was consulted and its advice followed in all domestic and business matters, and now everything went on prosperously. This female slave afterwards gained a great reputation for telling fortunes through the aid of her familiar spirit, and her fortune-telling was the means of making a great deal money for her master. She was consulted by people from far and near. Before the man Chu became a Christian he himself consulted her with regard to his child who was ill."*

* Compare Acts xvi, 16-18.

Note for page 393.

In regard to the prediction quoted from 1 Timothy iv. 1, 2, two things would seem to be properly implied by it. First, the spirits are described as *seductive* in the manner and effect of their approach to men. Their real character is concealed. They accommodate themselves to the known belief and disposition of men. They make no violent and obvious attack, but gradually insinuate a false impression, and one contrary to the word of God. Next, a form of demonic activity to which the heathen were always, and are still, subject, and which was no new thing in the world, would, in time, show a new outbreak among people who had become identified with the Christian faith. And some of these, heeding the plausible and flattering communications of spirits that seem, to use words quoted on page 313, "benign and optimistic instead of diabolical and hurtful," and failing to bring all such things to the only authoritative test of the divine oracles, are led to abandon "the faith once for all delivered to the saints." (Jude,3.) [Editor.]

APPENDIX I.
(e)
CASE IN EASTERN EN-CHIU.

In the year 1883 a boy eighteen years of age, named Liu Yao-kwe, from the village Tung en-tai, in eastern En Chiu, was received as a pupil in the High School at Teng-Chowfu, when in the following year he was taken ill of fever and died. The news of his death together with an account of his good deportment in school, the high esteem in which he was held by his teachers, the sympathetic care he had received during his illness, and the evidences he gave that he was a true Christian, were sent to his mother who was then interested in Christianity but not a church member. She was comforted by this in her great grief, and continued her preparation for baptism with increased interest and assiduity. About two months afterwards (as is reported and believed by the family and the neighbors), her two daughters-in-law were possessed by a demon, and this demon professed to be the spirit of the deceased boy. It gave the mother a harrowing account of what the boy had suffered from the hands of his foreign teachers, and assured her that he had died from starvation and ill-treatment. The mother believed the story, gave up Christianity and hated foreigners with a bitter hatred, supposing them responsible for the death of her favorite son. The father of the boy was not deceived, as his wife had been, and applied to Christians in the village to come and cast out the evil spirit from his two daughters-in-law.

They declined, however, on account of the unbelief and opposition on the part of the other members of the family. When we last heard from them this same state of things continued. This affair has had a great deal to do with checking and almost putting a stop to the progress of Christianity in that village.

APPENDIX I.
(f)
A CASE IN SOUTHERN SHIU KWANG.

In the spring of 1883 or 1884, a girl of fifteen of the family Chang, living in the village of Chang kia chwang in Southern Shiu Kwang, was supposed to be possessed by an evil spirit. While thus affected and having lost entirely her consciousness, she went to another village where lived her future mother-in-law of the Sen family, going directly to the door without a guide, though she had never been there before, and could not have known the way. A young girl going to the house of her future mother-in-law is entirely contrary to Chinese etiquette, and the last thing a betrothed girl in her sane mind could be induced to do. Her future father-in-law and mother-in-law were averse to receiving her, but were almost obliged to do so in order to avoid scandal. They were sure by her appearance that she was possessed by an evil spirit, and applied to two Christians, Changho-yi and Chaoyu-yieh, living in the same village, to come and cast it out. It was from them that I heard the story. When they went with Mr. Sen to try to cast out the demon it boldly defied them, saying, "I will not go. I once found a home in a family named Mu which spent 60,000 cash (about $50.), in their attempt to drive me away, but without avail; and do you think you can cast me out?" While the two Christians were offering a prayer for help the girl came to herself at once and immediately returned to her own home as anxious to be there as they were to have her.

APPENDIX I.
(g)
EXPERIENCES OF CHIU CHING.

Chiu chi-Ching is a prominent and highly esteemed native Christian living in eastern En Chiu. He was the first convert in that region, and the stations in that vicinity, now numbering seven, owe their existence mainly to his influence and labors. In cases of supposed possession by evil spirits, he was the person generally applied to in that neighborhood for assistance. He has given me at length his views and experiences, but there is in the main so little to distinguish them from each other, and from those that have already been narrated, that there is no occasion to record them. He states that he undertook this business with great reluctance, but feeling that he could not conscientiously decline it. He says that he has never failed in a single case, and the effects of his labors in this direction have been helpful to him in his evangelistic work. One case that greatly tried his faith and courage I give below as narrated by him, and in his own words,

"I was applied to one day by a man of a very respectable family to go to see his mother who was possessed by a demon which they could not by any means rid themselves of. When possessed she insisted on being provided with wine and meat which she took in inordinate quantities, though in her normal condition she never took wine at all. I went to the place in company with a few other Christians. Arrived at the house, we found a large number of relations and

419

neighbors assembled, and the woman wild and unmanageable, and several strong men with difficulty
kept her under control. It was with fear and trembling that I commenced the work before me. When I
addressed the demon demanding that it should leave,
the woman flew at me like a fury, exclaiming, 'Who
are you?' I knelt down in prayer, the sweat streaming from every pore, and oppressed with an awful
sense of personal weakness and responsibility. The
woman was at once restored, and with unaffected surprise and chagrin apologized for the condition in
which her visitors had found her and her house. She
was convinced of the truth and importance of Christianity and commenced studying Christian books, but
was afterwards restrained from continuing their study
by the influence of the male members of the family.
Her malady did not return."

APPENDIX I.

(h)

THE CASE OF A FAMILY IN EN CHIU.

In the year 1885 in visiting the mission station in Kin-tswen in south-eastern En Chiu, a family consisting of a man and his wife and five children, together asked for admission to the church. This is the story as given by the eldest son who acted as spokesman for the family. It was concurred in by the Christians in the village and neighborhood.

"For several months my mother was sorely afflicted by an evil spirit. The attacks were frequent and violent. She pined away until she was a mere skeleton. You see how thin and pale she is now, but she is well compared to what she was, and is constantly growing stronger. We applied to the Christians here to cast out the demon, which they did, but it as often returned. Then we following our Christian neighbors' advice determined as a family to believe on and trust in Christ. These attacks are now less and less frequent. Whenever they come on some one of us kneels down and prays to Jesus, and my mother is at once restored. Some days since she had an attack when no one was in the house except my little sister, (pointing to a little girl present about five years old), who immediately knelt down and commenced 'Our Father who art in Heaven, hallowed be thy name,' etc., when my mother darted towards her as if she would tear her to pieces, saying, 'You little wretch,' but she fell down insensible before she got to her; and **very soon** rose up well."

The members of the family have since **been baptized** by Rev. Mr. Laughlin, **of Wei Hein.**

APPENDIX I.

(i)

EXTRACTS FROM A LETTER FROM MR. SHI OF SHAN-SI.

The following are extracts from a letter received April, 1888, from Mr. Shi, a prominent Christian now connected with the China Inland Mission, whose home is in the province of Shan-si. Mr. Shi is a literary graduate of private means, well known and much respected in the part of the province where he resides. A few years since he fell in with missionaries and embraced Christianity. He is an earnest student of the Scriptures and a Christian of an unusually pronounced and aggressive type.

Having heard of his remarkable success in founding opium refuges on a plan devised by himself, and also in healing diseases by prayer, and in dealing with cases of supposed demon-possession, I wrote to him asking for information on this subject. The letter from which the following extracts are taken was his reply.

In the introduction of his letter he gives an interesting account of his conversion. He continues: "I had not at first the courage to confess Christ before others. But soon after this new experience I destroyed all the idols in my house, fitted up a room for Christian worship, had family prayers every day with my mother and my wife, and public worship every seventh day. One day my wife was very suddenly possessed by a demon. Assuming a violent and threatening manner, she attacked me, endeavoring to stop the

423

worship. At first I was put to my wit's end and knew not what to do. Suddenly I bethought myself of the words of Scripture in which our Lord gave to his disciples power to heal diseases and cast out devils, and in Christ's name, and with the laying on of my hands, I commanded the demon to depart. My wife awoke as from a sleep, and was immediately well, and joined us in worshiping aud praising God for his goodness. The faith of all my family was much strengthened.'

Then followed a detailed account of several cases of casting out demons very similar to those which are to be found in previous chapters of this book. The two closing cases with the conclusion of the letter will give a good idea of its general contents.

"In the village of Hu-tsai, less than a mile from my own home, lives a relative of mine named Han Yang-lin A servant of his Hieh Pei-Chwang believed and received baptism. Suddenly his young son was possessed by a demon, writhed in agony, foamed at the mouth and with a loud cry fell down insensible. The family were in great consternation. I was not at home at the time, but my wife hearing of the event, after prayer for help and guidance, went to the house and in the name of Christ prayed, with the laying on of hands. The child awoke perfectly well. Afterwards Han Yang-lin's own little boy was seized by a demon, and afflicted in the same manner. His mother immediately got into her cart with the boy in her arms, and came to my house to ask my wife to pray over him. My wife first exhorted her to believe in Christ and then prayed for the child when it immediately recovered. (Compare Mark ix, 17-29.)

"During the eighth month of the present year a man named Heo Tai-ts, living in the village of Hu-kia, was possessed by a demon which came and went. When it left him he was extremely weak owing in part probably to the fact that he was an opium-smoker. When the demon possessed him the strength of three or four men was not sufficient to control him. His mother applied to 'Wu-po' (exorcist) to expel the demon, but it answered them in a loud voice, 'I am not afraid of you. I am only afraid of the one great God,'* Their village was only about a mile from the village of Keo-si where lives a Christian named Liang Tao-yuen. He hearing of the matter exhorted Heo Tai-ts to believe in God and pray for succor. When he had recovered he started to go to my house. On the way while he was passing the home of Liang Tao-yuen, the demon took possession of him again in a most violent manner, and called on several members of his family to take him back to his home. Liang Tao-yuen followed him, and spent the night in praying over him. He was restored to his normal consciousness. The following day Liang Tao-yuen assisted him to mount a donkey to come to my house. I was absent in the city of Ho Chiu. My wife was at home, and exhorted him to depend on God rather than man, saying our Christian teachers cannot be always present with us, but our Lord is. A Christian, Jen San-yiu, went with him to his house and cast away his idols, and his mother and wife joined in prayer for his recovery.

"When Heo Tai-ts was at my house, the demon came and insisted on his returning home, but my wife prayed for him, in the name of the Lord, and the demon left him. She urged Jen San-yiu to pray with him, with laying on of hands and fasting, so that the demon would not dare to return any more. He soon recovered entirely, and also broke off the opium habit. He changed his name from Tai-ts, to Su-sing, (restored to life) in attestation of the Lord's having given him back to life again. The disciples brought to Christ from the region south-east of us

* Jas. ii, 19.

have come from this beginning. Five families were freed from the opium habit, cured of their diseases, cast away their idols, and gave themselves to the Lord.

"Numerous cases of this kind need not be repeated in detail; they are certainly unmistakable evidences of the power of Christ. Believers ought not to be distinguished as ancient and modern. At the present time the power to cast out demons and heal diseases, whether in China or other lands, is only from Christ. Without Him we can do nothing. When our Lord wishes to advance and hasten his kingdom, break down the power of Satan, and bring deliverance to his elect from their sins, He first makes one of those who believe on Him to give hearing to deaf ears, to open blind eyes, so that dwellers in cities and villages all may know that the worship of idols is an offense to the Most High, not only of no profit, but a snare and curse, and that only those who believe and trust in Christ, and look to Him for redemption, shall enjoy everlasting happiness and peace, both of body and mind.

"I well know that all we can do is only Christ's power manifesting itself through us, as his instruments, to the glory of our Heavenly Father. When you thank God for his grace and mercy I beg you not to attribute anything to us. We desire with the four and twenty elders of Revelation to cast our crowns before the throne and say: To our Lord alone belongs all honor and glory.* I close with respectful salutations, praying that Christ may ever be with you, completing through you whatever work He has assigned to you.

Your Brother,
SHI."

* Rev. iv. 10, 11.

APPENDIX II.

OTHER TESTIMONIES.

(1)

Austin Phelps, D. D. on Modern Demonism.

"If the Biblical demonology is a *fact* in the divine organization of the universe, and if demoniac craft is a *fact* in the divinely permitted economy of probation, what else would seem more natural than these marvels over which science despairs? What else is the demoniac world more likely to be engaged in? If it *may* be that sin, matured and aged, tends to reduce the grade of guilty intellect, what else is more probable than these frivolities and platitudes which make up much of the spiritualistic revelations? On the other hand, what else than the marvels bordering on miracle, which this modern theory offers to gaping curiosity, are more likely to be 'signs and wonders' which in the last times are, if possible, to deceive God's elect?"* *My Portfolio; pp. 170.*

(2)

Dr. Wm. Ashmore and Archdeacon Moule on Chinese Spiritism.

To the testimonies from China may be added some statements made by two more of the most widely experienced missionaries in that country. The first is the Rev. Dr. William Ashmore, who says as follows:

"I have no doubt that the Chinese hold direct communications with the spirits of another world. They never pretend that they are the spirits of departed friends. They get themselves into a certain state and seek to be possessed by these spirits. I have seen them in certain conditions invite the

*Matt. xxiv. 24.

spirits to come and inhabit them.   Their eyes become frenzied, their features distorted, and they pour out speeches which are supposed to be utterances of the spirits."

Quoted in *"Ancient Heathenism and Modern Spiritualism."* *By H. L. Hastings. Boston, 1890. pp. 211.*

The second witness is the Ven. Arthur E. Moule, B. D., Archdeacon in Mid-China.   After thirty years of residence in that country he says: "From my own personal observations I am inclined to believe that amidst a great preponderance of deliberate imposture, for the sake of gain, there is as much positive intercourse with the darker regions of the nether world as that professed or possessed by the Jewish witches of old."   See p. 231 of his *"New China and Old. London, Seeley & Co., 1891."*

(3)   See p. 285.

Mr. G. H. Pember and Charlotte Elizabeth on the Demoniac and the Medium as described in the Bible.

"An *obh* is a soothsaying demon, but by an earlier use the word is also applied to the person connected with such a demon.   Originally it signified a skin bottle, and its transition from this first meaning to its second may be clearly detected in the following exclamation of Elihu: 'For I am full of matter, the spirit within me constraineth me.   Behold, my belly is as wine which hath no vent; it is ready to burst like new bottles.' *Job xxxii. 18,19.*

"The word appears, then, to have been used of those into whom an unclean spirit had entered, because demons, when about to deliver oracular responses, caused the bodies of the possessed to grow tumid and inflated.   We may perhaps compare Virgil's description of the soothsaying sibyl (*Aen. vi. 48-51*), for he tells us that her breast began to swell with frenzy, and her stature appeared to increase, as the spirit, or the god, drew nearer.

"According to some, however, the medium was called an *obh* merely as being the vessel or sheath of the spirit; but in either case the term was afterward applied to the demon itself.   That the spirit actually dwells within the person who divines by it we may see from a previously quoted passage of *Leviticus*, the literal rendering of which is 'A man or a woman when a demon is in them,' etc. (*Lev. xx.* 27.) And in strict accordance with this is the account of the Philippian damsel, who had a Pythonic spirit. For Paul compelled the spirit to come out of her, and she instantly lost all her supernatural power. From the stories of mediæval witches, and from what we hear of modern mediums, it seems likely that a connection with an *obh* is frequently, if not always, the result of a compact, whereby the spirit, in return for its services, enjoys the use of the medium's body.

"Indeed there is reason to believe that a medium differs from a demoniac, in the ordinary use of the term, merely because in the one case a covenant exists between the demon and the possessed; whereas the frightful duality and confusion in the other arises from the refusal of the human spirit to yield a passive submission, and acquiesce in a league with the intruder." Pp. 260-1. Revell's ed. of *Earth's Earliest Ages.* By G. H. Pember, M. A.

"Against the sin of witchcraft, the acquirement of power or knowledge by means of Satanic communications, the law was very strict." (*Leviticus xx.* 27.)

"By this we see that Satan had contrived to obtain a footing among God's peculiar people, that he had seduced them into holding intercourse with his subordinates, for the purpose of sharing such supernatural gifts as he could impart."

"The case of those possessed with devils is represented as being nearly always one of great suffering. The exceptions seem to be those instances where the infernal inmate was a welcome confederate, for the sake of such supernatural powers as he could confer." (As the Pythian damsel, Simon Magus, Elymas the Sorcerer, and others.) Pp. 49, 64-5, of *Principalities and Powers.* By Charlotte Elizabeth. Am. ed., N. Y. 1842.

(4)   See p. 99.

Virgil's Cumæan Sibyl.

" 'Now to the mouth they come,' aloud she cries,
'This is the time, enquire your destinies.
He comes—behold the god!'   Thus while she said,
(And shivering at the sacred entry, staid)
Her color changed, her face was not the same,
Her hair stood up, convulsive rage possessed
Her trembling limbs, and heaved her laboring breast.
Greater than human kind she seemed to look,
And with an accent more than mortal spoke;
Her staring eyes with sparkling fury roll,
When all the god came rushing on her soul.
Swiftly she turned, and foaming as she spoke,
'Why this delay?' she cried, 'the powers invoke;
Thy prayers alone can open this abode,
Else vain are my demands, and dumb the god.'

*   *   *   *

"Struggling in vain, impatient of her load,
And laboring underneath the ponderous god,
The more she strove to shake him from her breast,
With more and far superior force he pressed,
Commands his entrance, and, without control,
Usurps her organs and inspires her soul.

*   *   *   *

"Thus from the dark recess the Sibyl spoke,
And the resisting air the thunder broke,
The cave rebellowed and the temple shook;
The ambiguous god who ruled her laboring breast
In these mysterious words his mind expressed,
Some truths revealed, in terms involved the rest.
At length her fury fell; her foaming ceased,
And, ebbing in her soul, the god decreased." '

From the *Æneid, Bk. VI.,* beginning with line 67 of Dryden's Translation.

(5)

William James, M. D., Professor, formerly of Physiology, and now of Psychology, at Harvard University, on the Medium Trance.

"We believe in all sorts of laws of nature which we cannot ourselves understand, merely because men whom we admire and trust vouch for them.

"If Messrs. Helmholtz, Huxley, Pasteur and Edison were simultaneously to announce themselves as converts to clairvoyance, thought-transference, and ghosts, who can doubt that there would be a popular stampede in that direction? We should have as great a slush of 'telepathy,' in the scientific press as we now have of 'suggestion' in the medical press. We should hasten to invoke mystical explanations without winking and fear to be identified with a by-gone *régime* if we held back. In society we should eagerly let it be known that we had always thought there was a basis of truth in haunted houses, and had, as far back as we could remember, had faith in demoniacal possession.

"Now, it is certain that if the cat ever does jump this way the cautious methods of the S. P. R. (Society for Psychical Research) will give it a position of extraordinary influence.

"Now, the present writer (not wholly insensible to the ill consequences of putting himself on record as a false prophet) must candidly express his own suspicion that sooner or later the cat must jump this way.

"The special means of his conversion have been the trances of the medium whose case in the 'Proceedings' was alluded to above.

"Knowing these trances at first hand, he cannot escape the conclusion that in them the medium's knowledge of facts increases enormously, and in a manner impossible of explanation by any principles of which our existing science takes account. Facts are facts, and the larger includes the less; so these trances doubtless make me the more lenient to the other facts recorded in the 'Proceedings.'

"I find myself also suspecting that the thought-transference experiments, the veridical hallucinations, the crystal vision, yea, even the ghosts, are sorts of things which with the years will tend to establish themselves. All of us live more or less on some inclined plane of credulity. The plane tips one way in one man, another way in another; and may he whose plane tips in no way be the first to cast a stone!

"But whether the other things establish themselves more and more, or grow less and less probable, the trances I speak of have broken down for my own mind the limits of the admitted order of nature. Science, so far as science denies such exceptional facts, lies prostrate in the dust for me; and the most urgent intellectual need which I feel at present is that science be built up again in a form in which such facts shall have a positive place.

"Science, like life, feeds on its own decay. New facts burst old rules; then newly divined conceptions bind old and new together in a reconciling law. . . . . Mr. Myers seeks to interpret mediumistic experiences and ghostly apparitions as so many effects of the impact upon the subliminal consciousness of causes 'behind the veil.' The *effects*, psychologically speaking, are hallucinations; yet so far as they are 'veridical' they must be held probably to have an 'objective' cause. What that objective cause may be Mr. Myers does not decide; yet from the context of many of the hallucinations it would seem to be an intelligence other than that of the medium's or seer's ordinary self, and the interesting question is: Is it what I have called the extra-conscious intelligence of persons still living, or is it the intelligence of persons who have themselves passed behind the veil? Only the most scrupulous examination of the 'veridical' effects themselves can decide."

From *The Forum* for August, 1892.

(6)

Rev. H. R. Haweis on the Persistence of Occult Phenomena.

"Face to face with certain alleged phenomena of an unintelligible character, repeated experience has at last placed one conclusion beyond dispute, viz., that it is unsafe to denounce what it may be difficult to examine, but still more risky not to examine what we propose to denounce. But it is a busy world, and you may fairly ask: 'Why should I attend to ghosts, or for the matter of that, any of those bogey phenomena, which I am told on excellent authority can be accounted for by fraud, credulity, hallucination, or misunderstanding?' I will answer that question first.

"We must attend to occult phenomena (were there no other reason) because of their obstinate persistency. That is Herbert Spencer's test of reality.   The broad backs of those much belabored but patient beasts of burden called Fraud, Credulity, Hallucination and Misunderstanding have at last refused to bear any more loading. Who's to carry what is left? for this obstinate residuum, it seems, cannot be destroyed. Comparative studies in these days are all the fashion. Will no one give us a comparative study of ghosts? Will no one even provide us with an introductory and concise study of occult phenomena in and out of the Bible, in history, ancient and modern, sacred and profane? Lastly, in a word, will no one after loading the four beasts as heavily as possible, produce the fifth beast whose name is Truth, and who will bear without hesitation or fatigue that puzzling residuum of indisputable but unintelligible phenomena?

"Is it not strange that the occult, or what we commonly call the miraculous, weathers age after age of scepticism? True, that at this very moment, we are living in an age of scientific ostriches, who mumble, with their heads in the sand, that no one now believes in miracles; that ghosts never appear; that second-sight and premonitions and dreams that come true, and prophecies that are verified, have all vanished before the light of knowledge, and the scrutiny of science. True also it is that never were there a greater number of intelligent people convinced of the reality and importance of these occult phenomena. The persistency of the occult is at any rate a fact, and a stubborn one. From age to age the same unexplained phenomena occur. In spiritualism more than in anything else history repeats itself. From age to age a number of supposed supernaturalisms are exposed or explained; from age to age a residuum cannot be exposed or explained. No, not by Crooks, or Wallace, or Lodge, or Flammarion, or the Berlin conjurer, Bellachini; or the French conjurer, Houdin; or the English conjurers, Maskelyne and Cook, or Sidgewick and the Psychical society, or any other society, or anybody else. 'This gives to reflect,' as the French say."

From the *Fortnightly Review*, February, 1893.

(7)
Lyman Abbott on Demon Possession.

"For reasons stated in my *Life of Christ*, Chapter xiii., I believe not only that there really was, but there really still is, such a phenomenon."

Outlook, Aug. 25, 1894, p. 314.

(8) See page 291.
Regarding High Magic.

The term *magic* may refer only to sleight of hand. But it has also been defined as "the art of putting in action the power of spirits, or the occult powers of nature." This definition offers an alternative. The magicians of Egypt and Babylon mentioned in the Bible belonged to a class of wonder-workers who perhaps have their best modern parallels in India, though they are still to be found in Egypt and elsewhere. In the highest forms of magic there is all the appearance of some superhuman agency. Whether such an agency may ever be involved is a question usually answered by the prepossessions of the person judging. Mistaken prepossessions are hard to dislodge, though sometimes with a sufficient range of facts, and a sufficiently candid mind, this may be effected.

It can hardly be doubted that in the Bible a degree of power to work miracles by the agency of Satan or of demons, is attributed to men. Apart from the old Testament, we have the prediction of the Saviour that false Christs and false prophets would arise, who would 'show great signs and wonders, so as to deceive, if it were possible, the very elect.'' (*Matt. xxiv, 24.*) The apostle Paul predicts the coming of a ''man of sin,'' a ''lawless one,'' ''after the working of Satan with all power of signs and lying wonders.'' (*2 Thes. II. 8, 9.*) John saw in vision ''another wild beast coming up out of the earth. And he doeth great wonders, so that he maketh fire come down on the earth in the sight of men; and deceiveth those that dwell on the earth by the means of those miracles which he had power to do.'' (*Rev. xiii. 11-15.*)

In *Rev. xvi. 13-14,* he describes ''three unclean spirits like frogs, . . . the spirits of demons working miracles, which go forth unto the kings of the whole world to gather them to the battle of that great day of God Almighty.''

In *Rev. xix. 20,* he speaks of ''the false prophet that wrought miracles before him (the beast), with which he deceived them that received the mark of the beast.''

Some of the wonders wrought by the high caste fakirs of India are narrated in the *North American Review for January, 1893,* in an article entitled ''High Caste Indian Magic.'' The writer, Harry Kellar, is a professional juggler of thirty years' experience, who has spent fifteen years in India and the far east. He says that he would be the last to concede anything supernatural in their power, having spent his life in ''combating the illusions of supernaturalism, and the so-called manifestations of spiritualism.'' But he also says that ''through a thousand years of rumor the high caste fakir has succeeded in preserving the secret of his powers, which have on more than one occasion baffled my deepest scrutiny and remained the inexplicable subject of my lasting wonder and admiration.''

He supposes these magicians to have ''discovered natural laws of which we in the west are ignorant,'' and to overcome ''forces of nature which to us seem insurmountable.''

He describes in particular three great feats which have been repeatedly witnessed, and well authenticated by other competent observers besides himself. These are "feats of levitation, or the annihilation of gravity; feats of whirling illusion, in which one human form seems to multiply itself into many, which again resolve themselves into one; and feats of voluntary interment."

The mysterious and even dreadful facts that Mr. Kellar details introduce us at once to the very heart of the province of high magic, and they are such as may well be viewed in the light of such other facts as those given in the present volume.

Once admit that invisible spirits have access to men, with power to communicate with them, and to produce in and through them mental, moral, and also physical effects, as the Scriptures evidently teach, and we have a theory that easily and naturally covers many facts that cannot otherwise be explained. And there are facts for which every other theory is only a promise to explain that has never been fulfilled.

These Indian phenomena are shown at length in the writings of Louis Jacolliot, a French author and rationalist long resident in India. Their discussion on Biblical grounds, together with many other equally marvelous facts, may be found in a book by an able English solicitor, Robert Brown, entitled *Demonology and Witchcraft with Especial Reference to Modern Spiritualism So-Called, and the "Doctrines of Demons."* (*London, John F. Shaw & Co., 1889.*) This work is not without faults. But it manifests legal acumen, Hebrew scholarship, uncompromising fidelity to the authority of the Bible, and a familiarity with those phenomena under discussion which are most extraordinary, and also most characteristic. It is a book that ought not to be overlooked in the study of this subject. Upon the assumption that demons have anything to do with this species of magic the matter forms a distinct department of demonology, of which here only this brief mention can be made.

The wonders narrated by Mr. Kellar may have excited his admiration, but they are well suited to excite the horror of most observers. The moral quality of the spirits concerned in their production, whether human only, or other than human, can be determined only by moral tests. Miracles of this kind have always been associated with and conducive to, the worst forms of pagan superstition, and the darker and more groveling the superstition so much the more terrible has been the form in which the wonders have appeared, as may be seen in Mr. Kellar's own account of the witch doctors in Natal. In all times they have been exhibited to support the claims of idolatrous worship. They have invariably tended to draw men from the worship of the supreme God, to the worship of intermediate beings, however called, "gods many and lords many," (*1 Cor.* viii. *5*) including the open and avowed worship of demons. And even in the most enlightened lands where, as among modern spiritualists, prodigies in any degree similar occur, their tendency and result are the same. God is ignored or becomes an impersonal pantheistic force, while the spirits are followed up with the devotion of a passionate infatuation. The moral law becomes despised, and the character of the devotees tends to grow more depraved and blighted to the end. There are apparent exceptions to this rule, but that this is the rule may be regarded as the verdict of history. Consult Dr. Joseph Ennemoser's History of Magic. 2 vols. London, 1854. H. G. Bohn; Narratives of Sorcery and Magic from the most Authentic Sources. By Thos. Wright, M. A., F. S. A. Am. ed. N. York, 1852. Redfield; Lenormant's Chaldean Magic. London, 1877. Bagster. These books lie within easy reach on the shore of the ocean of the literature of magic.

(H. W. R.)

(9) See p. 389.

Telepathy, Human and Divine.

See on this theme a fine passage in H. Gratry's *Guide to the Knowledge of God;* Roberts Bros., Boston, 1892; pp. 441-2. No work in pure philosophy has appeared in France in recent years nobler than this, which with honor to itself the French Academy has crowned.

See also Joseph Cook on Cosmic Telepathy. *Our Day,* *Oct., 1895;* and on Psychical Research, do. *Nov., 1895.*

(10) See p. 378; also pp. 276, 374, 392.

Heli Chatelain, late U. S. Commercial Agent at Loanda, author of Folk Tales of Angola; On the Prevalence of Spirit Worship.

"It has been my privilege to associate personally with missionaries laboring among all races, to have perused missionary records of many societies in the respective tongues, and also to mingle with the ignorant classes of most so-called Christian nations; and the more I ascertain and compare original facts, the more am I impressed with the fundamental unity of the religious conceptions of Chinese, Hindus and American Indians, as well as of nominal Moslems, Jews and Christians, with the African Negro.

"They all have a dim notion of a Supreme Being; they all serve him far less than they serve the spirits, the mysterious forces of nature, and the souls of deceased persons (ancestor worship, etc.), and put their trust in amulets, talismans, incantations, quacks, priests, soothsayers, spiritists, and the thousand and one manifestations and paraphernalia of the one universal disposition of mankind, known as superstition."

Conclusion of an article on African Fetishism, in the *Journal of American Folk-Lore* for October-December, 1894, p. 304. See also do. pp. 301 and 314-315; also in do. for July-September, 1895, pp. 181-184.

(11)

A Definition of Superstition.

To the above statements the present editor would add the following: What constitutes superstition is not the belief that the human race is surrounded and affected by an invisible race of spirits, a matter of evidence, but the putting of any finite being or object in the place of the Infinite. To invest anything, animate or inanimate, imaginary or real, with attributes, relations, prerogatives of worship, which belong of right to God alone, and to yield to such an object the fear, faith, interest, or attention that are due to him is the essence of superstition. It is well characterized in Romans i. 25.

BIBLIOGRAPHICAL INDEX.

An index of the books and authors consulted in the preparation of this volume, or referred to in it ; with a more particular account of some which are regarded as important to its theme, but insufficiently known, or which are insufficiently described elsewhere in its pages.

"Spiritual Manifestations." 302 pages, 8 x 5½ in. Lee & Shepard, Boston, 1879. "For the earnest expectation of the creature waiteth for the manifestation of the Sons of God." Rom. viii. 19.

This book, assuming the reality of spiritual manifestations, and the correctness of the Biblical view of them, interprets that view, and its wide bearing upon related matters, in a lucid, original, and highly suggestive manner. The earlier studies of the same author in this field were published in 1853, in a volume called, "A Review of the Spiritual Manifestations." Read before the Congregational Association of New York and Brooklyn. 75 pages ; G. P. Putnam & Co. Both books deserve to be read.

Among modern witnesses to the facts of possession, of exorcism, and of healing through believing prayer, Blumhardt may fairly be regarded as holding the first place. Perhaps no man of recent times has had a more intimate and practical acquaintance with these matters at first hand, and no student of them can afford to overlook his life and work. Subjected as these were to a searching and public scrutiny, and every test that friends or foes could make, this only resulted in a perfect vindication of his claims from all suspicion, and the wondering approval of those who came to know the facts. He was born in 1805, and died in 1880. He was graduated in theology at the University of Tübingen, a man of thorough cultivation and generous tastes. Familiar with the whole course of Biblical criticism, he yet always maintained an active evangelical faith. His character was strong, guileless, unassuming, magnanimous, and just. He had a singularly well-balanced judgment, rare penetration in his knowledge of men, executive power and unusual tact. Although a conservative Lutheran clergyman, he had world-wide sympathies. For many years he maintained a ministry of relief to suffering minds and bodies, with the most beneficent results, to which hundreds can still testify. He was so transparently noble, and his wisdom and influence so marked that, whatever explanation may be made of his work, it must still be of unique interest to a student, upon psychological as well as moral and religious grounds.

His biography in German has reached a fifth enlarged edition, which should be translated into English. A much briefer account of him exists in English, entitled, "Pastor Blumhardt and His Work," by Rev. W. Guest, with an Introduction by Rev. C. H. Blumhardt (a brother). Morgan & Scott, London, 1881. This contains a chapter by Henry Drummond, describing a visit to Blumhardt's institution in Bad Boll, and expressing confidence in the character and results of its work. The German biography is as follows: Pfarrer Johann Christoph Blumhardt. Ein Lebensbild, von Friedrich Zündel, Pfarrer. Fünfte vermehrte Auflage. Zürich, 1887. 552 pages, 9¼ x 6½.

"The Unknown God; or Inspiration among Pre-Christian Races," by C. L. B., author of "Gesta Christi," "Races of the Old World," etc. 336 pages, cr. 8vo. A. C. Armstrong & Son, New York, 1890.

"Memoirs of David Brainerd, Missionary to the Indians of North America," by Jonathan Edwards, D. D. and Sereno E. Dwight, D. D. Edited by J. M. Sherwood. Funk & Wagnalls, New York and London, 1885.

"Demonology and Witchcraft," with special reference to modern "Spiritualism," so-called; and the Doctrines of Demons. "In the latter days some shall depart from the faith, giving heed to seducing spirits, and doctrines of demons. . . . If thou put the brethren in remembrance of these things, thou shalt be a good minister of Jesus Christ." 1 Tim. iv. 1, 6. 354 pages, 7¼ x 5. John F. Shaw & Co., London, 1889. Also by the same author, "The Personality and History of Satan." 216 pages. S. W. Partridge & Co., London, 1887.

and Kingdom of Satan." (The Bishop Paddock Lectures for 1889.) 197 pages, 8¼ x 6. T. Whittaker, New York, 1889.

(1786-1862.) Graduate of Tübingen. "Geschichten Besessener neuerer Zeit." Beobachtungen aus dem Gebiete kakodämonisch-magnetischer Erscheinungen. Von Justinus Kerner; nebst Reflexionen von C. H. Eschenmayer über Besessenseyn und Zauber. Karlsruhe. G. Braun, 1834. 189 pages, 8½ x 5. Second edition, 1835.

These narratives of modern cases of possession, quoted by Dr. Griesinger, form perhaps the most important monograph exclusively upon this theme hitherto published. Kerner's best known book in this department is "The Seeress of Prevorst," first issued in Stuttgart in 1829. The fourth edition in 2 vols., 1846; fifth edition, 1877. This was translated into English by Mrs. Catherine Crowe, and an American edition issued by Harper Bros., New York, 1845, entitled, "The Seeress of Prevorst:" being revelations concerning the inner life of man, and the interdiffusion of a world of spirits in the one we inhabit. Communicated by J. Kerner.

Author of "Custom and Myth," 1884; "Myth, Ritual and Religion," 2 vols, 1887; "Cock Lane and Common Sense," 1894.

President of the Tung-Wen College, Pekin. "The Chinese, Their Education, Philosophy, and Letters." 319 pages, 12mo. Harper Bros., New York, 1881.

(1800–1870.) He was a brother of President James Marsh of the University of Vermont; studied medicine in New York with Dr. Valentine Mott, who was known as the "father of American surgery;" received his medical degree at Dartmouth College. After some years of practice he was, in 1855, "made Professor of Greek and Latin in the University of Vermont; and in 1857 was transferred to the Chair of Vegetable and Animal Physiology, which he held until his death. He was a man of singularly penetrative and independent intellect, widely read in general literature, as well as in his profession, and in the branches in which he gave instruction." It may be hoped that Prof. J. E. Goodrich, of Burlington, who makes the above statement for this volume, will prepare a new edition of the "Apocatastasis," which President Felton, of Harvard, pronounced a masterly work. The "Apocatastasis; or Progress Backwards, A new Tract for the Times." 204 pages, 10 x 6½. Chauncey Goodrich, Burlington, Vt., 1854.

The "Wonders of the Invisible World," being an account of the trials of several witches, lately executed in New England, to which is added a farther account of the trials of the New England witches, by Increase Mather, D. D., President of Harvard College, Boston, 1693. John Russell Smith, London, 1862. 291 pages, 7 x 4½, with portrait.

This is a comparatively recent edition of a famous book produced in the time and heat of the witchcraft excitement in New England. Men now write books to show what fools the forefathers were for supposing that anything besides human agency, credulity, or disease was involved in the curious phenomena connected with ancient witchcraft. But the opportunity remains of studying at first hand, in our own day, generically similar phenomena, and many forgotten books on witchcraft are full of data that may profitably be compared with existing facts.

following titles : "Spiritualism, What it is Not ;" Spiritualism Probably of Satanic Origin ;" "Ought the Pulpit to Ignore Spiritualism ? ;" "How Shall the Pulpit Treat Spiritualism ?" The first two are published as a tract : "Spiritualism, The Argument in Brief." Congregational Publishing Society, Boston, 1871. 35 pages. The last two form chapters XVII and XVIII in his´ volume, called "My Portfolio." Chas. Scribner's Sons, New York, 1882. 280 pages.

Especial value attaches to the testimony of Dr. Phelps from the fact that in his own father's house at Stratford, Conn., occurred the most remarkable series of occult phenomena which have ever been put on record in the United States. It would aid the cause of truth if an exhaustive monograph regarding those events might be prepared and bound in one volume with these four chapters. (See note on page 133.)

(1803-1858). Graduate of Princeton College and Seminary ; missionary of the A. B. C. F. M. in India, 1831-34. Pastor of the Cedar St. Presbyterian Church in Philadelphia, 1837-1857. A man learned in many languages, efficient, and fruitful in his ministry. His testimony to facts observed in India and elsewhere is largely that of a competent personal witness. In 1856 there appeared from his pen : "Spiritualism, A Satanic Delusion, and a Sign of the Times," edited with a preface by H. L. Hastings. "The God of Peace shall bruise Satan under your feet shortly." Rom. xvi, 20. 122 pages, 12mo. Peace Dale, R. I. Published by H. L. Hastings. Four or five thousand copies were issued. Recently Mr. Hastings has embodied the contents of this book with additional matter in a consecutive series of tracts, to be made, when complete, into a new volume. The series already numbers ten parts and 316 pages, 7¼ x 6¾. It is prepared with ability and much experience. The titles of the separate tracts are as follows :—

1. "Spiritual Manifestations : Their Nature and Significance," by W. R., 1888.

2. "Spirit Workings in Various Lands and Ages," by W. R., edited with additions by H. L. H., 1888.

3. "Familiar Spirits : their Workings and Teachings." 1888.

4. "The Mystery Solved : Spiritual Manifestations Explained," by W. R., 1888.

5. "The Depths of Satan : A Solution of Spirit Mysteries," by W. R., 1889.

6. "Trying the Spirits¦: An Examination of Modern Spiritualism," by H., 1889.

7. "Ancient Heathenism and Modern Spiritualism," by H., 1890.

8. "Primitive Christianity and Modern Spiritualism," by H., 1890.

9. "Witchcraft : Is it a Reality or a Delusion ?" by H., 1893.

10. "Necromancy," by H., 1893. Published at The Scripture Tract Repository, 47 Cornhill, Boston.

Professor of Comparative and Experimental Psychology in the *Collége de France*, editor of the *Revue Philosophique de la France et de l' Etranger*. Author of "English Psychology." From the French, London, H. S. King & Co., 1873. "German Psychology of To-day : The Empirical School." Translated from second French edition, by Jas. Marsh Baldwin. Preface by Jas. Mc Cosh. C. Scribner's Sons, 1886. "L' Hérédité ; Étude Psychologique." Paris, 1873. English translation, London, 1875 ; "La Philosophie de Schopenhauer," Paris, 1874 ; "Diseases of Memory," International Science Series. D. Appleton, New York. "Diseases of ¡Personality," authorized translation. Open

Former president of Columbian University, Washington, D. C. Cover title, "Physical Media in Spiritual
Manifestations," proper title, "The Physical in Spiritualism; or the Spiritual Medium not Psychical but
Physical." Illustrated by attested facts in universal
history, and confirmed by the ruling philosophy of all
ages. Presented in a series of letters to a young friend.
J. B. Lippincott Co., Philadelphia, 1881. This is the
last form in which the author has presented studies of
many years in this department, two previous volumes
being these :—

1. "To Daimonion; or the Spiritual Medium," by
Traverse Oldfield. Gould & Lincoln, Boston, 1851.

2. "Spiritualism Tested." 185 pages. 16mo. Gould
& Lincoln, 1860.

3. "Physical Media in Spiritual Manifestations."
1869. Among other of the more important works taking a view similar to that presented by Dr. Sampson,
are several by Baron Karl von Reichenbach (1788–
1869), who wrote largely upon animal magnetism, and
with whom originated the name and discussion of Od,
Odyle, or Odic force. Reichenbach's "Dynamics of
Magnetism" was translated by Dr. John Ashburner of

the Royal Irish Academy, and the American edition was published by Redfield, New York.

Count Agénor De Gasparin wrote "Science *vs.* Modern Spiritualism," a treatise on turning tables, the supernatural in general, and spirits. Translated from the French by E. W. Robert. Introduction by Rev. Robert Baird, D.D. 2 vols. 470 and 469 pages. 7¾ x 5½. Kiggins & Kellogg, New York, 1856.

Dr. E. C. Rogers wrote "Philosophy of Mysterious Agents, Human and Mundane ; Or the Dynamic Laws and Relations of Man," embracing the natural philosophy of phenomena styled "Spiritual Manifestations." 336 pages. 8¼ x 5½. John P. Jewett & Co., Boston, 1852. Also "A Discussion of the Automatic Powers of the Brain," being a defense against Rev. Charles Beecher's Attack [see Beecher] upon "The Philosophy of Mysterious Agents," in his "Review of Spiritual Manifestations. " John P. Jewett & Co., Boston, 1854.

Sargent, Epes.. **48, 361, 378**

(1812–1880). Author and Journalist. "Planchette ; the Despair of Science," being a full account of modern Spiritualism ; its phenomena and the various theories regarding it, with a survey of French spiritism. 404 pages. 6½ x 4½. Roberts Bros., Boston, 1869. Also "The Proof Palpable of Immortality," an account of modern Spiritualism, 2nd edition, Boston, 1876 ; "The Scientific Basis of Spiritualism." 372 pages. 16mo. Colby & Rich, Boston, 1880–'81.

Savage, Rev. Minot J..................................... **360**

Scott, Reginald **356**

Scott, Sir Walter.................................**355, 383**

Scott, Rev. Walter **131**

President and theological tutor of Airedale College, Bradford, Yorkshire. "The Existence of Evil Spirits Proved ; and their Agency Particularly in Relation to the Human Race Explained and Illustrated." 2 Cor. II, 2. The Congregational Lecture, 9th Series. Jack-

---

JOURNALS.

OMITTED FROM LIST OF BOOKS.

H. Gratry, Professor of Moral Theology at the Sorbonne: Guide to the Knowledge of God. A Study of the Chief Theodicies, Translated by Abby L. Alger. Introduction by Wm. Rounsville Alger. Pages 469, 8¾ x 6½. Roberts Bros., Boston, 1892.   •   437

BIBLICAL INDEX.

(Note for page 377.)

"It may be questioned whether idolatry as properly understood has ever prevailed except among the most debased and ignorant of races. It is not the emblem that is worshiped, but a power or being which the emblem represents. When the Apostle warned the Corinthian Church against participating in anything devoted to an idol, he was careful to explain that the idol in itself was nothing. 'But,' (he declared) 'the things which the gentiles sacrifice they sacrifice to *demons*, not to God, and I would not that ye should have fellowship with demons.' (1 Cor. x. 20.) This will afford an insight into the character of the predicted serpent worship of the last days. (Rev. xiii. 3, 4.) Satan's master lie will be a travesty of the incarnation; he will energize a man who will claim universal worship, as being the manifestation of the Deity in human form." For this, and further development of this thought, see *The Coming Prince, the Last Great Monarch of Christendom.* By Robert Anderson, LL. D., Barrister at Law, etc. Second edition. London & Toronto, pp. 207-8, *et passim.*

For a different view of the words in Corinthians, see Marcus Dods, D.D., in *The Expositor*, March, 1895; also see "Hat der Apostel Paulus die Heidengötter fur Dämonen Erhalten? Osterprogram der Universität Halle-Wittenberg. Verfasst von D. Willibad Beyschlagg. Verlag von Eugen Strien, 1894, Halle; pages 22.

PATHOLOGICAL INDEX.

A NUMERICAL INDEX OF THE CASES OF POSSESSION DETAILED IN THIS VOLUME. *

* Cases, in medical language, of Demonomania or Psychical Epilepsy.

[464]

GENERAL INDEX.

Absurdities and rubbish found equally in old and new literature of the occult. Each reader to do his own sifting, 353, 369.

Acupuncture in exorcism, 53, 54, 67.

Adjuration, its effect on demons. Tertullian, 129; Cyprian, 131.

Afflicted, the, in Salem witchcraft regarded as demoniacs, 304–311.

Africa, possession in, 156; witchcraft in, 301, 311.

Agrippa, Cornelius, 379.

Ahab, demons in case of, 269.

Ahriman, 372.

Air, the habitat of demons, 128.

Alford, Dean, his rendering of Gal. iii. 5, 289.

American Psychical Society, 385.

Angel, speaks, 124; power of, 129; guardian, 63; manifestations of good angels, 354, 271; literature of angelology, 353; Bible test of good, 391, 392.

Animism, Tylor on, 161–164, 373; Hammond on, 178; persistence of this view, 163.

A-priori reasoning upon the occult, 339, 341, 344; A. R. Wallace on, 344, 345, 370.

Apparitions, to G. Dittus, 112, 113; of Castor, 128, 129; of lambent lights, 322; James on, 432; Haweis on, 433; Kant on, 364; Positivist testimony as to reality of, 365; literature of, 363.

Appearance of demoniacs, 37, 48, 49.

Appendix, referred to, 92.

Apocatastasis, See Leonard Marsh, 133, 357.

Apollonius of Tyana, 379.

Apotheosis of departed spirits, 62, 63, 269, 374, 377, 378.

Asia, possession theory in S. E. Asia, 157.

Ashmore on Chinese spiritism, 427.

Astrology, 299.

Athanasius on exorcism, 131.

Augustine on Platonic view of demons, 270, 295, 296; on miracles, 337.

Aura, peripheral nervous, 196.

Aurelius, Marcus, use of word demon, 330.

Author (J. L. Nevius), Introduction. Explanatory Note. Arrival in China, and incredulity as to demons, 9, 10, 262. His teacher in the language the first witness, 9, 10. Removal to Shantung, Called on for exorcism, 138. Issues circular, 41.

Auto-hypnotism, see Hypnotism, and 229.

Automatic writing; case of Sydney Dean, 218; Myers on, 48, 69, 188, 204, 223, 233, 221. See Planchette, Mediumistic literature; 348, 360.

garded by many, 339; belong to class of prodigies, 340; pervade history, 340; experimental research in, 386; danger of this, 387; a fad, 386; duty of understanding it, 386; curiosity to witness it, 386; in Bible lands, 386; in heathen lands, 387; rising flood of in Europe and America, 387; Journalism of occult, 384; Haweis on persistence of the phenomena, 432.

Odic force, 150, 151, 366, 455.

Oracles, Greek, Delphic, 217, 293, 294; evidence of superhuman knowledge in, 296; tested by Crœsus, 296; and by Trajan; priestess same as witch and medium, 310, 311, 317. Tertullian on, 128; Cyprian on, 131; Dr. Tylor on, 153; Sibylline, 297; Kamtchatka, 154; Tahiti, 155; Guinea, 156.

Oudh, 101.

Pacific Islands, Wizard, 164.

Paganism identified with demon-worship, 270, note; 294, 374, 377, quoted.

Pagoda Shadows, 88.

Pantheism and Polytheism, their historical order, 170.

Patagonian Wizard, 153.

Pathology, literature of, 380.

Pathological explanation of possession, Tylor, 167–169, 174; Hammond, 175–186, 237–241; Fairfield, 195–197; Griesinger, 197–201; Baelz, 201–206; Gamanouchi, 107, 108.

Paul, St., his temptation, 269, law of the members and mind, 212; on connection of idolatry with demon-worship,

292, 377; on Greek worship, 270; his inventory of nature, 335.

Pember, 206, 269; on difference of demoniac and medium, 428, 429.

Personality, the new personality in possession, 107, 186–190, 144, 198, 203, 217, 218, 255, 53.

　Multiplex personality (may be more than two selves), 204, 257, 258, 120, 198, 188, 205, 206.

　Diseased personality, 189; alternate, 212–216, 224–227; a mask, 226; a concensus, 228; implications of, according to Dr. James, 211; contrasted with individuality, 226; assertion and recognition of new personality, 144, 258. (See Consciousness, Possession, Self, Soul.)

Pe-ta, 23.

Peter, St., his temptation, 268.

Phantom. (See Apparition.)

Pharisees, creed of, 391.

Phenomena, occult, how distinguished, 335, 336.

Phelps, Dr. Austin, 110, 126; on modern demonism, 427; basis of truth in Spiritualism, 318, 319; adaptation to its ends, 320, 330; value of his testimony, see Bibliog. Index.

Phelps, Rev. Eliakim, 125–127.

Philippi, damsel of (Acts xvi, 16), 293, 294.

Physical phenomena of demonism. (See possession.)

Ping-tu, 15, 395.

Planes of natural being, various, 335, 336.

Planchette, Chinese, 48, 69.

Plato on polyglottic powers of demoniacs, 192; conception of demons, 270, note.

SUPPLEMENT TO SECOND EDITION.

"Why then should witlesse man so much misweene
That nothing is but that which he hath seene?"

FAERIE QUEEN, BK. II.

For the convenience of those who may wish to follow up the subject of this volume, or to know how this discussion of it has been received, some extracts are here given from reviews of the first edition. These are preceded by two personal tributes to the author, Dr. Nevius, who died before the publication of his work was completed; also by passages from four letters regarding the book, and by some brief preliminary comments of its editor.

I.

PRELIMINARY.

A second edition of this work has been prepared one year from its first issue. Many minor corrections have been made in the typography, and a few in the text. Considerable material has been added to the footnotes and Appendix.

More may be done to improve the editorial part of the book in future issues, and the editor would gratefully receive from any source suggestions, criticisms, references and verified data which may be used to that effect. Adverse criticism often aids a writer more than the most friendly encomium, and, whenever made in good faith, will be entirely welcome.

The main conclusion of this volume is repugnant to the drift of opinion in our day, and, indeed, offers a respectful challenge to all that passes for modern thought, whether scientific or religious. It is one very easy to misjudge. Some violent antagonism it must arouse, but a strong division of sentiment may also result, and this has already appeared. Out of fifty reviews which have thus far come to the editor's knowledge, the most, however noncommittal as to the author's conclusions, exhibit a decided confi· dence in his statements of fact, and a surprised but emphatic conviction of the strength of his argument. Three of considerable length from medical sources speak in severe condemnation.

There will yet be a battle of the doctors, if not over this book, still over this subject; they will not all be found on one side.

Yet in general it may be said that, with notable exceptions, the clergy regard a doctrine of demoniac agency among men as an integral part of Christian theology, and believe that the phenomenon of possession was actually prevalent in the time of Christ; but they are loath to think that it has continued to our own time. Whereas physicians admit that if possession were a fact in the time of Christ there is no good reason why it may not be a fact to-day; but they repudiate the view that there was ever such a fact.

If the author be right his discussion is of great apologetic value to conservative theology; and even if wrong, his forty cases of the peculiar affection known in medical language as demonomania and psychical epilepsy will have their value for pathologists and psychologists. Thus far his adverse reviewers have not succeeded in correctly stating his actual premises. They have put some grounds under his argument which are not his. They have erected the familiar man of straw, and then knocked him down. They have not fully faced his facts, and however unwittingly or unintentionally, they have made serious misstatements about the book which would not be warranted by a careful reading.

This is not the place to point out the particulars of this disagreement, which any candid student may discover by a close comparison of their words with the text of the volume. But if an author is to be demolished he must first be understood.

They totally confuse the Christian and pagan views of demoniac agency, seeing the points of resemblance but not those of difference, and regard the doctrine in whatever form, and whether in the Bible or out of it, as only an effete and degrading superstition. They deride the author's Chinese witnesses, though these are numerous, belong to all parts of their country, and without possibility of collusion present a mass of testimony that agrees upon every important feature of the phenomena in question.

The double personality, figuring in every case described by the author, is spoken of by these reviewers as if it were always identical with "the central and most interesting phenomenon" of hypnosis, and as if it were easily explained without resort to any other than the contradictory and provisional theories now current among neurologists.

The evidence of superhuman knowledge is met by a flat denial, although this denial must either face or ignore an enormous array of evidence connected with similar cases, not contained in this book, but scattered through all literature and history from first to last. The evidence in this book should be judged in its cumulative character, and, if better so, by disconnecting the forty cases from their context, reading them consecutively through, and comparing them with the numerous cases to be found elsewhere, and abundantly in the literature referred to in this volume on possession. The corroborative evidence in this literature of the subject, and the events of the time, for every position that Dr. Nevius takes, may prove to be quite inexhaustible, and his implicit challenge not unworthy of regard.

The principal conclusions of the book have already the entire endorsement of two widely known and honored missionaries to China, the Rev. Arthur H. Smith of Canton, whose recent book on "Chinese Characteristics"* puts him in the first rank of writers upon that country; and the Rev. Timothy Richard of Pekin, who is engaged "in an important and exceptional work among the highest officials" of that capital.

Its value to theology and apologetics has been emphatically recognized by Drs. H. C.

*Published by F. H. Revell Co.

Trumbull and S. T. Lowrie of Philadelphia, by Dr. Joseph Cook and the editor of the *Watchman*, Boston, and in various religious papers of large influence.

Its value to missionaries has been shown in the *Indian Standard* of Allahabad. Without endorsing or denying its conclusions, Andrew Lang, a chief of folk-lore writers, has shown at some length in the *London Illustrated News* its importance to folk-lore. And so its use to psychology has been highly approved in the *Psychological Review* by Dr. William James of Harvard University, a physician whose eminence in psychology is international, whose writings are the most fascinating and most read in his field. Its relation to pathology has been treated as already described by editorials of some length in medical journals, from which passages will be given farther on.

Just as this writing goes to press there comes to hand *A History of the Warfare of Science with Theology in Christendom*, exhibiting the labor of years by Dr. Andrew D. White. Seventy pages of the second volume describe the final triumph of science over theology in accounting for the very phenomena which are considered in much more detail by Dr. Nevius. "Thus has been cleared away," says Dr. White, "that cloud of supernaturalism which so long hung over mental diseases, and thus have they been brought within the firm grasp of science." (II., 166.)

When it is remembered how often an important advance of medical science has been made in the face of contemptuous conservatism, and almost insuperable prejudice on the part of its own profession; how the dogmatism of science exemplified in its history was never surpassed in any field beside, unless that of theology; how "despitefully entreated" by the medical faculties of every time have been many of their chief discoveries; how slow and late has been the admission of facts in every new department; how recent and limited still is the serious study of the whole region occupied by trance, clairvoyance, clairaudience, hypnosis and cognate things; how symptoms and conditions receive names, and then those names are used as if everything were explained; how the schools of hypnotism are divided still, how confident are the adherents of each, and how few physicians belong to either of them—when these things are considered we may gauge the strength of that grasp which material science has upon the facts of psychical epilepsy and demonomania.

Theology, with Dr. White, has no standing whatever as a science, and the worth of any conclusion which may be proposed as a part of material science theologians are not regarded as competent to dispute. What they have done to hinder the progress of knowledge is displayed in full, what they have done to promote it is not emphasized; while their human nature appears in so much worse light than that of other men as to be by far the principal source of the intolerant bigotry which has disfigured and retarded the advancement of the race.

The work of Dr. White will be profitable to theologians, who, like other men, need at times to be humbled by the record of their own past follies and mistakes. It will be hurtful to many who do not know theology, and who may suppose that all the story is here told; who when they listen to the prosecuting attorney will think that his tone of finality is the voice of the judge. Very little mention is made in this labored polemic of some far more masterly irenic works in its own field.

The doctrines of demoniac agency and possession, which form a consistent and integral part of Biblical theology from Genesis to Revelation, and which, as there shown, concern every period of human history up to its approaching consummation, have been grievously distorted, and hurtfully misapplied, alike by devout believers and by wicked men. They have been taken out of their relation to the entire system of which they form a part, and by perverse isolation and mischievous misconstruction have been made to aggravate the miseries which they were intended to diminish, and to protect mankind against. Nevertheless, those teachings of Holy Scripture have not been invalidated by their abuse. And now they are reaffirmed and reënforced by such illustration of their significance for human life in this latest century as may, perhaps, convince an honest mind both of the danger to which the race of man is subject, and of the adequate defense provided for all those who choose to take it.

And furthermore, when the means of this defense are rightly apprehended, it makes that very danger seem a privilege which compels us to seek shelter in a refuge so sublime. No evil spirit can be so near to any man as is that Eternal Spirit in whom and from whom we have our being.

> "Speak to Him thou, for He hears,
>   And Spirit with Spirit can meet—
> Closer is He than breathing, and
>   Nearer than hands and feet."
>
> (TENNYSON.)

He may not help us if we will not trust him, because he desires sons, not slaves; and because the very purpose of all our proving is to make us understand our dependence on his help. But by him the Lord Christ cast the demon out, and he is ready still to save those who put their confidence in him.

The curse becomes a blessing. His victorious faith makes the believer acquainted with the Captain of his Salvation, introduces him to another army set for his defense, shows him that he is not alone in the awful conflict with a hidden foe, interprets the purpose of this conflict in the perfecting of that faith which is necessary to his own complete perfection, brings him to the munitions of rocks, and into the secret pavilion and gracious presence of the Lord of Hosts, the King of Glory, whose Angel encampeth round about them that fear him, and delivereth them.

"A mighty fortress is the Lord our God." The hymn that rang from the Wartburg three hundred years ago is still the shout of a triumphant people, and will be till the new song takes its place.

If the devil who contested every step of Martin Luther's progress was but a phantom of his mind, engendered by superstition and disease, then Jesus Christ himself was but a victim of hallucination. Many are ready to admit that Jesus plainly taught this doctrine, so obnoxious to their minds, who do not think that his authority adequately guarantees its truth.

There are preëminent crises in the history of man when the devil, if there be a devil, seems unusually active and conspicuous. Are we coming upon such a crisis now? Does he know that his time is short? We all may freely admit that, if there be a devil, to suppress the fact of his power and existence would go far with the mind of this age towards accomplishing his ends.

Put any truth in a false setting and it becomes a lie. Ignore a truth that we ought to know and it becomes a peril. Suppress a truth of which we have good evidence, and, like the stone of stumbling and rock of offense, it may fall upon us by and by, and grind us into powder.

HENRY W. RANKIN.

East Northfield, Mass., May 12, 1896.

II.

PERSONAL TRIBUTES TO THE AUTHOR.

From an Obituary which appeared in Woman's Work, Jan., 1894.

It is no common blow that has fallen on the Shantung Mission. Like the shock on the air when some monarch of the forest is felled to the ground, came tidings of Dr. Nevius' death to the Mission House. He was among the foremost missionaries in all China. At the great Conference in 1890, he was chosen Moderator on the first ballot, by delegates from every missionary society in the Empire, and was put on their committee for translation of the Bible. Questions were laid up for reference to him by workers all over China and America, and, after forty years' experience, he was looked to, with his catholic spirit, great learning and childlike attitude towards the truth, for his ripest service in the next ten years; for he was a vigorous man and only sixty-four years old. Apart from Dr. Nevius the missionary, the remark of one that "he was a prince among men" will be appreciated by many who saw him during his recent furlough in this country.

———

William A. P. Martin, D.D., LL. D. President of Imperial Tungwen College, Pekin. Author of "The Chinese, Their Education, Philosophy and Letters" (Harper Bros., N. Y., 1881), and of "A Cycle of Cathay" (F. H. Revell Co., 1896). In his introduction to "The Life of John Livingstone Nevius, by his wife, Helen S. Coan Nevius." (F. H. Revell Co., N. Y., Chicago and Toronto.)

It was obvious that he possessed that "concord of

harmonious powers" required by the career that lay before him. A strong body, a vigorous and well trained intellect, a sound judgment, and a firm will—these were the corner stones of a character which, abounding in natural magnetism and penetrated by the grace of God, was marked out for usefulness of no ordinary type. His inborn dignity compelled respect from the highest; his kindly sympathies were such that the lowliest might approach him in confidence. Serious, but not morose, at times mirthful, but never frivolous, he was the most genial of companions. His society was sought by the worldly, though most appreciated by those who could enter the sanctuary of his religious affections.

III.

EXTRACTS FROM LETTERS.

Rev. Arthur H. Smith, Author of "Chinese Characteristics." (Fourth edition, F. H. Revell Co., 1896.) In a letter to the present editor under date of March 9, 1896, Oakland, Cal.

I have just finished reviewing it (Demon Possession) for a journal here, and am about to write a more extended notice for the Shanghai press. It is evident that the subject ramifies into a practical infinity. All of it is very interesting, especially that portion which relates to Shantung cases. When I traveled with Dr. Nevius over a part of his field nine years ago I was unacquainted with the details of most of these cases, and should not have accepted his explanation; did not, indeed, when he related the most striking instances to me. But now I am quite prepared to accept the view which he advocates as essentially a reasonable one, and much more philosophical than one which consists mainly of stalwart negations.

I have no expectation that the theory of the book will find general acceptance at present. We are in the midst of a highly material age, when a "law" is of more consequence than Deity itself. It is only by being forced to admit that "law" does not explain all, or nearly all the real phenomena, that the candid will be compelled to admit that there is a law above recognized law, and that perhaps the account which God has himself given us is as good as one at which we can arrive by shrewd and contradictory guesses.

———

Rev. Timothy Richard of Pekin, in a letter to Mrs. Nevius, under date of Nov. 20, 1895. Pekin.

This wonderful volume will form one of the indispensable books, not only of every efficient missionary in China, but, I should say, of every efficient minister at home. It should be a textbook in the theological colleges. In this way they will be better equipped to deal with these mysterious questions than by anything I have ever seen before.

———

Rev. J. F. Dripps, D. D., of Savannah, Ga., in a letter from that place to the editor, of date March 5, 1895.

I have been unable to lay it aside, so fascinated have I been with it. The position taken as to "spiritualism" is just that to which I was led by my own experience in a community of spiritualists; the Salem Witchcraft mystery finds here the only real solution, I am sure; and it is of absorbing interest to get such clear light on the more obscure points of gospel demoniac narrative. It is so original and so powerful that thoughtful men everywhere must surely welcome it for its light on scripture and science and on man. It is serious work to live among such forces as are here revealed. "But thanks be to God who giveth us the victory through our Lord Jesus Christ."

———

Dr. Nevius' manuscript was submitted to the late D. Hayes Agnew, M. D., LL. D., of the Medical Faculty of the University of Pennsylvania. Dr. Agnew wrote of it as follows to the Rev. Samuel T. Lowrie, D. D., of Philadelphia:

I have gone over, with some care, the manuscript of Rev. Dr. Nevius on demoniacal possessions. The subject has been treated very ably by the Doctor. He has brought out very clearly the differential points between "possessions," and epileptic, cataleptic, and hysterical disturbances of the nervous system. I believe these demoniacal seizures, mentioned in the New Testament, fall within a realm which has never been invaded by the studies of the pathologist.

Yours very sincerely,
D. HAYES AGNEW.

IV.

EXTRACTS FROM REVIEWS.

Talcott Williams, Editor of the Press, Philadelphia, in Book News, April, 1895.

It is now over half a century that Williams noted the Polynesia phenomena which he deemed due to demon possession. Repeatedly, and in many countries, missionaries—most of them educated men, many of them physicians, and some of them men of considerable scientific attainments—have noted like phenomena, and their exorcism in the name of Christ. My own experience is that nearly every one who examines these phenomena at first hand is very chary of asserting their easy explanation on natural grounds. Dr. Nevius collected a wide array of facts in many countries bearing on this subject. (His volume) has been edited with care. (The editor) has added a chapter on the literature of the subject, and a bibliographical index. This renders the work most valuable for reference, and it will long remain a magazine of information on its topic.

———

The Tribune, New York, Dec. 13, 1895.

Dr. Nevius was a careful and accurate observer, and has gathered together a body of facts and stories relating to obscure psychical phenomena, that will be of value to the student of the occult.

———

Prof. William R. Duryee, D. D., of Rutgers College, N. J. In the Christian Intelligencer, April 24, 1895.

The Christian world is so much interested in Biblical investigation at the present day, and the occult is receiving so much attention in the fields of general literature and of jurisprudence, that we feel sure the work of Dr. Nevius must find many readers. For ourselves its general conclusions seem established by the facts brought so carefully together, and sifted so thoroughly by the judicious author.

———

The New York Observer, June 13, 1895.

The first ten chapters are given to detailed instances of demon possession studied in China and elsewhere; five chapters consider the various theories which attempt an explanation of it; two chapters contain an historical sketch of demonism, and a study of spiritualism; and the editor of the book adds an excellent chapter on the facts and literature of the occult, and supplies appendixes and indexes which are of no small value.

Whatever may be thought of the evidence adduced for demoniacal possession in China, as a book of curious lore, as a collection of facts made by careful hands, as an able exegesis of the Gospel accounts of possession, as a polemic against unscriptural theories, especially against the psychological and pathological, and as a thesaurus of general views scientific and popular of the occult sciences, this volume will take a high place.

The Christian Intelligencer, N. Y., April 17, 1895.

It may be commended as the most comprehensive treatise accessible on demon possession.

The Christian Observer, Louisville, Ky., March 27, 1895.

The book will be of great interest to the scientist and the student of the occult. Four indexes complete the volume, and their range is so wide as to render it an encyclopedia on the subject of Demonology.

Western Recorder, Louisville, June 6, 1895.

Much patient and wide study is manifested, along with great ability.

Rev. James H. Brooks, D. D., in The Mid-Continent, St. Louis, March 27, 1895.

Altogether the best book that has appeared on the subject of Demonology.
(*Also in his Magazine called The Truth, F. H. Revell Co., May, 1895, Dr. Brooks says again:*)
The ablest book that has appeared on the subject. . . . . It is needless to say that those who believe in the Word of God have no hesitancy in accepting his conclusion as true. . . . . The Bible from first to last teaches the real existence of demons, and their infernal power over men. The habit of thinking that this

was owing to the ignorance of the age, and that epilepsy and lunacy were attributed to demons, comes perilously near irreverence and blasphemy. Again and again our Lord Jesus Christ spoke to demons and evil spirits, cast them out with his word, and carefully distinguishes between them and all forms of physical and mental disorder. Demons are mentioned nearly seventy times in the Gospels, and in not a single instance as a disease, but as an awful fact of possession by evil spirits, afflicting, debasing, tormenting. Precisely the same thing is true of the Old Testament, where demons appear under the name of familiar spirits and devils, and God's abhorrence of them is shown in his command, "A man also, or a woman, that hath a familiar spirit, or that is a wizard, shall surely be put to death." Lev. xx. 27. Just as this is written the testimony of Sir Monier Williams comes to hand, showing how deep-seated and wide-spread is the conviction that people are still subject to demon possession. (He says:) "The great majority of the inhabitants of India are, from the cradle to the burying ground, victims of a form of mental disease which is best expressed by the term demonphobia. They are haunted and oppressed by a perpetual dread of demons. They are firmly convinced that evil spirits of all kinds, from malignant fiends to merely mischievous imps and elves, are ever on the watch to harm, harass and torment them, to cause plague, sickness, famine and disaster; to impede, injure and mar every good work."

But it is not heathenism alone that swarms with demons; our own land is filled with them. Look at the atrocious and frightful crimes that are increasing more and more, and that are properly called "devilish." Tricky lawyers speak of the scoundrels as "paranoiacs," a convenient dodge to escape responsibility. (Quoted further on p. 290.)

Rev. H. D. Griswold, in The Indian Standard, Allahabad, July, 1895.

This is a valuable book, dealing with a series of facts which have been too much neglected by Christian scholars. . . . Thus there is no doubt of the existence of such phenomena, and the fact that the manifestations noted in China agree in all important points with those described in the pages of Griesinger and Tylor, as well as in the New Testament, is a sufficient proof of their general credibility. . . . . The book is rich in suggestiveness. The author attempts to correlate the occult of every age and country, e. g. sorcery, magic, New Testament demon possession, Indian devil dancing, Salem witchcraft, modern spiritualism, etc., as a means of discovering general facts and principles. The book will serve as an excellent handbook on the occult phenomena of Scripture. Many a reader who is not at all given to rationalizing the New Testament accounts of demon possession, nevertheless inwardly confesses to a certain embarrassment in dealing with them. This is a book which will greatly help all such.

Further, the book ought to stir up the Indian missionaries, who do district work, to a more careful, unprejudiced examination of any phenomena which are akin to those described in this book. The method pursued by the author is inductive, and the fact that no other hypothesis is adequate to explain all the phenomena shuts up the author to the hypothesis of demon possession.

The conclusion is of apologetic value in regard to the Scriptures. On the whole the book is a most useful one, and worthy of a place in every missionary's library.

———

The Outlook, N. Y., October 26, 1895.

This is a remarkable book for the nineteenth century. It shows the powerful reactionary forces at work beneath the surface of modern Christianity. . . .

There is considerable material in this book for the study of the "night side of nature." . . . . There is a point of view other than religious from which one can see that this book is not without some value. The names on its title page should secure for it a respectful examination. . . . . We should like to commend it to the attention of the Society for Psychical Research. Dr. Nevius's testimony will not be impeached in the point of veracity, but there may be some question as to the accuracy of his interpretation of the facts.

———

Bibliotheca Sacra, Oberlin, January, 1895.

What the author shows beyond question is that in many countries there are observed many cases in certain respects like those described in the New Testament as caused by demoniacal possession; and his inference is that they are thus to be explained. . . . . That in many cases these possessions are the result of nervous disorder seems to us unquestionable, but there is an unexplained remainder. We prefer to treat the matter of this volume as the author intended, as material for induction, awaiting a more careful investigation of the relations of bodily and mental states than has yet been made

———

The Christian Leader, Cincinnati, April 2, 1895.

It is very evident to us that epilepsy, hysterics, hallucination and melancholia, and not personal possession of demons, as in the apostolic age, are the factors which must give finality to this question. Nevertheless the book is well worthy of close study.

———

The Advance, Chicago, April 1, 1895.

Whatever may be thought of Dr. Nevius's conclusions, his book is a very strong presentation of the subject, and throws the light of modern fact on the gospel narratives.

———

The Toronto Daily Globe, December 14, 1895.

Dr. Nevius's inductive study of the pathological phenomena which he is pleased to entitle "Demon Possession" is an instance of how a man may part too easily with the sheet-anchor of his reason, and give himself over to vain imaginings. . . . The book . . though somewhat incoherent, is a readable exposition of the spiritistic point of view.

———

Hartford Seminary Record, for June–August, 1895.

Whatever may be one's prepossesions, he will have to confess that the author has made out a very strong argument. He pursues a thoroughly scientific method. He first investigates the facts, and then inquires what explanation best fits the facts. He was at first disinclined to believe in the present occurrence of demon possession, but changed his views under the pressure of observed and well attested facts.

———

Andrew Lang, in the London Illustrated News, June 29, 1895.

That Dr. Nevius is always logical one cannot affirm; nor that he has a very wide knowledge of his subject; but he is always fair and honest in controversy. This singular merit his book has—that it shows us in contemporary China exactly the state of things described in the New Testament. The Chinese recognize the existence of madness, epilepsy and nervous disorders; but to one particular set of symptoms they give the name of diabolical possession. . . . Of these mental phenomena explanations have been suggested by many physicians. The explanations, as Dr. Nevius shows, do not explain anything. . . . The *Folklorist* finds himself in very well known country, *quod semper, quod ubique, quod ab omnibus*. But what it is that causes this ubiquitous and uniform belief the *Folklorist* does not pretend to know. (Quoted further on p. 206.)

Rev. Robert Aikman, D.D., of Madison, N.J., in the Madison Eagle, March 15, 1895.

The absence of the dogmatic spirit is one of the features of Dr. Nevius's book.

The Congregationalist, Boston, April 25, 1895.

Dr. Nevius has written in a temperate, self-restrained manner, with no purpose of making one kind of impression rather than another, but simply to state the facts ascertained by him, letting them make their own impression; although he naturally draws some conclusions which have occurred to him. . . . He discusses the subject from the scientific as well as the religious side, has much to say about spiritualism, and has made a significant and impressive volume. In our judgment all candid readers will feel bound to admit that his position is probably correct.

Central Christian Advocate, St. Louis, April 24, 1895. Editorial.

Dr. Nevius does not attempt to decide dogmatically the exact nature of the 'possession,' but, after marshaling all the theories which have been constructed whereby to account for these phenomena, he shows very clearly that there are good reasons for believing that men and women in China are still possessed by demons, in the same way as people in Palestine were in the time of our Lord.

The Presbyterian Journal, Philadelphia. Editorial, July 25, 1895.

There is evidence of great caution pervading the entire work. The basis of the book is a splendid collection of indisputable facts, drawn from real life, which are carefully guarded and fortified.

———

The Church Calendar, Kansas City, Kan., Nov., 1895.

No cheap and flippant criticisms can easily demolish the positions taken by this author.

———

The Watchman, Boston. Editorial, May 23, 1895.

Recounting the concurrent collateral testimony of travelers in distant lands, and explorers in every realm of human life and history to the reality of the phenomena in question, and considering in detail the various theories, evolutionary, pathological and psychological, offered to account for them, he returns to the Biblical narrative as affording the only credible and consistent explanation of facts now occurring, identical in almost every detail with those there described. . . . . The resultant opinions of Dr. Nevius are characterized by great carefulness, impartiality and intelligence, and, while not absolutely positive in assertion, are of more value because of their evidently conscientious reserve of decision until the evidence has been fully sifted and weighed. They ought to lend new and far more impressive significance to the phenomena which, under the name of "spiritualism," are so rife among us. A very valuable chapter on the "Facts and Literature of the Occult" has been added by the editor.

———

The Journal and Messenger, Cincinnati, May 9, 1895.

This is a remarkable book which we would like to

see in the hands of every pastor. One approaches the subject with prejudices against it; he is likely to end with a hearty endorsement. . . . His book is what it professes to be, "an inductive study" of the subject, carried on through many years under favorable circumstances.

———

The Medical News, Philadelphia, July 13, 1895. Editorial.

Nothing but the evident sincerity and devoted philanthropy of the author . . . would enable us to take it seriously. . . . The only original part of the book is the small portion of personal experiences, and responses to a circular letter, and is of a most disappointing nature. . . . It seems well nigh incredible that any man of his intelligence and education could extract the smallest atom of solid conviction from such a frothy mass of self-evident ghost stories, and fairy tales, or could even relate them with seriousness. The only way it can be accounted for is the influence of a life-long exposure to an atmosphere of belief in them. . . . Even the missionary is unconsciously tinged by the heathenism among which he spends his life. . . . Not only should our missionaries be medically educated, but they should have practical and clinical courses in mental disease. A course of scientific study, however limited, would teach the differential diagnosis between demon possession and mental abnormalism. Psychiatry kills superstition.

———

The Medical Record, New York, August 10, 1895.

This is a curious book and one written with such sincerity of purpose, and painstaking attempt at accuracy, that we feel somewhat disarmed in an attempt to criticise it. An author who at this period of our civilization sits down deliberately to establish a thesis that demoniac possession exists, certainly awakens our wonder. The idea. that human beings are at times possessed by spirits, evil or good, has certainly never been held by even the average theologian of late years, much less by men who have studied the question medically. The medical view of these cases, in which people are supposed to be demoniacally possessed, is that they are suffering from epilepsy, hysteria or insanity. This interpretation is abundantly supported by facts, and is sufficient to explain the phenomena; sufficient, at least, for most minds. Dr. Nevius, however, thinks that in certain parts of China demon possession exists, and in proof of this he collects a large number of stories of various people who were, as the people believe, possessed of spirits. The theory of demon possession is ingeniously supported by quotations from the works of medical authors and psychologists, and by the teachings of Scripture. There is also appended a chapter upon the facts and literature of the occult.

In fact the book contains a great deal that is curious and interesting to all persons interested in psychology, particularly pathological psychology, and it will have its use even for those who do not, and cannot at all believe in the theory that the author tries to maintain.

———

The Nation, New York, August 22, 1895.

How the belief in demoniacal possession (which is one of the most articulately expressed doctrines of both Testaments, and which reigned for seventeen hundred years, hardly challenged, in all the churches) should have become the utterly dead letter which it now is in Christian countries, is an interesting historical question on which the present reviewer is unable to cast light. Its decay is far less intelligible than the decay of the belief in witchcraft, which Mr. Lecky has so vividly attributed to an unreasoned alteration of the intellectual fashions of the age, for most of the old witchcraft accusations rested on direct demon-testimony, and the phenomenon which announces itself as demon possession has never ceased since men were men, and is probably as frequent at the present day in New York and Boston as it ever has been at any time and place in history. It follows at all times the local and temporal fashions and traditions, and, from causes which, once more, would form a highly interesting problem to unravel, it has with us assumed a benign and optimistic, instead of a diabolical and hurtful form, constituting what is familiarly known to-day as *mediumship*. It differs from all the classic types of insanity. Its attacks are periodic and brief, usually not lasting more than an hour or two, and the patient is entirely well between them, and retains no memory of them when they are over. During them, he speaks in an altered voice and manner, names himself differently, and describes his natural self in the third person as he would a stranger. The new impersonation offers every variety of completeness and energy, from the rudimentary form of unintelligible automatic scribbling, to the strongest convulsions with blasphemous outcries, or the most fluent "inspirational" speech. Imitation is a great determining factor, and suggestions from the bystanders are readily adopted and acted out. Exorcisms of various sorts often succeed in abolishing the condition, and the possessing spirit often makes treaties and compacts with the bystanders and carries them faithfully out. The condition may become epidemic, as in our own "developing circles," or in those Alpine villages whose "hystero-demonopathy" has recently been so well described by the French and Italian medical officials Constans, Chiap, and Franzolini; but more often it is sporadic and individual. At any rate it is a perfectly distinct and it may be a perfectly spontaneous "morbid entity" (as a Frenchman would say), or natural type of disease, and its essential characters seem to have been quite constant in every age and clime.

Of its causes, apart from suggestion and imitation, absolutely nothing definite is known, the psychical researchers being the only persons who at present seem to believe that it offers a serious problem for investigation. The Charcot school has assimilated it to hysteria major, with which it unquestionably has generic affinities, but just why its specific peculiarities are what they are, this school leaves unexplained. The name hysteria, it must be remembered, is not an explanation of anything, but merely the title of a new set of problems. The tendency to prophesy, to profess to reveal remote facts, to make diagnoses and heal diseases, are among the commonest features of the demonopathic state.

Dr. Nevius is vouched for by the two editors of the book before us (he having died before its publication) as a singularly learned, versatile, and accurate man. His volume contains, in addition to a large amount of comparative natural history of the subject and a mass of biography, a number of interesting first-hand observations made in China. As in the Grecian oracles, in India, Japan, Polynesia, and elsewhere, the possessed person is in China prone to speak in the name of a god. This god often demands a shrine, worship, incense, food, and burnt-offerings from the household, and throws the patient into convulsions if these are withheld Sometimes, again, a departed relative or other human being announces itself as the possessing spirit. . . . Such as it is, Dr. Nevius's book is one of the best contributions to the natural history of the subject, and a stepping-stone towards that not yet existing book which some day will treat this class of phenomena in a thoroughly objective and unprejudiced way, bringing it into comparison with all the other features of the "sublime" life of which it is one modification.

The American Journal of the Medical Sciences, Philadelphia, October, 1895.

The author's claim, however, that he has made an inductive study cannot be allowed for a moment. He states that he went to China a disbeliever in demon possession, and yet he acknowledges that he always believed in a literal interpretation of the demonology of the New Testament. What can be expected from an "inductive" philosopher who assumes everything in his premises? He claims that his study is based upon observation, whereas the argument is based upon a tissue of the crudest and most transparent superstitions and ghost-stories of an ignorant peasantry. These tales were accepted upon the testimony of native and foreign Christians who evidently were as superstitious as Dr. Nevius himself, and were confirmed by replies to a circular letter from other missionaries who were of the same type of mind. The "phenomena," in brief, were of the conventional kind —haunted houses, strange noises, destruction of dishes and furniture, table-rapping, bad luck, and last, and alone important, quite typical hysterical and hypnotic manifestations, with which we alone are concerned. All these phenomena were accepted by our "inductive" missionary as so many incontrovertible proofs of demon possession. No adequate attempt was made to investigate them in a rational spirit; on the contrary, the author of this book was promptly converted to an implicit belief in this heathenish diabolism, and upon this mass of misinterpreted facts he has written one of the most extraordinarily perverted books of the present day. The only original part . . . is in the first few chapters, in which he narrates very inadequately, and with absolute credulity, incidents of the so-called possession. This part, which might have been expanded into a most interesting and valuable exposition of fetish-worship and hystero-hypnotic manifestations . . . is written in such a prejudiced spirit, and with such absolute disregard for all the rules of scientific criticism, that it presents material of practically little value to the anthropologist, and of such a kind as can only be accepted after much winnowing from chaff, and after careful comparison with studies by more reliable observers—which we hope may yet be made. . . . The so-called personality is the central and most interesting phenomenon of hypnotism, and is now so well known that it has even become a part of the stock in trade of the average novelist. . . . . As for the "new" knowledge—as, for instance, the faculty of speaking in an unknown tongue—we believe that there does not exist an instance in which this alleged power has not been found on careful investigation to be the result of precedent psychical states and impressions. It is significant in this connection that this alteration of personality was so realistic in these remote and densely ignorant Chinese provincials that it gave the vivid impression that the victims were really possessed by personalities not their own, and that this impression was so strong, that it completely deceived an educated man like Dr. Nevius, and converted him to a belief in peregrinating devils. Surely no stronger or more unique proof can be needed of the genuineness and completeness of these hypnotic manifestations! But if the distinguishing marks upon which Dr. Nevius relies for "differentiation" are identical with the symptoms of hypnotism, what becomes of his differentiation? . . . Dr. Nevius, instead of converting the heathen, was perverted by them. Such a book would be impossible for any man who had not himself been far removed for a long period from the best civilizing influences. When Christian educated ministers lead in such a demoralizing witches' Sabbath as is depicted in this book, then does the gap between orthodox theology and pure science seem wide indeed. The influence of the book cannot but be wholly bad.

The Standard, Chicago, March 28, 1895.

The author's method in presenting facts, and in his study of them, must satisfy the fair-minded reader of his candor, and win respect for his judgment, whether his conclusions be in all respects accepted or not.

———

Prof. W. G. Moorehead, D.D., of the Theological Seminary, Xenia, O., in The United Presbyterian, Pittsburg, Pa.

The book is a genuine example of the inductive method of investigation. The facts are set forth first, then the explanation of the facts is submitted. One thing that impresses the reader of this strange and fascinating volume is the obvious fairness and candor of the author. He can hardly be said to have a theory of his own as to demoniacal agency and influence. The *facts* are beyond dispute, if human testimony is worth anything. . . . Dr. Nevius gives twenty-four points of resemblance between the Chinese cases of possession and those recorded in the New Testament, and no one can read them without being profoundly convinced of the almost complete parallelism they present.

———

The Sunday School Times, Philadelphia, Nov. 2, 1895.

The author next takes up the attempts to explain these facts, either by sociologists like Tylor, or physiologists like Hammond, Griesinger and Baeltz. He discusses these in a calm, scientific spirit, showing that they raise more questions than they answer, and that their proffered explanations are often "words, words, words" which do not fit the facts. . . . From these makers of hypotheses he passes to the Scriptures, showing the wonderful correspondence of the occurrences in Galilee in our Lord's time with those in other lands in our own day. The Bible offers an explanation which does explain; the men of science beat about the bush, and do not face the facts.

Dr. Nevius feels that his experience read in the Bible's light goes far to explain the residuum of fact in the phenomena of Spiritualism.

———

The Evangelist, New York, March 28, 1895.

Marked throughout by extreme candor and caution, the statements of this book must be taken at their full face value. They cannot be set aside with a mere wave of the hand, albeit they will seem to many to belong wholly to the past. The volume strikes us as of exceptional intellect and importance; but even at its lowest valuation a mass ʾof material is furnished for students of body and mind, evolutionists, pathologists, psychologists, in the field of double-consciousness, hypnotism and what not, at once novel and striking.

———

The Journal of Comparative Neurology, Evansville, O., March, 1896.　Editorial.

The volume . . . . challenges criticism. It is moreover a book destined to create a considerable amount of interest in various circles. Unlike most recent attempts to discuss this most perplexing subject, it at least claims a degree of preparation on the part of writer and editor which hardly permits of an *a priori* waving of its claims. It demands a serious hearing, if for no other reason, because it claims to fairly represent the calm judgment of all but an insignificant minority of the educated occidental missionaries at present actually living among the Chinese and other oriental people. [The book makes no such claim; see pp. 134–139.—EDITOR.] If this is indeed the case it may give rise to serious reflection, or even to the query, whether the reaction of barbarism on the missionary is not as great as his influence on the barbarism in the opposite direction. [Assumes that the Christian and heathen

doctrines of spirits are the same, and equally a base
superstition. ED.] We admit to a feeling of grave responsibility in dealing with such a work, and while
we feel that scientific truth leaves us no alternative, it
is hoped that the reviewer may be credited with no antagonism to the cause in the interest of which the
volume was sincerely written. Even more, it is because the reviewer believes that the false views here
promulgated will do great injury to that very cause
that he does not feel justified in holding his hand. At
the outset it is freely granted that the entire honesty
and credibility of the author and his witness is assumed in all that follows. The author has displayed
not only praiseworthy industry, but considerable skill
in the gathering of facts, and discussing their significance, and when we are forced to add that he seemed
singularly lacking in critical and scientific discrimination it does not follow that the value of the facts is invalidated. . . These so-called possessions are not in
any material way different from phenomena with
which modern pathology is dealing every day at home
with no doubt of their pathological character. That
they have been generally referred to devils is as forci-
ble an argument as it would be to adduce the universal belief that scrofula was due to the evil eye in a
modern medical consultation. [The author's conclusion is not grounded on this prevalent belief, which is
only one item in his cumulative induction. But he
searches the grounds of that belief to judge how far
it is warranted by the facts on which it is based. ED.]
. . . It is gravely stated that the possessed shows supernatural powers of speech, and gaining information
There is, however, no case given where such powers are
proven. [A careful, consecutive reading of the forty
cases of demonomania detailed in the volume will
show the cumulative character of the proof that *superhuman*, not *supernatural* power of this kind exists. ED.]

Fifteen cases are given from China, and we must

give up our plan of analyzing them. [Thirty-two cases are given from China, out of a far greater number collected, and forty cases in all, which call for close, consecutive comparison. Further quotations from this nearly nine-page article cannot be given here. It is written in wholly courteous terms, and with no desire to quarrel. But it is based on a too hasty reading, and very inadequate apprehension of the author's real position. It denies or ignores well attested facts, both in and out of this volume, while the explanations substituted for the author's, even of the facts that are admitted, would obviously fail to cover those facts in the eyes of any but a pathologist who ignores many things in history and psychology. —ED.]

William James, M. D., Professor, formerly of Physiology, now of Psychology, in Harvard University, in the Psychological Review, September, 1895.

This interesting contribution to mental pathology would probably fifteen years ago have gained for its author a reputation for nothing but mendacity or childish credulity in scientific circles; but now, thanks to the "apperceiving mass" which recent investigations into trance conditions have prepared, probably few readers of this journal will be seriously tempted to doubt its being a trustworthy report of facts. . . . Epidemics of possession like those recorded in Savoy by Constans and Chiap e Franzolini are not related by Dr. Nevius. The phenomena are among the most constant in history, and it is most extraordinary that "science" should ever have become blind to them. The form which they take in our community is the benign one of mediumship. Dr. Nevius is a believer in the reality of the alleged demons, and in the objectivity of their driving out in the name of Christ, etc. Such questions cannot be fairly discussed, however,

till the phenomena have been more adequately studied.
Dr. Nevius gives a large amount of collateral material
and bibliographical information; and we have to
thank him for an extremely good contribution to a
really important subject.

———

*Rev. Samuel T. Lowrie, D.D., in the Presbyterian and Re-
formed Review, July, 1895.*

The title is enough to attract readers; and also to
repel many who ought to read the book. The reputation of the author may assure the latter that a theme
which has become repugnant to them, as it was originally to him, is here treated in a fashion that does
justice both to their sentiments and also to the subject. . . . The book is scientific and apologetic, exactly
as books that report geographical explorations and
archæological excavations in Bible lands. It is a
valuable scientific acquisition when a "find" clears up
some occult matter of human life. It is a valuable
contribution to Christian apologetics when the find
corroborates Bible statements of fact that have been
discredited. The apologetic value is the popular interest. The purely scientific value interests a narrow
circle.

The facts produced in this book may be classed with
those finds in Bible lands that corroborate Scripture.
But they concern a very different subject from the
usual ones, viz., demoniacal possession. The Biblical
representations on this subject might be thought incapable of similar corroboration. . . . But this book
reports, what may convince the reader, that in China,
that land of so many origins, the identical plague of
demon possession has existed and still exists, though
now disappearing before Christianity as it did in
Palestine. That plague has great prominence, and
therefore great importance, in the New Testament.
It appears there as a familiar thing, which only per-

plexes present day believers the more, because to them
it is as unfamiliar and incredible as solid water is to
an ignorant inhabitant of a tropical island.

Under the circumstances skepticism has much apparent advantage, and spiritualists claim, with a
logical force hard to resist, that believers in demon
possession are bound to admit the pretensions of
spiritualism. All these matters are relieved, and embarrassment is exchanged for satisfaction, by the facts
as they are reported and applied in this book. Its
readers should be as many as the reflecting persons
who have felt the embarrassments and perplexities
just referred to.

———

*Joseph Cook, LL. D., Boston, in Life and Light for Woman,
July, 1895.*

Three things make Dr. Nevius' book on demon possession a remarkable contribution both to the literature of modern psychology and to that of the Christian
evidences. 1. It is written with the utmost coolness,
impartiality, and judicial balance of mind, and in a
style of great clearness and precision. 2. It is based
on original investigations undertaken without any
preconceived theory, and, indeed, with prepossessions
inclining the author to adopt a strictly naturalistic
explanation of the amazing phenomena forced on his
attention during a missionary experience of nearly half
a century. 3. It offers exceedingly significant, if not
conclusive evidence, that demoniacal possession is a
modern fact. Experiences almost precisely parallel to
those detailed in the gospel narratives as to possession of human beings by demons, are here recorded, as
they yet take place in the vicinity of pagan temples in
China and elsewhere among a people of somewhat low
intellectual and moral development.

Dr. F. F. Ellinwood, the distinguished Secretary of
the Presbyterian Board of Missions, after more than a

quarter of a century of acquaintance with Dr. Nevius, says that he regards him as a man peculiarly fitted to examine so intricate and difficult a subject. "His philosophic insight, his judicial fairness of mind, his caution, and his conscientious thoroughness, his mastery of the Chinese language spoken and written, his intimate sympathy with the people, and his correspondingly true interpretation of their innermost thought and life, rendered him capable of ascertaining the real facts in the case, and of forming accurate judgments upon them." (Introductory Note, page iii.)

The Rev. Arthur H. Smith, whose brilliant book on "Chinese Characteristics" has won such high praise in all quarters, has written on the flyleaf of the copy of Dr. Nevius' book owned by the present reviewer, the following words: "I am personally acquainted with the Shantung field described in this work, knew, admired, and loved the distinguished and honored author, and am convinced that his book is a record of realities, and embodies a true explanation of fundamental and vital facts."

Prayer in the name of Jesus, and a command from genuine Christians given in his name to the evil spirit to depart, has again and again effected exorcism. In one case the spirits cast out seemed to enter the bodies of inferior animals, as in the New Testament narrative of the Gadarene swine. Casting out demons in the name of Christ was one of the proofs given by the apostles of the Divine origin of their message.

Our Lord himself promised that the Apostles should have power to cast out evil spirits in his name. Mr. Arthur H. Smith read this wonderful promise on a certain occasion to the present reviewer, and claimed most solemnly that it is fulfilled to this day in the experiences of faithful missionaries and native preachers in China and elsewhere. As it was in the first generations reached by Christianity, so now the casting out of demons in the name of Christ is an evidence, readily appreciated and understood by the masses, of the presence and power of our ascended Lord, "thus convincing men of the Divine origin and truth of Christianity, and preparing the way for its acceptance" (p. 259).

Anti-supernaturalistic criticism of the Gospel narratives concerning demon possession appears very arbitrary and superficial in presence of the experiences narrated in Dr. Nevius' book. Immense importance attaches to the substantiation of the reality of the intercourse of disincarnate spirits with men, whether the communications received from beyond the range of ordinary human consciousness appear to come from evil spirits or from good. The scriptural direction is that we are to try the spirits to ascertain whether they are of God.

It is highly important to notice that Dr. Nevius is no spiritualist, but he, like Prof. Austin Phelps, or Prof. Theodor Christlieb, or John Wesley, is inclined to be a Biblical demonologist. He quotes many defenders of the psychological theory offered in explanation of the abnormal phenomena he discusses, but he adheres himself to the Biblical theory as far more coherent, satisfactory, and scientific than any other.

On the whole, we commend this book as an important contribution to current discussions of the Christian evidences, and of psychology in some of its most strategic and alluring departments. Let the positions taken by Dr. Nevius in this volume be once securely established, and the materialistic philosophy which denies the reality of the supernatural is overthrown, the Gospel narratives concerning demon possession are shown to be plain statements of matters of fact, and a flood of light is thrown upon some of the most vital and fundamental religious truths hitherto scouted by science, falsely so-called, and yet affirmed in the Holy of Holies of Revelation.

CPSIA information can be obtained
at www.ICGtesting.com
Printed in the USA
BVHW011619150620
581522BV00007B/533